5.49
12/17

PORTFOLIO

BLUESTREAK

Barbara S. Peterson is senior aviation correspondent at *Conde Nast Traveler,* where she has reported on airlines and other aviation related topics since 1998, and the coauthor of *Rapid Descent: Deregulation and the Shakeout in the Airlines.* Her articles have appeared in *The New York Times, The Wall Street Journal,* and the *San Francisco Chronicle.* She is the winner of the 2005 Gene DuBois Award for Excellence in Travel and Aviation Reporting. She lives in Hasting-on-Hudson, New York.

bluestreak

INSIDE JETBLUE, THE UPSTART THAT ROCKED AN INDUSTRY

barbara s. peterson

Portfolio

to my parents,

robert and marie sturken

PENGUIN BOOKS
Published by the Penguin Group
Penguin Group (USA) Inc., 375 Hudson Street, New York, New York 10014, U.S.A.
Penguin Group (Canada), 90 Eglinton Avenue East, Suite 700, Toronto, Ontario, Canada M4P 2Y3
(a division of Pearson Penguin Canada Inc.)
Penguin Books Ltd, 80 Strand, London WC2R 0RL, England
Penguin Ireland, 25 St Stephen's Green, Dublin 2, Ireland (a division of Penguin Books Ltd)
Penguin Group (Australia), 250 Camberwell Road, Camberwell, Victoria 3124, Australia
(a division of Pearson Australia Group Pty Ltd)
Penguin Books India Pvt Ltd, 11 Community Centre, Panchsheel Park, New Delhi–110 017, India
Penguin Group (NZ), cnr Airborne and Rosedale Roads, Albany, Auckland 1310, New Zealand
(a division of Pearson New Zealand Ltd)
Penguin Books (South Africa) (Pty) Ltd, 24 Sturdee Avenue, Rosebank, Johannesburg 2196, South Africa

Penguin Books Ltd, Registered Offices:
80 Strand, London WC2R 0RL, England

First published in the United States of America by Portfolio, a member of Penguin Group (USA) Inc. 2004
Published in Penguin Books 2006

10 9 8 7 6 5 4 3 2 1

Copyright © Barbara S. Peterson, 2004
All rights reserved

THE LIBRARY OF CONGRESS HAS CATALOGED THE HARDCOVER EDITION AS FOLLOWS:
Peterson, Barabara Sturken.
Blue streak : inside JetBlue, the upstart that rocked an industry /
Barbara S. Peterson
p. cm.
ISBN 1-59184-058-9 (hc.)
ISBN 1-59184-111-9 (pbk.)
1. JetBlue Airways—History.   2. Airlines—United States—History.   I. Title.
HE9803.J48P48   2004
3887.7'42'0973—dc22   2004053404

Printed in the United States of America
Designed by Jaye Zimet

acknowledgments

Blue Streak grew out of an article I wrote for *Condé Nast Traveler* and from numerous reporting assignments I have had since then as a contributing editor. For their encouragement and support, I thank Tom Wallace, Clive Irving, Kevin Doyle, Deborah Dunn, Krista Carothers, and Peter Frank, whose early enthusiasm for the material led me to consider a book in the first place.

Many friends and colleagues generously stepped forward at critical junctures with suggestions and support. Jeanne Martinet is a gifted editor and loyal friend who gave perceptive editorial advice when I needed it the most. Deborah Gaines, Bill McGee, Don Phillips, and Joe Brancatelli lent their expertise as writers and fellow travelers.

Richard Severo inspired me, as a teacher and a friend; the late Paul Grimes was generous with praise and support.

Louise Story, Johanna Piazza, Sam Rudykoff, and Mike Haney provided excellent research assistance, and Mike Denneny and Amy Mintzer gave expert editorial guidance. Lisa Pistorino was a godsend, cleaning up my drafts on short notice. I also wish to thank Barbara Lopez for her transcripts and Joshua Brown and Gigi Fresiello for guiding me through countless computer mishaps.

At JetBlue, and in the aviation world in general, so many lent their expertise and time that I apologize for the inevitable omissions in the following roster of helpers and enablers: Ellen Arcia, Carol Archer, Todd Burke, Amy Curtis-McIntyre, Gareth Edmondson-Jones, Jonathan Kriebel, Doreen Lawrence, Brian Manubay, Dean Melonas, Fiona Morrisson, Greg Trevor, Eric Tremblay, and Cathy Westrum; at JetBlue U, Lenka Brady, Jonathan Cillick, Katrien Ceragioli, Matt Kliff, Shaine Hobdy, Scott Robillard, and, above all, the entire class of 07–03. SH&E gave me access to its library and to its expertise. And thanks to Mark Greenberg for his wonderful photographs and good humor, and to Bryan Baldwin for helping track down elusive photos and clippings.

I never could have contemplated this book, much less completed it, without the unflagging efforts of my agent, Joni Evans, whose representational skills are exceeded only by her talents as an editor. To her, and to Jay Mandel for his insightful comments on the manuscript, I am truly indebted.

At Portfolio, Adrian Zackheim and Stephanie Land saw early on how to shape the story and were strong supporters of this project all along. Thanks also to Megan Casey, Will Weisser, and Allison Sweet.

My family was, as always, a constant source of encouragement: my sister, Marita Sturken, and brother-in-law, Dana Polan, my brother, Carl, and sister-in-law, Cheryl Anne Sturken, and my parents, Bob and Marie Sturken.

Above all, I could not have embarked on this book without the unconditional support of my husband, Bill Peterson, who was always there to read and critique drafts I dared show no one else, and who patiently withstood the inevitable dramas such a project inflicts on those closest to it. He and our daughters, Leigh and Moira, got me through it all with humor and affection.

contents

introduction
drinking the blue kool-aid

I am in the aft galley of a JetBlue airplane, thirty minutes into a flight from New York to Florida. Before me, a mass of humanity: 141 souls, lulled into a semicatatonic state by an equal number of tiny, flickering television screens. You can size up the crowd by the radiating images; this one is equal parts stock ticker and Scooby Doo. Jack, the crew member whom I am assisting, hands me a list of items to retrieve from the catering bin: We are ready to deliver that infusion of sugar and salt that will further numb our charges into forgetting where they are—in an aluminum tube, five miles above terra firma, hurtling through the air at 525 miles an hour.

First, an explanation: I'm here on a mission, a subversive one at that. Fresh from sitting in on a three-week JetBlue flight training course, I will try to muddle through a few simple chores and convince customers that I'm the real deal, a true convert to the JetBlue cause. I can't wear one of the airline's Prada knockoff uniforms lest I mislead anyone, but my dark-blue suit and my JETBLUE U badge from training will convey a bogus authority.

I am really here to get a backstage view of the "JetBlue experience," that intangible essence so many companies are chasing as if it were the secret formula for Coke. On its face, the notion that this could be anything special is absurd. We're on, after all, a coach flight on a narrowbody jet crammed with the usual cross section of bargain seekers, and lacking in hot meals and other supposed staples of in-flight comfort.

But the JetBlue experience is also defined by the absence of something else, the culture of discontent, that indifference bordering on hostility, which has created something akin to the Stockholm syndrome among fliers: You're almost suspicious when it's not there. One oft-heard customer query at JetBlue is: "What are you guys on?" Apparently air travelers are so inured to abuse that they can't believe it's possible to be nice without relying on copious amounts of controlled substances.

The training course, which mixed the required safety drills with a kind of benign brainwashing, is designed to banish such thoughts. Inside the company, it's called drinking the blue Kool-Aid, an expression with macabre origins for it refers to the mass suicide, via cyanide-laced punch, of hundreds of People's Temple followers in a South American jungle in 1978. It became an airline in-joke thanks to the disenchanted pilots of the defunct People Express, the fast-growing budget airline that had a wild ride in the early 1980s only to tank spectacularly before the decade was out. Now the catchphrase as well as some of People's communal culture have surfaced, minus the dark edge, at JetBlue.

It's tempting to think of JetBlue as a corporate version of a cult, and its improbable journey from start-up to major player is hard to explain without falling back on this well-worn metaphor. The cult comparison is also made more credible by the presence of a powerful personality in the form of David Neeleman, JetBlue's founder and CEO, whose profound influence is felt throughout the company. But Neeleman is no messianic leader; in person, he is plainspoken, direct, and with so little artifice that it has the effect of almost diminishing his achievement by making it appear so simple. He's fond of spouting aphorisms such as "You treat your people right, and they'll treat your customers right," which, again, is so self-evident that it seems remarkable so few of his competitors have grasped its import. Neeleman likes to tell the story of the time a Delta Air Lines flight attendant accused him, not entirely in jest, of "stealing all the *nice* passengers." No, they're the *smart* passengers, he retorted. "They know we'll treat them fair and give them a fair deal." Consistently delivering on that promise, as many would-be imitators have found, is maddeningly difficult to pull off.

That is what I am doing on Flight 27: attempting to deliver the experience as well as deconstruct it. But in deference to the very real possibility that I might embarrass myself as well as JetBlue, I'm traveling with an experienced in-flight supervisor, Jonathan Kriebel, who flies frequently to observe how attendants are upholding the credo. Kriebel is an ideal travel companion; he's kind and unflappable, politely fielding oddball requests and complaints with a sangfroid he's honed from flying for twenty-five years with airlines like TWA and US Airways. Awaiting boarding, he had shared war stories; he had been through it all—layoffs, strikes, and countless flights from hell—before finally landing at United Airlines in a management post in the mid-1990s. On the afternoon of September 11, 2001, he was on vacation in Israel with his wife and infant son when he got word that two of his employer's planes had been turned into guided missiles by terrorists. By the time he arrived back in the States, his job had been eliminated. After nearly a year, he started over again at JetBlue, taking the same training course I just had.

It's a story I hear often in my research: Many of those charged with delivering the JetBlue buzz are veterans of the very companies that have given air service a bad name. Indeed, when JetBlue first came on the scene, Neeleman had imagined that much of his in-flight crew would come from different fields, the thinking being that those coming from other airlines would be too jaded. The first recruits were a sitcom-worthy group, comprised of a sixty-year-old retired New York City fire-fighter, a nightclub singer, and a mortician. By the time I joined my class (about the fortieth since the airline started), the trainees were about evenly divided between laid-off airline employees and retreads from other fields, all of whom had to compete with many others like them-selves. In one recent year, JetBlue received 130,000 applications for 2,000 positions; the odds of snagging a job offer today are 80 to 1.

I surely wouldn't make the cut for my instinct that morning had been to reach for the Xanax when I first spied the motley parade of pas-sengers I would help serve that day. I had picked what I thought would surely be a slow flight, a Tuesday afternoon two weeks before the De-cember holiday crush, forgetting that this is an airline where flights are so full that employees often can't use their free travel passes. We were al-ready twenty minutes behind schedule, the plane having arrived late from Rochester. There were 14 travelers in wheelchairs (although that was nothing compared with the flight we heard about in training in which 43 of the 160 passengers were wheelchair bound). A gaggle of others marched down the jetway hauling SUV-sized carry-ons; it was, to my eyes, a flight from hell.

I have my JetBlue manual with me, a souvenir from flight school, so I flip to the chapter on service, page 10. "Think in terms of difficult situations, not difficult people," it exhorts hopefully. It's no accident that it does not refer to "passengers": That word has been banished from the JetBlue lexicon and an employee would be fined a dollar for forgetting that "customer" is the preferred term. The lingua franca that accompa-nies the cause, confirming that everyone here *is* different, sometimes gets a bit much: All employees are "crew members," supervisors are "in-flight support specialists," and so on. But David Neeleman, who speaks to every new class of flight attendants, does believe these semantic exercises make a larger point:

"A 'passenger' is somebody who is just a piece of baggage. I think there are actually people who work for airlines who get up in the morning and say, 'If we could just do without those annoying passengers at the airport, my job would be a whole heck of a lot easier. Hey, if we could fly empty it would be even better.'"

It's all part of the process of distancing ourselves from what has come before; there are some within JetBlue who think the company shouldn't even call itself an airline.

And so, with this in mind, for the two and a half hours we are in the air, I dutifully get with the program, doing my bit to add to the bottom line. In a sense, this single flight is, in microcosm, the whole Jet-Blue formula at work: a process that has been so fine-tuned that each component becomes a small cog in the profit-making machine.

During flight training, we learn, for example, that the fact we can help customers stow their carry-ons in the overhead bins, which work rules prohibit at most other airlines, can shave as much as ten minutes off the boarding time. We study the behavior of "spinners," that's airline parlance for that subspecies of traveler who gets on a plane and is so flummoxed by where to put his gear that he simply spins around, in place, causing a bottleneck that can delay not just one flight but ripple through the system all day long. Treat that one symptom and your punctuality goes up, we are told.

Then there's the drink service drill: First off, we serve snacks, not meals, which is an enormous cost saving, and we don't serve off rolling carts, which clog the aisle and slow down the service. Instead, when we hit an altitude of 10,000 feet, we're out taking drink orders. That saves time, eases claustrophobia. And it prevents accidents: The massive serving carts used by other airlines are one of the biggest causes of on-the-job injury to flight attendants.

Then there are those seat-back TV screens. When JetBlue first started, a debate was still raging over whether to charge customers for using them. One of the planes had working TVs, the other did not. Company insiders quickly learned they could tell one from the other just by looking at the faces of customers as they got off the plane; the functioning one got nicknamed "the happy plane," and company managers who track such things noted that lavatory use "went way down" when the TVs were switched on. The talk of a fee was dropped.

It is with this mix of couch potato comforts and solicitous service that JetBlue has upended an industry.

Flight 27 was, in effect, the end of a journey that for me had begun nearly five years earlier in mid-1999, when I first interviewed David Neeleman and his closest associate, president Dave Barger, for an article I was writing on new airlines. At that point they had little more than a paper airline: They had no planes, no name, and no license to fly. Their long-shot notion of starting a new airline that would combine low fares with high style had yet to be discovered by the arbiters of cool. In fact, their plan was on its face so outlandish that it drew outright derision from the airline establishment, whose members pointed out that of the fifty-eight jet airlines that had started up after the 1978 deregulation of the airlines, all had gone bust except one, Midwest Express (American West is still operating but only after going into, and emerging from, bankruptcy). But this was the nineties, and capital was being flung at all sorts of ephemeral concepts. By the time Neeleman announced his plans for a new airline in early 1999, he had raised more than $100 million for his new venture by shrewdly pointing out that the big airlines, which at that time were earning profits in the hundreds of millions, were ripe for a challenge.

Five years later, those same airlines had become a collective basket case, racking up losses of twenty billion dollars since the year 2000. By mid-2004, JetBlue had made money in more than sixteen consecutive quarters. At the end of 2003, it was also one of the most on-time airlines in the country and the most full—two achievements that rarely come in tandem.

There are even predictions that the big airlines that so dominated the business in the later 1990s will go the way of the dinosaurs. Warren Buffett once joked that capitalism would have been better served if someone had shot down the Wright Brothers at Kitty Hawk a century ago, so difficult is it to make money in the business. The drawbacks are considerable: Airlines have high fixed costs (a scheduled flight, after all, has to take off whether it's full or empty), enormous expenses such as jet fuel that can't be controlled, and an extreme vulnerability to the ups and downs of the economic cycle. The airlines have lost a hundred thousand jobs in the past two and half years, and not all of the devastation is attributable to the attacks of September 11; the airlines were already weakened by the recession. And it has always been thus: It is a business whose margins are so razor thin that a couple of passengers on each plane can spell the difference between profit and loss and where a one-cent rise in the price of jet fuel can cost the industry an added $180 million a year.

So, why is it, then, that so many people have plunged into this insane environment but only a handful—notably Neeleman and Southwest Airlines chief Herb Kelleher—have gotten it right?

The answer may lie in the particulars of Flight 27.

Forty minutes before we are to begin our descent, it is my turn to go out in the aisle, unchaperoned, for the critical task of picking up garbage, er, "service items." (I have memorized the phraseology: One must say, "Can I take that for you?" and not "Would you give me that trash?") This is more essential than it sounds because once we arrive in Fort Myers we're going to try to "turn" the plane in twenty minutes, about half the time it would normally take to unload the plane and fill it back up again. So the faster I can scoop up snot rags and junk food wrappers, the faster we'll be on our way, back to New York City, then back to Rochester for yet another quick turnaround. A typical JetBlue plane will perform this quadrille six or seven times in one day. You've seen this routine on other airlines, but JetBlue's crews attack this chore with an uncommon zeal—we're also responsible for cleaning up after the travelers exit and have a real incentive to get as much of this out of the way before landing.

So I grab a bag and start marching. It goes slowly: I chat with some customers, heeding the warning (manual, page 11) to avoid "controversy" and discussions of company business. It's not easy: One woman beckons me over to opine that the news she's watching on the CNN channel is too "biased," asking why we don't show Fox News instead. We're getting perilously close to politics here, but before I say anything, a man in a black jogging suit and sunglasses blindsides me with a question about the gyrating price of JetBlue stock. He is an investment banker and is eager to tell me that he once met David Neeleman at a financial conference, a fact he confides in reverent tones one might reserve for an account of a papal audience.

Thirty years before, flight attendants were actually encouraged to converse with their customers in flight; some were even given conversational openers, so important was it to airline managements. Something like this—minus the flirtatious overtones of the past—is now happening at JetBlue. In training, we were told that we don't process people; if we have time, even in the post–September 11 climate of suspicion, we can spend it getting to know the people aboard. It is Neeleman's great insight to seize on these modest gestures to draw a stark contrast between his way of doing things and his rivals'.

So here on Flight 27, I'm getting to know the man sitting in seat 13C. He'd mentioned he'd stockpiled one million miles in his American Airlines frequent flier account. He had no intention of using them. "I'm never flying American again," he said, without elaboration. His wife, a sleek, well-dressed blonde who would be at home in any airline's first class, grimaced in agreement. Apparently they'd withstood a series of horrors that had sent them firmly to the JetBlue camp.

It is not oversimplifying matters to say that the Mr. Million Miler's allegiance to an upstart airline is one of the biggest threats to the existing airline order that the industry has ever seen. Just five years ago, fewer than 10 percent of the air travelers in the United States flew on a budget airline, and of those—90 percent were carried by one airline, Southwest. In 2004, fully 30 percent of all passengers were flying on a low-fare airline— and JetBlue, in just four years, is ranked among the top ten airlines in the country.

By 2005, JetBlue will be growing to the point where it expects to add seven to ten employees each day, which means that each month it will add the same number of people that made up its entire payroll on the day it began operating. In short, it's adding the equivalent of a small airline every few weeks. And it will do so without resorting to a merger or acquisition, which is exactly the strategy that so roiled the industry during the 1980s and, it can be argued, is still giving agita to consumers today. And as I write, a new class of airline aspirants is taking flight around the world. And yes, like countless others before them, they will attempt to copy the spirit of a unique group of people engaged in a singular enterprise. Only this time it is not necessarily Southwest Airlines, the mother of all low-fare upstarts, that they are seeking to emulate.

This book, then, is the story of how a small band of believers took on an establishment and beat the sizable odds against them, not only in one of the world's toughest businesses but also in one of the worst periods in that business's history. This is not an authorized account but the outgrowth of research and on-scene reporting that began with that first story I wrote, which appeared in *Condé Nast Traveler* two months before JetBlue began flying. My original idea had been to follow several airline start-ups, hedging my bets in case one of them flamed out prematurely. Sure enough, one other newcomer I followed, an all-first-class airline out of Texas called Legend, didn't make it past its first year. My editors at the magazine were so skeptical about the premise of the article that the headline read: BUT WILL IT FLY? I shared the general pessimism. "The odds that any of them will be flying five years from now . . . are slim," I wrote.

I continued to follow Neeleman and company, as they repeatedly made fools of the naysayers. Ultimately, I interviewed more than seventy-five people involved with the JetBlue story, as well as many others outside the company—in the federal government, at airports, and at some of the company's competitors. Right before September 11, 2001, I'd been taking flight training classes at JetBlue for a story on air rage that I was researching for my magazine that was spiked, for obvious reasons, right after the terror attacks. But it was clear this aspect of the airline was so integral to the story that I eventually took the entire three-week course.

It may be premature to declare with certainty that JetBlue will be an enduring success, and, in fact, David Neeleman was initially opposed to anyone's writing a book, saying that it is far too early in the story to write the definitive account. While the story is not over, it has ripened to the point where it can be told. JetBlue is about to enter its fifth year of existence, and for an airline, that marks a coming of age: It's when the Federal Aviation Administration regards an upstart as mature enough to be removed from the safety watch list that began after the fatal ValuJet crash in 1996. JetBlue is the first postderegulation airline to reach major airline status in so short a time; Southwest Airlines' growth rate, by contrast, was glacial. As the company begins another chapter, its planes will age, as will its workforce; with its increasingly high profile will come increasing scrutiny, for no other reason than that is the inevitable side effect of longevity. For that reason, it is a good time to assess how it got to a place where one can even speculate, with confidence, about its next five years.

Someday, perhaps, Neeleman will write the definitive memoir, but what I set out to do was something else—to depict that weird, intoxicating rush that comes with seeing your idea come to fruition and to chronicle not only the giddy start-up phase but the more perilous process of making it stick. JetBlue may now be an unassailable brand, in a business where brand loyalty long ago ceased to exist, but even if it was to disappear tomorrow, it has already wrought far-reaching changes in the airlines and beyond. Neeleman showed people that the notion of figuring out what your customers need, and giving it to them, is possible, even in a business that rivals the IRS for its perceived indifference to same.

And so when I finally return to the galley with a bulging sack of refuse and some drink orders to fill, Jonathan nods approvingly. I flush with pride, and then with embarrassment, because somehow along the way, I apparently bought into the notion that my trash-collecting talent was a tiny, but vital factor in the difference between profit and loss that day.

I'd done it. I'd drunk the Kool-Aid.

one
flying home

At around 6:30 on the evening of November 17, 2000, David Neeleman headed down the concourse at Salt Lake City Airport to await an incoming flight. He appeared oblivious to the odd looks he was drawing from passersby, who no doubt were riveted by the sight of a strikingly attractive man shuffling awkwardly in a pair of bedroom slippers and a set of baggy blue pajamas, from which a sales tag still dangled. Like everything else he had done since arising at 5:00 A.M., his last-minute purchase of this costume had a precise place in that day's order of business. In a few hours, he would host a "slumber party" at a departure gate to usher in a new red-eye flight, an overnight trip on which no real slumber would be possible as it would take only four hours to get to New York. Aside from the profits it would rake in—for these bare-bones runs are the proverbial gravy in the airline business—it would give him a small measure of personal satisfaction. If he could just get through the next few hours, the hundreds of people who worked for him in Salt Lake would no longer have to fly into their hometown on an airline other than their own.

JetBlue Airways had been in business for nine months, and it was doing nicely for an airline with ten planes, selling some $1 million worth of tickets every day. Neeleman had been maintaining the sort of peripatetic routine that was closer to that of a politician on the campaign trail, "opening" a new city every few weeks. That meant arriving in a new place, getting to know the local pooh-bahs, and shuttling between newspapers and television stations, repeating the now-familiar outlines of his life: his early failures, his later successes with small airlines in Utah and Canada, and how he had moved thousands of miles away to create the hottest new airline in memory, all before he turned forty. Here, the story was the hometown angle and it was infused with respect for his family: Neeleman's father was a prominent media executive; his uncle Stan Neeleman was a well-known lawyer and professor; their roots in Utah went back more than a hundred years.

Neeleman wasn't reveling in any of this. He was, instead, agitated, barely able to conceal it as he made his rounds in this friendly territory. He'd woken up that morning to find out that his reservations computers had crashed and that the million or so dollars they should have been raking in that day were, by early afternoon, roughly zero. Between his rounds to talk to his staff and the deferential sit-downs with the press, he'd been on the line to the computer programmers, trying to sort it out. There was another irritant here: The reservations company was one that he himself had founded in the early 1990s to capitalize on one of his innovations—the paperless airline ticket.

Later in the day, while rushing off to Old Navy to pick up the pajamas he suddenly realized he was lacking, he was even joking to his colleagues that the "curse of inaugurals" would assert itself in some particularly obnoxious way. In his experience, something inevitably went wrong when the cameras were rolling. Just a few weeks earlier as Neeleman cracked a bottle of Champagne over his newest plane at West Palm Beach, a mechanic operating a moving staircase became distracted and crashed into the plane in full view of the assembled television crews and civic leaders, damaging the plane as well as the mood.

Back at the terminal, his cell phone rang, and, almost as if summoned by his fears, it was the bad news he had been awaiting: The incoming plane, which should have been in the air long ago, was still sitting on the ground at Kennedy Airport in New York. One of his executives who was to travel on the flight from New York explained that JetBlue had been sabotaged by its policy of not stranding passengers like the other airlines. They had held the plane for six customers connecting from a late flight from Buffalo and then had lost their place in the take-off queue.

"Boy, we really screwed up," Neeleman said. He wasn't angry, his tone was flat, but the message was one of profound disappointment. "We should have put the people up for the night. Now we've really blown it."

He started laughing, in a punchy, adolescent sort of way, a tribute to the futility of the situation. "We should have put them on Delta; in first class!"

There was a mordant side to his crack: Putting them on Delta, for Neeleman, was the equivalent of sending them to the enemy camp. Delta Air Lines was the biggest airline in Salt Lake City and it had been, seemingly, a constant presence in Neeleman's career as an airline executive, and hardly a positive one. Back when he had started up his first small budget airline, Delta had come after his company, and Neeleman became convinced it was using underhanded means to drive him out of business. He'd even gone to Washington to complain, testifying before a special presidential commission on airline competition. The Justice Department had sent investigators to look into the charges, which became moot when David sold his airline to Southwest Airlines.

Now he had other things to worry about. The local television crews were not going to hang around waiting for the first JetBlue plane to touch down, and they were already decamping for more fruitful pursuits, a fire, a highway crash. Even worse, Neeleman's parents were flying back from a trip to Mexico City and planned to join the party. Surely the vision of their son's standing there to greet them in his jammies was going to be even more bizarre if his plane had gone AWOL.

He wandered off to the departure lounge, where a television screen above beamed CNN, showing the 24/7 news story of the day: the Florida recount in the presidential election. Neeleman had spent much of the day talking about the effects that the final outcome might have on his company as he made the rounds with local newspapers. His airline had been, in a sense, a special project of Bill Clinton's Transportation Department, which had adopted JetBlue as a poster child for its efforts to inject some competition into the airlines. Neeleman had expected that the team that had midwifed his upstart airline would remain in place. Now it looked like he'd be spending a lot of the next few months in Washington.

It was one of those times that called into question what had lured him to a business he himself had once dismissed as a "stupid." Whatever it was that propelled him, it had begun just a few miles away from where he was now sitting.

David Neeleman was born in São Paulo, Brazil, on October 16, 1959, but his roots in Utah stretched back to the mid-nineteenth century. On his mother's side, he is seventh-generation Mormon. One of his forebears, Sally Hulett, was among the original pioneers who trekked west in the beginning of the Mormon migration to Utah in the 1850s. The Neelemans, Dutch immigrants, settled in the West many decades later. Gary Neeleman, David's father, had a traditional Mormon upbringing and went to Brazil as a teenage missionary, fulfilling the expected stint of volunteer service for the church. Less predictably, however, he soon returned to South America with his wife, Rose, to become a reporter for United Press International, rising in a few years to become bureau chief in São Paulo. David was the second child of what would eventually be seven children; when he was five, his parents decided that Utah might be a better place to raise their growing family. A reporter's salary did not go as far in the States as it had in Brazil, where the family had lived a comfortable expatriate life, and a few years later, Gary moved from journalism to the business side, taking a sales job with UPI and, later, with the Los Angeles Times Syndicate.

Neeleman has recalled his childhood as contented, amid a large close-knit family. He spent summers at his grandfather's ten-thousand-acre ranch on the edge of Zion National Park in southwestern Utah, and occasionally the family would pile into a station wagon, driving across the desert to visit another branch of the family in Southern California. Later, he would use this family ritual to make a point: We couldn't afford to fly back then, he said, so we had to drive this barren, sun-baked stretch of highway for ten hours instead.

As a child, David was eager to please, his family recalled, always volunteering to take out the garbage and perform chores no one else wanted to do. The restlessness and impatience that would become defining traits were evident early on. Gary Neeleman has said that even such prosaic childhood pastimes as fishing were challenging for David, who would get bored or distracted after a couple of minutes. This was well before the day when children would be subject to the diagnosis du jour, and David's oddities didn't strike anyone as abnormal. It would be years before he confirmed that he had attention deficit disorder, but his schoolwork suffered noticeably, and his teachers suggested that he repeat third grade. His parents refused to keep him back, but by fourth grade, he still wasn't reading. Gary Neeleman sought advice from a teacher, who gave him a dubious assessment of their son's prospects: He was very bright but so unpredictable that his chances of success were iffy unless he hired a very competent assistant.

One person who did see some promise in David was his paternal grandfather, Johnny Neeleman, a local entrepreneur who owned several local restaurants and convenience stores. The son of the first Neeleman to emigrate frrom Holland, Johnny had quit school in ninth grade and delivered loaves of bread during the Depression, and eventually scraped together enough money to form his own modest chain of mom and pop coffee shops and markets, which bore names like the Chubby Lunch and the Pine Cone café. His main operation was the Miniature Market in downtown Salt Lake City, and when David turned nine, he started his first job there, one of only two in his life, he said, where someone else paid him a salary. He was too small to reach the cash register to check people out, so his grandfather put a milk crate behind the counter, and David would stand there for hours, discovering a facility with numbers that his teachers had missed. He stocked shelves, swept floors, and learned the arcana of pricing your product above costs, but not so much so that you risked a competitor coming in to undercut you. His grandfather also spoke often about cultivating customer loyalty, and he developed a minor cult following for his overstuffed sandwiches and rich desserts. "He wanted to please everyone," David said, recalling that if a customer asked for something they didn't stock, then Johnny would distract them with a doughnut and coffee while David or someone else would race through the back of the store to the Safeway market down the street to pick up the missing item.

By high school, however, David had slipped far behind his peers academically; while he managed to graduate on time, he entered the University of Utah in 1978 with serious self-doubts. "I couldn't write well; I couldn't sit down and read a whole book. I thought, 'How am I ever going to be successful in anything if I can't read and write?'" But he now had a respectable alternative: At age nineteen he headed to Brazil, as his father had, for two years of missionary work for the church, which is expected of most Mormon men. Unlike most of the other missionaries, David possessed a Brazilian passport and a decent grasp of Portuguese, and he moved quickly into a more active role in the church's growing organization in the country. After living in the state Espírito Santo, north of Rio, he was told that as a dual citizenship holder he had to report for military service in the country. It was understood that he would not have to serve, and he was soon made a zone leader, with added responsibility, and then was made assistant to the head of the Mormon mission for the country, which required him to move to São Paulo. While he was profoundly disturbed by the poverty he found, he was moved, he said, by the generosity and dignity of those he met. And David exceeded in his tour beyond anyone's expectations. He baptized two hundred converts, which is an unusually high number for one of these volunteers, whose tallies normally run in the single digits. He returned to Utah with a surfeit of the self-confidence that had eluded him during his school years. "It was the first thing in my life that I really excelled at," he recalled later. "I had not succeeded at school; I had not succeeded at sports and it gave me a success that I had not experienced before. I think back on those people who lived in abject poverty, and how their lives changed and how my life changed." David would continue to have a bond with the country of his birth, and his father was so involved with charitable work there that he would become known around Salt Lake as the honorary consul of Brazil.

Before departing for South America, David had begun seeing Vicki Vranes, a tall, dark-haired beauty who was the sister of a college friend. They kept up an intense correspondence during his absence and married soon after he returned in 1980. Their first child, Ashley, was born the following year and by the time he was twenty-two he had another baby on the way.

He went back to studying accounting at college but, as anyone who knew him could have predicted, he was soon bored. If there was a precise moment that David's airline career began, it was likely a day in 1982 when he began seriously looking at the potential of the airlines, which were just then undergoing the first convulsions of the deregulated era. Gary Neeleman remembered that he was sitting in his office when "David called and said he'd just read a piece in the *Wall Street Journal* saying that deregulation of the airline business presented a lot of opportunity." Around that time the business press was reporting extensively on how the old order was shifting. Already some major airlines were on life support, having been ill prepared for the end of forty years of economic regulation, and Braniff had shut down, becoming the first high-profile casualty. However, the disruptions were also an opportunity for smaller regional airlines such as Southwest, and to newcomers such as Midway Airlines in Chicago, which were run more efficiently, had lower costs, and could essentially undercut the major airlines and still turn a nice profit.

"I remember David telling me, 'Dad, I think we should get into the airline business,'" Gary recalled. "To which I responded, 'How on earth do you think we could do that? Airplanes cost money.'"

But David wasn't thinking of buying airplanes, at least not initially. Both men do recall that they sat down to lunch soon after this conversation and talked about how to get into the travel business, not via the scheduled airlines but through less capital intensive ventures, such as packaging tours.

One day, a college classmate mentioned offhandedly that she knew someone who had bought four hotels in Hawaii and had converted them into condominiums. The country was in a recession, however, and the man was having trouble selling them. David saw an opportunity. He would rent out the condos for short stays for customers craving a quick cheap escape. So he got on the phone to the owner and made a pitch: He would pay him his maintenance fee, about $100 a week, for each empty unit. Then he could mark up the price and collect the difference. He scraped together $100 and ran an ad in the paper that said "$50 a night for your condo in Hawaii!" The response, he recalled, was "incredible." "People said, 'Wow, what a great deal,'" and it was equally so for Neeleman: He cleared $250 on each weekly rental. School suddenly seemed even less interesting. "I started doing this practically all day and started making $500 a day and then $1,000 a day. And here I am in college."

The nascent venture took off, but there was a problem: Clients often had trouble getting good air fares to Honolulu out of Salt Lake on scheduled airlines. Neeleman reasoned he could do even better by buying airline tickets from a charter or budget airline, packaging the whole vacation under one price. He checked out a few lines, found the cheapest one, Hawaii Express, also known as the Big Pineapple. It flew a single 747 between Los Angeles and Honolulu. Neeleman's clients had to make the long drive to LA themselves, but "they'd do it," he said, "because we gave them such a good deal." To handle the air tickets, he formed a travel company, Independent Flight Services, and christened himself president. He had a modest family car at the time, but a company president needed something more distinguished, he thought, so he splurged on a BMW sedan. He also dropped out of college in his junior year because by then he was too busy running the business, which had twenty employees and eight million dollars a year in sales.

In late 1983, it all came apart, with no apparent warning. Hawaii Express went bankrupt and suddenly ceased flying, taking with it a substantial amount of deposits from Neeleman's agency, which had bought blocks of seats in advance to resell as part of his packages. Neeleman, in turn, had no money left to refund his customers' deposits. He had no choice but to file for bankruptcy.

"And I had one hundred fifty thousand dollars in the bank and no debts, and if I had just had a few hundred thousand dollars more I could have saved the company. We were about to sign with a charter airline to fly directly to Hawaii from Salt Lake, and we wouldn't have had to go through this . . . if we could have just hung on a little longer." The realization that he could have made it with a rather modest cash cushion made a lasting impression.

"I was devastated," he said. "Here I was, twenty-four years old, driving a Beemer, which I've never driven since because I learned my lesson. I had a house, a wife, and two kids. And I went from up to down just like that; I lost everything overnight."

Humbled, he went back to stocking shelves and manning the cash register at his grandfather's grocery store. That didn't strike his family as an appropriate career path, so David's uncle Stan contacted a few of his well-connected friends. One of them was June Morris, the owner of the largest travel agency in Utah. "Stan called me, and he's a very old friend, and our family attorney, and he said 'Look, I've got this nephew who is very smart, and he's had a really bad break here, and can you do anything for him?' I said sure I'll call him. Actually, I knew about him already. I'd been watching what he was doing and he was even cutting into some of my business, so I was certainly aware of him. And I thought he was a very nice, very capable young man."

When she called, however, David turned her down flat; and both agree that he did so particularly ungraciously. "I never want to work in travel ever again," he told Morris. "I hate that business, it's such a stupid business." Morris couldn't change his mind, and so she blurted out an impulsive offer that was more an act of charity: He could park himself at her office for six months, and she'd pay him a salary, no matter what he chose to do.

June Morris was more than a kind family friend; she was a local business leader. As a young divorcée trying to support a child, she'd gone to work as a sales assistant in a travel agency and ended up as CEO of her own $50 million-a-year business. She was the sort of person who'd invite employees to tea and deliver birthday gifts personally to their desks. Michael Lazarus, a venture capitalist from San Francisco who was an early investor in Morris Air, described her as "a cross between Mary Kay and Aunt Bee." June and her second husband, Mitch, who worked with her, took a liking to David. "He was like a son to me," she would often say, although her own son by her first marriage, Richard Frendt, also worked in a senior level job at her agency. Apparently Frendt did not object to working alongside a surrogate son, and Neeleman was soon back at what he said he would never do—selling package tours through an arm of the agency that would soon become known as Morris Air. It was basically the same principle as his Hawaii gig except that it was now under the umbrella of a far more established company. To lessen the risk to the core business, however, they incorporated it separately. David was able to save some money and put in $10,000. In two years, the division was handling thousands of customers a year and his stake was worth $239,000. Neeleman was the second largest shareholder in the fledgling company, and he was constantly searching for ways to expand its reach. June Morris was by all accounts a benevolent boss who gave Neeleman a free rein. Yet, mindful of his earlier fiasco, he always worried about whether the company had adequate capital.

Neeleman didn't fit the usual profile of an aspiring airline chieftain; he wasn't a member of the "scarf and goggles" crowd, the self-styled flyboys whose adolescent fascination with flying carried them into the more pragmatic pursuit of making it work as a business. Given his flealike attention span, flying lessons were out of the question. "It was really this 'deregulation thing' that he was very excited about," his father said. What appealed to the salesman in him were all the potential customers he imagined out there, people like the Neeleman clan, who drove rather than pay the extortionate fares charged before deregulation.

Those early years spent behind the counter at the Miniature Market were also an influence. "He thinks like the customer," said Michael Lazarus. "He had an understanding of what it takes to run a service business." And he sensed what economists had long been arguing: An airline is actually more akin to a supermarket than the uninitiated might imagine. It all goes back to the basic principle that you have to fly the plane on a published schedule, no matter how many seats are filled. Thus, an empty seat on a flight is that most perishable of commodities: Once the plane takes off, the opportunity to sell that seat—at any price—is forever lost. Neeleman would find ways to stem the spoilage.

His sales pitches sometimes went comically overboard and he was known to hawk honeymoon packages at wedding receptions he attended. But in most other ways he was conservative. The airline began slowly, with a few charter flights to the usual tourist haunts of Hawaii and Mexico, with a couple of leased airplanes. Soon it became clear that there was a bigger market out there for people who didn't have an economical way to fly to places like San Francisco or Seattle. Salt Lake City, as Neeleman had observed, had been missing out on the supposed low-fare revolution; start-ups like People Express were concentrated mainly in the East. It was not a stretch to think that Neeleman, with a few extra planes, could do something about it.

Tom Kelly, a partner of Stan Neeleman's, started doing legal work for Morris Air in 1984, then became full-time general counsel in 1990. Kelly was close in age to Neeleman, but was a stark contrast in temperament. A graduate of Harvard Law School, where he edited the *Law*

Review, he was as cautious as Neeleman was impulsive, and soon became a sober-minded sounding board for his new colleague. By the late 1980s, Neeleman was itching to branch into less familiar turf, the sorts of markets that were normally reserved for the big airlines. "If you want to know where the whole idea of JetBlue really got started, it was with our flights between Salt Lake and Los Angeles," around that time, said Kelly. That was a route Neeleman had studied closely ever since his driving vacations with his parents, and he knew well that the air fares charged were way out of proportion to the distance of the trip. Eventually, Los Angeles became Morris's biggest market. Neeleman arranged for a plane to fly a couple of daily round-trips, and undercut the other airlines by about 70 percent. The other airlines soon matched Morris on price. The "walk up," or undiscounted fare, which had been $600 one way before Morris arrived, plummeted to $118.

Soon, Morris Air had more than one thousand employees and was flying to a dozen cities in the West, but it was still officially defined as a public charter. In effect, it was a virtual airline; it leased its planes and crews from various airline leasing companies, which bore the ultimate responsibility for making sure the planes were airworthy and met the rigorous standards of the Federal Aviation Administration. That had advantages: It spared Morris the substantial expense of having to acquire its own fleet and obtaining a license from the FAA. The main drawback was the lack of flexibility in dealing with customers. A public charter was a curious creature: It was created by regulators in the mid-seventies to encourage some backdoor price competition in the then tightly regulated airlines. But precisely because they lacked a tangible infrastructure, public charters had to comply with lots of strict rules on handling passengers' moneys; they couldn't accept credit card payments and had to keep all funds segregated in escrow accounts. Customers were even supposed to sign a written contract before any money changed hands. These formalities were not a burden for a niche operator, but Morris was getting big enough to draw attention from unexpected quarters. Some of Morris's ads failed to mention prominently their charter status; a minor distinction to a customer, perhaps, but a major infraction in the eyes of regulators. Federal authorities were tipped off by an annoyed official at Alaska Airlines, which resented Morris's expansion into its home turf of Seattle and Anchorage.

Neeleman had, technically, violated federal rules. But the damage to consumers was negligible, he argued; in fact, it stemmed from the company's desire to make things easier for its customers. Consumers were hardly likely to complain about a lack of red tape—indeed, none had—and Neeleman thought this looked more like a case of a jealous competitor setting the dogs on them over a minor technicality.

The bureaucrats in Washington ultimately agreed. Neeleman and Tom Kelly had already decided it was time to formalize the airline's status, and so a compromise was reached: The Transportation Department slapped them with a two-hundred-thousand-dollar fine for the infractions but suspended half of it in exchange for the company's cleaning up its act and moving ahead with the process of getting a real airline license. In December 1992, it was granted a certificate that gave it the right to fly as a scheduled airline anywhere in the country.

It was not the big leagues but now they were the genuine article, a bona fide airline. June Morris had made history as the first female founder of a jet-service airline, and Neeleman's title of company president actually carried some clout. Neeleman could see the day when it could be, say, a smaller version of Southwest Airlines. The Dallas discounter was something of an obsession of his: It was widely admired as one of the best run and profitable airlines to flourish under deregulation. Indeed, as People Express and other budget champs had flamed out in the mid-1980s, Southwest had grown into one of the ten largest airlines in the country. It was also propelled by the outrageous antics of its chain-smoking, bourbon-swigging chief executive, Herb Kelleher, who culti-vated an outlaw image by riding a Harley and dressing up in Elvis costumes at company events. Neeleman wasn't about to imitate that side of Southwest's success, but he set about copying its formula, decid-ing on the Boeing 737, an efficient 130- to 180-passsenger plane that is still regarded as the workhorse of the industry and is the only jet South-west flies. He slavishly copied Southwest's trademark features, down to its signature plastic color-coded boarding passes, which are reusable; its peanuts-only cuisine; and its enviably swift turnarounds, in which the crews manage to offload an arriving plane, clean and refuel it, and take off again with a new payload in a mere twenty minutes.

Neeleman's aversion to paperwork, which might have contributed to the problems in Washington, was also prompting him to innovate, and it would help usher in one of the most far-reaching changes in the way airlines do business: electronic ticketing. One day soon after they got their license, Neeleman heard someone musing about "Why can't we be more like a hotel, where you just show up with your confirmation number and get your room? Why go through all this ticketing nonsense?" Neeleman picked up on the thought: Why *couldn't* an airline simply take reservations and charge people's credit cards, and when they got to the airport, they'd get their boarding pass? If he had asked the question at a large airline at the time, he would have likely been dismissed as deranged. The airline distribution system had evolved over forty years and was de-signed to ensure that travel agents, who then booked around 85 percent of all airline tickets, could act as middlemen. That allowed agents to collect payments from their customers any way they wanted and remit the moneys to the airlines through a complex network of regional banks that acted like clearinghouses, so that airlines often got paid weeks after the ticket was reserved. But it made sense; it allowed airlines to sell their product through thousands of outlets without having to staff them.

Neeleman figured that customers flying on $49 fares to Seattle didn't necessarily need to deal with a travel agent; they could deal directly with the airline for such a simple transaction. So he put a couple of technically adept colleagues on the case, and they came up with a way that would allow someone who paid in advance with a credit card to appear at the airport, identify himself, and get on the plane. There was another important advantage: Morris got paid right away—it didn't have to wait for weeks. Neeleman wasn't the only one in the airlines who saw the advantages; ValuJet, a new discount line just starting up on the East Coast, was considering experimenting with electronic tickets as the rush to automate was spreading to everything from banks to grocery stores. But Morris had Neeleman as its indefatigable pitchman, and he took it on himself to spread the save-the-forests gospel. "This was heresy at the time," said Frankie Littleford, who was then running the airline's reservations department.

David was delighted with the results of his experiment, but, as Tom Kelly relates, he also saw a negative side, one that bothered him personally. He sensed that if electronic ticketing ultimately caught on in the industry and encouraged customers to buy tickets directly from airlines, it could wipe out a lot of travel agencies. The major airlines, however, sneered at Neeleman's innovation, seemingly oblivious to the fact that they stood to benefit far more than Morris would, potentially saving hundreds of millions of dollars in expenses. "Our customers will never go for this; they want to have something to hold in their hand," a spokesman for the airlines trade organization, the Air Transport Association in Washington, was quoted as saying. The big lines' reticence was understandable; a five-billion-dollar-a-year behemoth couldn't change its ways so easily. This was one of the earliest cases where Neeleman saw clearly how he could exploit his small size and experiment with ideas it would take the big guys years to copy. Morris, by 1992, had the lowest costs in the entire airline industry—around six cents for every mile a passenger flew. Delta's was more like thirteen cents.

One less salutary result of Morris's gaining legitimacy as an airline was that its more established rivals suddenly stood up and paid close attention to the interloper. In a strange vestige of the ham-handed regulation that had governed the airlines for forty years, Neeleman now found he had to report reams of data on his operations to the federal government every month, including how many tickets he sold and how many passengers were carried on which flights, information that could prove very useful to a competitor. That wasn't the only place where airlines had to divulge publicly the kinds of details on their business that in many other industries would be considered highly confidential. Any airline that participated in the airlines' clearinghouse for ticket sales could learn which travel agencies were giving your rivals the most business by examining the sales reports that retail agents processed. In June 1993, this obscure aspect of the airline business became the center of an unsavory attempt to undercut Neeleman by his counterparts at the airline giant across town.

It all began when David Neeleman and June Morris started hearing rumors of some arm-twisting by Delta of agents who were deemed too friendly to the upstart airline. They soon got hard evidence from several large travel agencies that Delta salespeople were, in effect, attempting to cajole them to steer business to Delta and away from Morris. Delta salespeople would take note of which agencies were giving a fair amount of business to Morris and then would offer those businesses a lucrative deal. If they would promise to switch this business to Delta, they would get a substantial bonus on top of their normal 10 percent cut. That is known as an override commission, a perfectly legal practice, although using it to bludgeon competition is questionable.

That month, Neeleman traveled to Washington to lay out the charges against Delta in public. He was invited to testify at a hearing before a joint congressional and White House commission on airline competition, the typical Washington response to a problem that everyone acknowledges exists but no one quite has the courage to tackle head on. It was Neeleman's first appearance on the national stage. Aside from a respectful account of his testimony that appeared that day in the *Salt Lake Tribune,* it drew little public attention. Nonetheless, it was gutsy, if not foolhardy, for Neeleman to speak up at all about Delta's bullying. A few weeks later it did appear that someone in the U.S. Department of Justice had been listening. The department let it be known that it would investigate Delta's tactics for evidence of a possible antitrust violation, and it sent a team of investigators to Salt Lake to start interviewing potential witnesses.

Around then, Neeleman was spending a lot of time with someone who would become something of a mentor to him. Dan Hersh, a shrewd investor who had held executive jobs at several short-lived start-up airlines, ran a boutique investment firm out of Denver that specialized in advising smaller airlines. He was also one of the rare people who had made money in the airline business. Hersh was an insider's insider, with an encyclopedic knowledge of the business that had attracted a steady stream of consulting clients. During the transition period for Morris, Neeleman had called on him to help with the certification, and Hersh took to flying to Salt Lake City several times a week, spending long days at his client's side. Hersh was a skillful practitioner of what he called the dark arts of the industry, the esoteric matter of timing schedules to squeeze out the maximum amount of revenue from each flight. Neeleman was an indefatigable learner, he recalled. "He was just like a sponge," he said. "He was constantly asking questions and wouldn't give up until he was sure he understood it." Hersh would return home exhausted by Neeleman's persistent debriefings.

Hersh was concerned, however, about Neeleman's seeming tendency to get mired in detail. "He would get really upset when something went wrong, and if a flight was delayed, he would take it personally. He's a creative guy, and I thought he shouldn't be devoting all his energies to making the planes run on time." Hersh began to see that Neeleman was essentially running the airline himself, and he began to pick up on the fears of June and Mitch Morris that they might have taken on too much in becoming a full-fledged airline.

June was sixty-one, Mitch was in his seventies, and they hadn't necessarily bargained for this. "June and Mitch were just paranoid about what an airline like Delta could do to them. Ultimately, I just don't think they had the stomach for it," said Hersh. June Morris was further disturbed when she got some evidence that Delta's bullying of travel agencies was having an impact and that Morris Air had clearly lost business on some heavily traveled routes the two shared. It was payback, of course, for what Neeleman had pulled off: From Salt Lake to Seattle, for example, Delta had been flying twelve thousand passengers a month with no competition. After Morris came in, that number slid to eight thousand.

Morris and Neeleman could rightly point out that they ended up flying fifty thousand passengers a month on that route, pulling in a lot of people who wouldn't be flying at all. That wasn't how Delta saw it. The airline controlled half the air travel out of Salt Lake City, a position it had gained from buying Western Airlines in 1987. Its attitude was that even one passenger lost to Morris was worth fighting over. "We are going to compete with them very aggressively," warned a Delta officer when asked about Morris's incursions onto its turf. "I think she found out what it's like to swim with the sharks," a local travel agent was quoted as saying in an *LA Times* profile of June Morris.

Neeleman wanted to stay in the ring; with the Justice Department to keep the heat on Delta, he was making ambitious plans. He had become friendly with Michael Lazarus, the investor whose firm, Weston Presidio, had sunk in fourteen million dollars into Morris. Lazarus's confidence in the Morris team had been vindicated; Neeleman had put the investment to good use, and Morris's expansion and its low costs and high profits were now attracting bankers interested in backing an initial public offering. Morris was in good shape; it now had annual sales of two hundred million dollars. Lazarus realized that he stood to quadruple his investment in an IPO.

Morgan Stanley was brought in as the investment banker, and it looked like a deal would go forward. With the capital they would raise, Morris could be a formidable competitor to Delta.

It was not to be. June Morris was exhausted and was starting to think it might make more sense to sell the company. There was, she thought, only one logical buyer on the airline side and that was Southwest. She was acquainted with Kelleher and made a tentative overture. Then she learned she had developed a rare, and highly lethal, form of breast cancer.

Neeleman was stunned to learn of Morris's diagnosis, even more so when he found out the type of cancer she had. Morris was told by the first doctor she consulted in Salt Lake that she had no more than six months to live. Neeleman went to the library at a local medical school, again betraying the intensity he could summon when roused, and spent hours learning about the disease and searching for the names of leading specialists in its treatment. A doctor in Dallas, one of the top experts in the field, agreed to see her, and Neeleman joined Morris's family in urging her to go immediately to the hospital for surgery.

Lazarus remembered that word was getting out that selling the airline was inevitable, but he was skeptical about Southwest as a partner. Acquiring an airline was not Herb Kelleher's style. In 1987, the cover of the Southwest annual report bore a single line: "In 1986, we didn't merge," the point being that nearly every other airline had, with disastrous results. The mergers and acquisitions binge of the 1980s had left most companies saddled with huge debts and labor strife, and Kelleher's resistance to the trend had been vindicated.

But in 1993 Southwest was facing a new threat. United Airlines, then the largest airline in the country, if not the world, apparently had concluded the Texas renegade needed to be taught a lesson. In short, as one commentary put it at the time, "United Airlines will attempt to do what no airline ever has done: Beat Southwest at its own game." The plan was this: Create an airline within an airline under the rubric of "Shuttle by United," a nimble competitor with lower wages and more efficiency than the parent company. Then it would set that clone free to go against Southwest on the routes where it was cleaning United's clock.

"We knew little about Morris at the time," said John Owen, then Southwest's treasurer. "But we also knew United was about to attack us. And here Morris comes along, with the perfect airport locations, and the planes, and the opportunities . . . and we were ready to fight the battle."

In October, the two entered into formal talks. Southwest offered to buy Morris for $129 million in stock, and by early December, it was over; Morris would no longer exist as an independent airline. After less than a year of getting his license, the airline Neeleman had helped to build was about to be sold out from under him.

On the other hand, Southwest's offer would give him a stake worth around $22 million. Even better, he was offered a high-level job at Southwest that would allow him work alongside Kelleher. He felt he could leave now that June Morris was undergoing cancer treatments and, despite the discouraging prognosis she had been given months earlier, was expected to make a full recovery. Along with her husband and son, June, who obviously did quite well in the merger deal herself, would stay in Salt Lake and ensure that the merger went smoothly.

"It was a big day for him, because he worshipped Herb and Southwest," said John Owen. "And for him it was like going to Mecca. And he'd say, 'Wow, I'm going to go work with Herb.' He couldn't imagine anything better than that."

two
love field

Early in 1994, David Neeleman escorted Herb Kelleher to Salt Lake City's Temple Square, the carefully tended, ten-acre compound in the heart of the city that is the Mormon Church's equivalent of Vatican City. Neeleman was eager to quell any fears among the locals about the brash Texan coming to Utah and had taken it upon himself to arrange an introduction to the coterie of mostly septuagenarian men who ran the Church of Jesus Christ of Latter-day Saints. Kelleher admittedly knew next to nothing about the dominant force in the city he proposed to turn into a Southwest stronghold after the merger with Morris Air. And so it fell to the thirty-four-year-old Neeleman, young, fit, an advertisement for clean living, to remind Kelleher, a dissolute sixty-seven, that his five-pack-a-day cigarette habit and his open love of the bottle might not go over so well in this part of the country.

Neeleman remembered the encounter this way: "I said, 'Uh, Herb, could you go a little easy on the smoking and the drinking?'" He knew that Kelleher could take the kidding. Beneath the louche exterior was a cunning strategist; he had been, after all, a trial lawyer before he'd gotten near an airline. Kelleher had promised during the merger talks that he would do everything possible to protect the jobs of Morris's workforce, which had swelled to two thousand. But there was a particularly sensitive matter he'd have to deal with, where business realities might run afoul of the values espoused by the church leaders he was about to meet. It was the workforce of stay-at-home moms that Neeleman had trained to handle Morris Air's reservations, many from the confines of soundproof basements. Neeleman knew firsthand that most Mormon wives, his own included, were college educated, bright, and would make fine employees, except that they were expected to forgo careers when they married and started raising children. As with his e-ticketing idea, Neeleman became seized with an idea that had apparently eluded all others: Train a team of women who would have their own terminals at home, and he'd have a highly motivated and loyal workforce. Morris would save money by not having to operate a full-fledged reservations center and would have more flexibility to match staffing with demand. If a storm hit and flights were delayed, for example, Neeleman could immediately call on agents from a list of those willing to work overtime, without waiting for them to trek into a distant office.

It did work as he had hoped, and soon Neeleman had more than two hundred of what were inevitably referred to as the "agents in fuzzy slippers." Whenever a reporter happened to stumble over this unusual arrangement, he would get an earful from the agents about the delights of being able to work from home. (Of course, telecommuting was becoming increasingly common around the country, but it hadn't spread to the airlines.) Now, everyone was nervous about Southwest, which had no telecommuting option and whose reservations agents were unionized.

Frankie Littleford remembered the day when they learned about the merger deal. "It had been a very closely guarded secret," she said. "And we got a message that we were all to report to a hotel downtown. We all assumed it was the IPO. And then we found out we were going to be absorbed into Southwest. We were in complete shock."

On the surface, the Southwest–Morris merger was bound to be

fairly painless as these transactions go; after all, Neeleman had fashioned Morris as a sort of Herb Kelleher fan club. But the cultural divide was apparent early on.

Michael Lazarus recalled a dinner that Southwest hosted to mark the closing of the deal, at the Palm Restaurant in Dallas. "We were in one of these banquet rooms, with a big U-shaped table, and on one side are all the Southwest people and all the Morris people on the other. And in the first twenty minutes Herb came and found me and he's had four Wild Turkeys, and I'm thinking, the cultures couldn't be more different. You've got the Mormon people who don't smoke or drink and then you have these wild Texans who all smoke and drink. . . .

"And so I go to sit with the Southwest people. And here's Herb, working the room like a bar mitzvah, and he was being very attentive to these two matronly women. I thought, they've got to be some important people in all this and then I find out they were two secretaries who'd put in some very long hours on the transaction documents. And that was Herb, he had the touch."

Whatever their differences in background, Lazarus noted, "David and Herb were really kindred spirits in that sense."

For Morris, the reality was that decisions were now being dictated by people in a distant corporate headquarters. Morris's employees were told, in short order, that while they might get jobs at Southwest, they would have to reapply and go through the full Southwest hiring process just to hold on to their current positions. The bunny slippers brigade would likely have to start getting dressed for work and report to a real office, if they wanted to keep their jobs. Most refused.

David Neeleman, though, was already on his way to Dallas. The fact that he had been given a high-ranking position was an indication to some that he was possibly being groomed to be Herb Kelleher's successor. But he was also leaving the protection of his longtime mentor, and

June Morris worried that her protégé's eccentricities might cause him problems. Right before he moved, she and Tom Kelly sat him down for a talk. "We told him, 'Please, David, don't talk . . . just listen.'" Morris recalled. But Neeleman apparently could not imagine that a company that had been praised on business pages as "the best place to work in America" would be anything less than welcoming.

To get to Southwest's headquarters at Love Field Airport, just outside downtown Dallas, a visitor often has to navigate a seedy strip of topless bars and tattoo parlors, punctuated by billboards blaring slogans like FREE AS A BIRD! or GUMBO JETS. Subtlety is a scarce commodity in these parts; the "Love Airline" theme is flogged so mercilessly—the stock symbol is LUV, passenger snacks are "Luv bites"—that the city appears to have forgotten that the airport was actually named after aviation pioneer Lt. Moss Lee Love.

Entering the main lobby at 2702 Love Field Drive, you feel as if you are in a shrine, an unabashed tribute to the cult of Kelleher. The headquarters' walls are covered with thousands of photos and other memorabilia, including such bibelots as a ventriloquist's dummy of Herb, holding the inevitable cigarette. The company has a team of employees whose only job is to maintain the displays with the reverence of a museum curator. But it is on the wall on one of the boardrooms that you can glimpse the most sacred relic, what amounts to the airline's first business plan, reduced to a scribble on a cocktail napkin. As in so many aspects of the Southwest saga, it was informed by a generous dose of whiskey.

The legend of Southwest began on a December evening in 1966, when a Texas businessman named Rollin King, who ran a small commuter air service out of San Antonio, invited his friend and lawyer Herb Kelleher to join him for drinks at a local bar. King had been following the goings-on in California, where an upstart airline called Pacific South-west was charging low fares and making money. It had thrived because it flew only within a single state, putting it beyond the reach of federal regulators. King thought that Texas, where fares were much higher than on flights of similar length in California, was surely big enough to merit its own home state airline. As the story goes, King grabbed a cocktail napkin and sketched a rudimentary route map, connecting Dallas with Houston and San Antonio, the so-called golden triangle. Engraved on the plaque bearing the original napkin is this bit of repartee: "HERB, LET'S START AN AIRLINE"; "ROLLIN, YOU'RE CRAZY, LET'S DO IT." No one seems to care whether these now-famous words were actually uttered; they're part of the Kelleher hagiography.

King and Kelleher would likely have shredded the napkin if they'd known what awaited them. Braniff and Trans Texas airlines, the two lines that laid claim to the state's airspace, immediately ran to court to block Southwest, assuming correctly that they'd get a few friendly judges to fend off the intruder. The legal fight took more than four years and dozens of lawsuits to resolve, because the airlines hadn't counted on Kelleher's determination. After he went through the fledgling line's meager war chest, Kelleher dipped into his own savings, pursuing the case all the way to the U.S. Supreme Court, which finally cleared the way for Southwest to begin flying.

On June 16, 1971, two days before the launch, the incumbents found yet another pliable Texas judge who issued an order grounding South-west. Kelleher was outraged and flew down to San Antonio and found an appellate judge who would agree to hear his appeal the following morning, hours before the first flight was due to take off. Spending all night in a law library, he arrived in court the next morning, disheveled but prepared: That judge reversed the ban and Southwest was free to fly. Kelleher called back to Dallas to tell them the news, but his colleagues weren't convinced it was all over. "What if the sheriff shows up any-way?" he was asked. "Then you roll right over the son of a bitch and leave our tire tracks on his uniform if you have to," Kelleher shot back. This homicidal urge proved unnecessary, but it was then that South-west's in-your-face culture was born.

There were other wars to come. In the late 1970s, Kelleher had to fight for the right to remain at Love Field; all other airlines were re-quired to decamp to the-then brand-new Dallas/Fort Worth Airport, thirty minutes away in the suburbs. Kelleher knew that Southwest's whole reason for being—short flights to close-in airports like Love—would be destroyed if he joined the exodus to DFW, and so he per-suaded authorities to allow him to remain as an intrastate airline. Then deregulation came, and Kelleher, understandably, wanted to take ad-vantage of his new freedoms by flying from Love to cities in other states. That infuriated the big lines, which ran to Congress and persuaded then-House majority leader Jim Wright of Fort Worth to ram though a ban on interstate service from the airfield. Eventually a compromise was reached allowing Southwest to fly to a few nearby states, but more than twenty years later, the so-called Wright Amendment was still in effect, preventing Southwest from flying out of Love to places like Chicago or Los Angeles. Kelleher has maintained an uncharacteristic silence about all this; after all, the flip side of this peculiar limitation is that it has given Southwest a near monopoly on the most convenient airport in one of the busiest air travel markets in the country, which it exploits by offering some 160 flights a day, most of them packed. All of this had to be fasci-nating to Neeleman, whose orientation was from the standpoint of an airline that had snuck in under the radar and whose skirmishes with Delta were, by contrast, rather mild stuff.

One got the sense that Kelleher privately relished the attacks on his company: What he liked to refer to as the "Battle of Britain" mentality was essential to the esprit de corps that allowed him to whip the competition. Most of his employees worked for less than they would make at a big airline and didn't have the traditional fixed-income pensions that many other airline workers considered their birthright. But they had profit sharing, and unlike its larger brethren, Southwest had been profitable for twenty-five consecutive years.

In many ways, the Southwest that Neeleman found in 1994 was like the Southwest of the early 1970s, still milking the underdog status as if it were a two-plane operation. However, it was now ten times the size of Morris Air; it had twenty thousand employees, most of them unionized, and a fleet of more than two hundred planes. To prevent it from becoming your average large, soulless corporation, Southwest had fixated on the notion of "fun" as a sort of extreme sport. In a promotional pamphlet for job seekers, the "company benefits" were listed as follows: "chili cookoffs, Friday afternoon deck parties; Halloween celebrations, spontaneous celebrations, parades . . ." Departments even got their own budgets for partying. *Fortune* magazine had dubbed Herb Kelleher the "High Priest of Ha Ha" for his singular devotion to the work-is-play credo. There was virtually nothing Kelleher would not do to gain a little free publicity. Not long before Neeleman arrived in Dallas, Herb had engaged in a much-hyped arm wrestling contest with the chief of a small air cargo shipper, Stevens Aviation, over who owned the slogan "Just plane smart." It was a classic Herb hustle: He rented a Dallas arena, packed it with employees of both companies, and then called in the TV networks, which merrily collaborated in the buildup with stories about Kelleher's "training regimen" of cigarettes and whiskey. The actual bout was over in one minute, Kelleher's younger foe easily trouncing him, but the news carried only the shots of a smiling Kelleher being carried out on a stretcher.

He encouraged a similar lack of inhibition in his staff; flight attendants would occasionally hide in overhead bins, popping out to startle passengers; they'd honor passengers' birthdays by presenting them with rolls of toilet paper; their stand-up style in-flight announcements were legendary ("Flight attendants, prepare your hair for arrival" was a typical one-liner).

What Neeleman admired was Southwest's perceived lack of hierarchy, which he had attempted to reproduce at Morris Air. John Owen remembered that one day while visiting Neeleman in Utah during the due diligence period, he couldn't find the name of a senior Morris executive in the company directory until he realized that it listed people alphabetically by *first* names. It was a minor but telling detail. "That did it. I knew he 'got' the culture," said Owen.

All the institutionalized zaniness hid a larger issue: Kelleher was genuinely worried that his precious spirit would be suffocated by layers of bureaucracy. Out of this came a "culture committee," charged with spotting any signs of burnout. People from various departments would be tapped to serve on the team for two-year stints, during which they'd visit Southwest stations, pitch in with tasks, deliver meals to maintenance crews working overtime, and the like. Kelleher would frequently cite these ad hoc cheerleaders as among the most critical people at Southwest. They were his "fire watchers," he would say. "The most important person in prehistoric times was the one who made sure the fire didn't go out," he said.

In hindsight, the idea that David Neeleman would fit in at Southwest was as realistic as Herb Kelleher becoming a devout Mormon. "He didn't know much about office politics or how to behave," said Owen. "He had never had much in the way of a boss. If you look at bureaucracies, with the Pentagon being ten, Morris Air would be zero and Southwest would be a one . . . but for David, going from zero to one was a very big deal."

Flush with his success at introducing electronic ticketing at Morris, he decided he had to convert Southwest to the paperless cause, and he fully expected everyone to embrace the idea enthusiastically. Southwest had always been a fairly low-tech place; due to the simplicity of its operations, managers saw no need to acquire a lot of fancy computer software and for years it had a rudimentary reservations system. When Neeleman argued that Southwest was an ideal place to test the ticketless philosophy, he was virtually ignored, and it would take several years before Southwest finally would come around. (When it did, in 1995, it made such a big fuss over "their" innovation that "you'd think they had dreamed it up themselves," Neeleman snorted.)

"David literally came in with an idea a minute, particularly about technology, and the people there thought they were doing pretty well themselves, thank you," said Ann Rhoades, who at the time was heading human resources, or the "people department," in Southwest nomenclature. "He forgot these were people who had a personal investment in this place." Neeleman also went after Southwest's resistance to giving customers assigned seats. Neeleman not only thought this policy was unfair to passengers, but it also stood to hurt Southwest in the long run as it expanded to places where customers were unaccustomed to the stampede that was the Southwest boarding drill. Again, he was rebuffed. From time to time, Kelleher would ask someone to study the costs of giving passengers advanced seat assignments and inevitably the answer would come back: It would cost too much in time and money to justify any perceived benefit to customers.

Neeleman was unmoved. He started speaking out in the strategy meetings he attended, where Southwest was planning the next five years, airing ambitious plans for spreading eastward, how it would fight the big lines and their loopy attempts to clone the Southwest formula. "We'd be debating something, and he'd say, 'What you need to do is this!'" Owen remembered. "And everyone would be thinking 'Who is this new guy?'" It didn't help that Neeleman apparently saw nothing wrong with barging into people's offices without knocking.

"What to do with David" became a frequent topic of discussion, and June Morris spoke often on the phone with Kelleher and his closest associate, Colleen Barrett, who had started out as his secretary in the 1960s but was now executive vice president in charge of customer services. Barrett was a grandmotherly sort who wore her long mane of hair pulled into a braid; Morris hoped she would take David under her wing. However, Barrett was fiercely loyal to her own people, some of whom were put off by Neeleman's tactlessness.

"Basically, David drove the people at Southwest crazy and the people at Southwest drove David crazy," said Owen. "And I didn't think it needed to be that way. He needed a mentor, and everyone was too busy with the acquisition. But it was pretty clear he wasn't bonding with the group."

Things went south from there. Neeleman said he would sit in meetings, restraining his urge to speak by scrawling "DSAW," for "don't say a word," over and over on a notepad. Cathy Westrum, a vivacious brunette who worked in the customer service department next to Neeleman's office, recalled that many people just stopped talking to him. "Herb and Colleen just stuck him in this little office, I think it was eight by eight feet. It was like he was being punished." But of course "he couldn't sit still for a moment; he was always zipping around," she said. One day Westrum looked up from her desk to see Neeleman, grunting and struggling with a gumball machine she had placed right outside her office. Westrum started laughing: Neeleman had folded a dollar bill into a small square that he was attempting to jam into the coin slot. The two struck up a friendship, and Neeleman would often go to her office to air the ideas no one else wanted to hear.

Although he chafed under the rounds of interminable meetings and his increasing isolation from the top brass, Neeleman was intent on sticking it out. He had found a house in the affluent Highland Park section of town and was planning to move Vicki and his children—he now had six—down to Texas. Moreover, if he quit, he would sentence himself to a long exile from the only business he knew. Kelleher had cagily persuaded him to sign a five-year noncompete agreement when the merger was finalized. That was considerably harsher than the standard two-year term. But Neeleman had signed it, against strong advice, he said, because he was convinced he would succeed at Southwest.

Kelleher didn't think he was being unreasonable, because Southwest's first chief executive, Lamar Muse, had started up a competitor, quickly dubbed "Revenge Air," after he had resigned from the company following a dispute with the board in the early 1980s. Muse was a formidable personality who had virtually run the airline for much of its early years while Kelleher continued to work in his law practice. (One fact that many of the Kelleher chronicles omit is that he wasn't fully involved with the day-to-day running of the company until ten years after Southwest had begun.) The eponymous Muse Air did well for a while, but when it faltered Kelleher snapped it up, ran it briefly as a separate company, then eventually shut it down.

So Kelleher likely thought that Neeleman would find another calling if he was cut off from the airlines for five years. So one day in mid-May, Kelleher invited Neeleman out to dinner to break the news he wasn't working out. He didn't mince words, as Neeleman recalled: "He told me, 'Everyone here thinks you are a pain; even your biggest supporter, Jim Parker, told me he thinks you're a pain.'" Jim Parker, then Kelleher's general counsel, was a soft-spoken straight man to Kelleher who would later be tapped as CEO. This unflattering review of his performance apparently stunned Neeleman. "And I guess I cried a little. I'd never been fired before, and it was hard." Neeleman went into the office the next day in a state of shock to go through the motions of cleaning out his office. A few months later, Cathy Westrum received a large package in the mail. She opened it to find a model of a Morris Air 737, with a handwritten note from Neeleman. "You were always one of my favorite people at Southwest," he wrote. He was, he said, planning to start up a new airline of his own and when he did, he hoped she would join him.

Neeleman has since said that what would ultimately become JetBlue began the moment he cleared out his desk at Love Field. While he had been there only five months, he had gotten a rare look inside the company at the highest level, one that many other entrepreneurs would have killed for.

First, however, he would have to get over the pain of having been dumped so unceremoniously. When he moved back to Salt Lake City in the summer of 1994, he admittedly fell into a funk. "It was almost as bad as when my company went broke," he recalled. "I had twenty-five million dollars and I lived in Salt Lake City, and you can buy the whole town for that money. And I was completely miserable. I wanted to build a company again and I had signed that [noncompete] agreement because I trusted Southwest Airlines."

He had a choice: He could challenge the five-year stranglehold in court and would in all likelihood prevail. It was, after all, unusually restrictive; Neeleman couldn't work in any capacity at any airline in the United States, nor could he recruit Southwest employees (aside from informal notes to friends like Westrum). But he was still in awe of Herb, and he couldn't imagine suing him in court.

This long sentence, however, wasn't totally without benefit. It would force Neeleman to think hard about what he wanted to do next. He also had time to ponder what went so wrong at Southwest. He knew that his impulsive habits were causing him some trouble as he moved beyond the protective fold of those who understood and tolerated his quirks. Vicki Neeleman was constantly cleaning up after him; once, Neeleman had disappeared during the middle of a cookout, leaving the meal to burn. Around that time, his youngest brother began having some problems, doing poorly in school, smoking marijuana. He was soon diagnosed with attention deficit disorder. Neeleman studied up on the syndrome and the more he read, the more convinced he became that he, too, suffered from ADD. He declined to seek treatment, however, fearing it might dull his senses. While some of his family—including his wife—encouraged him to try Ritalin, the most commonly prescribed medication for the disorder, Neeleman resisted. "I'll take some pill, and then I'll be just like the rest of you," he would say.

By early 1995, Neeleman was ready to get back to work. He made a few halfhearted attempts to break into other fields, investing in a new burn treatment product that he licensed from its South African patent holder. All that did was burn up cash, as did another failed venture, a pretzel bakery. The only times he succeeded were when he stuck close to his airline roots. He incorporated a small company called Open Skies, licensing the electronic ticketing and reservations software he'd developed at Morris Air with the help of David Evans, a technical whiz who'd developed it at Morris Air. He got his friend and former colleague Tom Kelly to join, and together they found an office in Salt Lake and put out the word.

Forming Open Skies was a clever move. The airlines were recovering from one of the worst downturns in their history, brought on by the first president Bush's Operation Desert Storm and the attendant rise in fuel costs. The industry in aggregate had posted losses of thirteen billion dollars during 1991 and 1992, an unprecedented amount at the time, and was looking for any way to cut costs. One of the biggest items on the airlines' expense ledgers has always been the cost of getting the airline tickets into the hands of customers; in fact, many outsiders are surprised to learn that it can outpace what airlines spend on aircraft. Travel agency commissions typically ran into the hundreds of millions per year, and even the mundane matter of printing and delivering tickets devours millions in expenses.

The other advantage of this venture was that it kept him in the loop. Kelleher might have blocked his admission into the airline club for a few years, but Open Skies gave him a back channel to the close-knit aviation community, where his youth and his ease with technology distinguished him from the computer-phobic geezers who then dominated the top ranks of many airlines. It was the smaller airlines he was going after, however, not the major lines that had invested hundreds of millions in developing massive computer reservation networks. Soon, emissaries from niche airlines began making the pilgrimage to his offices in Salt Lake City. Smaller airlines often had to pay big lines substantial fees for the privilege of getting reservations through their systems. Neeleman's system could help break them of this dependence on their rivals. (Neeleman would ultimately sell Open Skies to Hewlett-Packard, and his new airline would become a client.)

He then heard from a group of investors in Calgary who wanted to start a Canadian knockoff of Southwest to take on Air Canada, which enjoyed a near monopoly thanks to its status as a state-run "flag" airline. They needed someone who knew the secrets and yet was independent from the Dallas crowd. Neeleman fit that description perfectly, and he began shuttling between Salt Lake and western Canada. It was as close to revenge as he could have imagined: He could work on a start-up and share in its success, and by crossing the border he was beyond the reach of Kelleher's control.

The new airline, WestJet, took flight in February 1996.

He was back.

three
the virgins

In the mid-1990s, few rational entrepreneurs were venturing near the airlines. After all, the companies that did survive the convulsions of the first few years following the deregulation of the airlines were now stronger, the weak sisters like Pan Am and Eastern had conveniently disappeared, and virtually all of the brave souls that had challenged the existing order had vanished.

If there was one individual who personified this sorry saga it was Donald Calvin Burr, who in a short five years went from supremely confident visionary, the youthful founder of uber-upstart People Express in 1981, to one of the most prominent failures in the annals of the modern airlines. There are many reasons why he crashed so spectacularly, not the least of which was Burr's own blinding overconfidence. But during its heyday, People Express was such a success, with its $29 air fares that were said to be cheaper than driving, that Burr landed on the cover of *Time* magazine and was said to be seriously considering running for president. Burr had more than a bit of Elmer Gantry in him. Like Neeleman, he'd been a teenage missionary of sorts for his Congregational church in Connecticut and had considered becoming a minister. He, too, was a masterful salesman who spoke of "making a better world" through his practices, which included employee ownership and job sharing, to the point where pilots would occasionally do shifts checking in bags, and executives would clean airplanes. Then a succession of blunders— an ill-conceived merger, a rash purchase of aging 747s that flew nearly empty to places like Paris and Brussels—brought the whole thing to an abrupt end.

In 1987, after he had lost his airline, Burr retreated to Martha's Vineyard to write a book, and for a long time there was little word on what had happened to him. One day in 1996, though, he showed up at David Neeleman's office in Salt Lake City.

Burr had contacted Neeleman to investigate whether his Open Skies reservations system could be adapted for a new airline he wanted to start, People Express II. Burr was keenly aware that his demise had been caused in no small part by the primitive reservations system he'd used. It proved no match for the might of the majors' powerful computers, which could adeptly juggle pricing with demand. As Burr told Neeleman, when American Airlines had come after him in 1985 with rock-bottom fares—carefully calibrated to siphon off People's business where the two competed—the percentage of seats filled on his flights plummeted rapidly from 80 percent to 30 percent. But Burr had had plenty of time since to contemplate what had gone wrong, and, as he told Neeleman, he was ready to stage a comeback.

Even with Neeleman's technological aid, Burr could not build an exact clone of his old company. Newark Airport, which People's had transformed from a blighted backwater into the busiest airport in the New York area, had become too successful; it was effectively closed to newcomers. Continental Airlines had absorbed the carcass of Burr's airline and had turned Newark into a huge hub that was now straining at the seams, and it was frequently cited as having one of the worst on-time records in the country.

No, it was Kennedy Airport in New York that he was looking at and Neeleman, who had been casting about for locations in the East, had already put it on his short list for his new airline. Kennedy's reputation was so off-putting that most airline chiefs avoided basing any domestic operations there; more than fifty international airlines flew there, but it was rightly regarded as inhospitable territory for anyone seeking to offer high-frequency, low-fare service à la Southwest. And there were other reasons why Neeleman would hesitate before staking his claim there. "Unwelcoming, unaesthetic, and next to impossible to drive to and from" is how author James Kaplan described it in his 1994 book, *The Airport,* a vivid and, ultimately, depressing profile of the once-great jetport. As Kaplan reported, the airport had been on a downward slide for nearly twenty years and was, oddly, a microcosm of the worst of the city it had once proudly claimed as its own. It had a growing crime problem, a sizable homeless population, and, in popular lore at least, its cargo hangars functioned as a sort of ATM for organized crime. The image that came across in the press, Kaplan wrote, was one of a "depot from hell, a sinkhole of civic and moral turpitude." And that was just how locals saw it. Frequent travelers routinely voted Kennedy their most hated gateway, the airport of last resort, and with Newark having caught up, they could easily bypass it. After the Port Authority of New York and New Jersey had failed to get support for a one-billion-dollar plan to rebuild the airport around a central terminal, a lot of airline managements simply crossed it off the list.

Don Burr and David Neeleman weren't particularly interested in what platinum cardholders thought of Kennedy; they saw something else. The key to making a low-fare airline work at JFK was that, unlike LaGuardia Airport, Newark, Boston Logan, or indeed any of the other possibilities, the airport was practically empty for a good part of the day, before the flotilla of foreign airplanes began to alight. "You know, most of the time Kennedy is so quiet that you could go bowling on the runways," Burr told Neeleman.

Bowling on the runways. That was the kind of evocative image that could get people excited. As Neeleman sat down to outline his own plan, he began to visualize a place where his new airline could thrive, far from Dallas, Salt Lake, and other Kelleher battlegrounds. In the end, Burr's reputation was too toxic for the potential investors he had approached, and not long after their meeting, he called Neeleman to let him know he was giving up; there would be no second act for People Express. Kennedy was Neeleman's to exploit.

Back in the mid-1990s, Burr at least had something of a cult following left; he was well known in the industry. Neeleman was still searching for reasons that would persuade people to read past the first page of the business plan he was then hashing out. At the outset he had to explain why he could start up yet another low-fare airline when the public had been burned by so many flameouts. This was no place for humility, he thought. As he worked with Tom Kelly on a draft, he came up with the hook: The key was to start out *big*. He would set out to create "the first mega-start-up in aviation history." Of course it would be making history simply if it survived. In a very real sense his opposition wasn't the existing airlines; it was the spectre of People Express and the other fifty-eight airlines that had started up and failed since deregulation of the airlines. By any objective measure, it was laughable that these unknown guys from Utah, in their mid-thirties, with scant experience running a scheduled airline, thought they could succeed where far more seasoned businessmen had failed.

When he wasn't working on Open Skies or one of his screwball investment ideas, Neeleman would stroll into Tom Kelly's office and the two would sit together for hours. He would talk about his ideas for the perfect airline, and Kelly, acting as Neeleman's factotum, would take copious notes.

First, Neeleman and Kelly set about dissecting the reasons why start-ups fail. It was a familiar cycle: At the time, you could enter the airline industry for a relatively paltry ten million dollars. In fact, Neeleman had more than enough money to bankroll a new airline without any outside investment. That would be enough to scrounge a few planes, hire the pilots and crews needed to fly them, and pay a few months' rent at the airport.

But, as he would later point out in his first formal business plan, you couldn't get brand-new planes for that price, so you'd end up renting a few clapped-out DC-9 jets from, say, an obscure foreign airline, slap a new coat of paint on them, and begin flying. You would start up modestly, with a few flights and little publicity—figuring that the rock-bottom fares you'd charge would generate a windfall of free advertising once word got out.

Already, though, you'd be hamstrung by high fixed costs. Small airlines lack the clout to negotiate airport leases on good terms and often are overcharged for such necessities as fuel and insurance. You could gain an edge only by charging sharply lower fares and hope that you'd fill enough seats to break even. And then the downward spiral would start: Your aging planes would break down, you'd get a reputation as cheap but unreliable, and then the behemoth whose turf you'd invaded would decide to get even. More precisely, it would lower its fares to yours, and your customers would be only too happy to defect for the familiar comforts of an established line, the frequent flier miles, meals, and all the other frills the challenger lacked. This is the classic predatory pricing scenario, which typically ends with the challenger's heading off to the airline dust heap while the bigger line triumphantly raises its fares back to extortionate levels once the coast is clear.

Neeleman would need, then, a well-funded war chest to survive the sorts of draining wars of attrition that, unless he could hire Herb Kelleher as his pro bono attorney, he would surely lose. "How do you make a little money in the airline business? Start out with a lot," an old joke goes. Neeleman's insight was that he could stand that joke on its head by amassing such a huge cash pile that it acted as a buffer against that syndrome. That was not just double or even triple what most new airlines normally raised, but ten times that amount, an almost unimaginable two hundred million dollars. Neeleman would put in the initial seed money of two million dollars—later upped to five million dollars—and Kelly and a few other partners would pony up a like amount but ultimately they envisioned giving a sizable slab of preferred stock in exchange for backing from other outside investors. Neeleman was admittedly still "paranoid" from his early debacle in Hawaii and felt so strongly about this point that he insisted they insert a footnote saying that if they couldn't make their fund-raising goal, they wouldn't proceed.

What they proposed to do with their pile of cash was even more startling. They would buy a fleet of all new planes, something that no postderegulation start-up had ever done before. Brand-new aircraft would mute public resistance to a start-up, they figured, and would also save costs since new planes are more reliable and cheaper to operate and maintain. They would have to pay a lot more to acquire new planes, but if they ordered enough of them, they surely would get a break on the price. This meant that they'd need to grow fast, and steadily. Southwest had long ago turned the David and Goliath cliché on its head; when Kelleher entered a market, he typically started up with a plethora of flights to establish a beachhead quickly. The effect was usually so dramatic—

sometimes doubling air traffic out of the city—that it had the added result of discouraging airlines from beating up too badly on the newcomer. Neeleman's plan assumed they'd grow to more than thirty planes in less than three years.

The third point was to have the lowest costs in the airlines. They'd seen how the "Costs are king" mantra had worked at Southwest. And they were much more comfortable with using technology than Kelleher had been; they would rid the airline of unnecessary paperwork, all reservations would be electronic, and they'd experiment with flying their planes overnight.

By early 1996, a decent interval had passed since Neeleman's banishment from the business, and he and Kelly began testing the waters. They dropped a few hints to Michael Lazarus, who quickly flew out to see them in Salt Lake. Over breakfast, the pair announced they were preparing to form an airline the very moment Neeleman's noncompete agreement expired in January 1999. Then they told him, quite calmly, that they needed roughly $130 million, for starters.

Lazarus at first was less than thrilled. "I'd promised my partners I'd never get involved with an airline again," he said. Yes, he'd done well with his Morris Air investment, but given the generally dreadful results for new airlines, that could have been a fluke. "I'd batted a thousand with the first one, and figured what are the chances that we'd succeed with another?" But Neeleman had done his homework and convinced Lazarus that basing the airline in New York City was the key. The more than eighteen million people living in the metropolitan area hadn't had a low-fare airline to call their own since People Express had tanked. Lazarus recalled that Neeleman's rationale for where to base his new airline evoked Willie Sutton's explanation of why he robbed banks. "Why New York City? Because that's where all the people are!" was Neeleman's deadpan pitch.

On May 11, 1996, everything changed. Moments after taking off from Miami International Airport, ValuJet Flight 582 crashed into the Florida Everglades, killing all 110 people aboard. The Atlanta-based airline was one of the few successful low-fare start-ups of the 1990s, but in the months before the accident, its rapid growth had begun to alarm safety regulators in Washington. Not until after the accident, however, was the airline grounded, and for two months its fleet of aging jets was put under the microscope.

The investigation was concluded and didn't blame ValuJet directly but rather a series of missteps by the airline's subcontractors. In a series of blunders, each compounding the last, a carton of highly flammable oxygen canisters had been mistakenly labeled and thus improperly loaded onto the plane, where it caught fire next to a pile of rubber tires and caused a conflagration powerful enough to bring the aircraft down within minutes. Nevertheless, the crash was seen as a direct result of deregulation and its pressure on airlines to cut costs in order to cut fares. "Valu-Jet burned and crashed not because the airplane failed, but the airline did," author William Langewiesche wrote in his elegiac essay on the crash in *Inside the Sky.* The increasingly common use of temporary contract workers by ValuJet and others "was their contribution to our cheap flying," he wrote, amounting to an ethical lapse by the company managers. While Langewiesche and others also singled out the FAA for its lax supervision, the public continued to shun ValuJet, which eventually had to change its name to AirTran, a smaller airline with which it merged, in order to survive. As Neeleman and Kelly contemplated their next move they realized that all the new planes and cash in the world couldn't overcome the public's resistance to getting on a plane bearing an unfamiliar name. Only a strong brand, they concluded, could erase the stigma.

They studied a partnership with Time Warner. Warner Bros., they wrote, could supply entertainment content for their flights. They looked at Planet Hollywood, thinking they could use their flights as vehicles to hawk movie-related merchandise. They even considered approaching companies as disparate as Pepsi and Nike. Being especially cautious, they inserted a caveat in the proposal, asking if an "Air Nike" airplane crashed, would it not only harm the airline company, but also the entire brand? They figured they'd better raise the safety question before anyone else did and concluded that Nike was such a powerful brand that it would survive any mishaps unscathed. However, Nike did not necessarily share that optimism. An airline would really do very little for its brand identity, and while the prospect of a crash was remote, it was a risk that did not seem worth taking.

It's hard to envision David Neeleman as CEO of, say, a Planet Hollywood Airlines, flying polyester-clad vacationers to the overrun oases of Las Vegas or Orlando, reduced to a footnote in the annals of airline marketing, somewhere between Hooters Air and MGM Grand (the latter being the bauble that financier Kirk Kerkorian lost millions on in the 1980s). That Neeleman even considered running his airline as an adjunct to a cheesy chain of theme restaurants is a telling detail for it reveals just how daunting it was, in 1997, for a virtual unknown to succeed with a start-up airline.

Neeleman and Kelly had already hit on the solution. Virgin Group founder Richard Branson had a powerful brand, and he also had an airline. Clearly, he was their best hope; in fact, they had already been inspired by Branson to propose that their new airline have individual seat-back screens at each seat, just like the Virgin flights did. So the two inserted a sly teaser in their proposal. "Our strategy is to join forces with a well-recognized and respected company and use its existing brand-name as part of the name of the airline," they wrote.

"For example, Richard Branson has been very creative and aggressive in extending the reach of the 'Virgin' brand that he has created . . . the prospect of a startup carrier named 'Virgin America' seems extremely appealing," they gushed. While they inserted a disclaimer saying that they had "not yet contacted Mr. Branson," they were already sending out feelers to Branson, whose European budget airline, Virgin Express, had recently become a client of Open Skies.

To say that Branson had been "aggressive" in stretching the Virgin label to its tongue-in-cheek limits was an understatement: He'd opened Virgin "bridal" shops, a line of condoms, Virgin life insurance, and he was preparing to launch a Virgin cola in an improbable quest to take on Coke and Pepsi. Branson was also an outsize figure, one of the original rock star CEOs, and, by the mid-1990s, he was also the ninth wealthiest individual in Great Britain. He had made his initial mark in the music industry with Virgin Records—so named because he was a business world virgin—branching out into the airlines as a sideline when an opportunity fell his way in the mid-1980s. The powerful marquee value of an international airline made up for the cyclical downturns of the airline business, as his scarlet-hued wide-body planes were flying the Virgin logo halfway across the globe, to Los Angeles, New York, Tokyo, and South Africa.

What Neeleman and Kelly likely did not know was that Branson had met privately with Herb Kelleher several times in the past two years. Mostly these were long, boozy lunches prompted by the suggestion of mutual friends. But Branson had been eyeing the domestic airline business in the United States, and his tête-a-têtes with Kelleher only whetted his interest.

It was of course improbable that Virgin—with its three classes of service, its onboard manicures and massages—would team up with a Spartan operation like Southwest. But these two divergent styles would indeed come together, in a way that neither Branson nor Kelleher could have imagined.

The unlikely go-between was a recent college graduate who had just missed bumping into David Neeleman in the corridors of 2702 Love Field Drive during an internship at Southwest around the time the Morris Air merger had first surfaced. Alex Wilcox was what the British call a "petrol head"; a pilot since the age of sixteen, he was so hooked on the smell of jet fuel that he had briefly dropped out of the University of Vermont to work as a baggage handler and a dispatcher for a commuter airline at Burlington Airport. After college, he had talked his way into a customer service job at Virgin Atlantic Airways in Miami, using his British passport—he had been born in London to a Swiss father and American mother—to impress the Virgin station chief that he was a sophisticated world traveler, when in fact he'd spent most of his life in Vermont.

Wilcox was smart and ambitious, and he was quickly promoted up the ranks. When he arrived in New York in 1996, he caught the attention of David Tait, an urbane Briton who had opened Virgin Atlantic's U.S. operations in a town house in Greenwich Village. Tait had been a protégé of Freddie Laker, who had become a folk hero to millions of backpackers by introducing a low-fare Sky Train across the Atlantic in the mid-1970s after years of battling big airlines and obtuse government regulators. By the mid-1990s, Laker and his ilk were long gone and Tait had moved beyond ministering to the needs of budget travelers. He moved Virgin's offices to Connecticut's Fairfield County from Manhattan and brought in Wilcox to help him come up with increasingly over-the-top marketing ideas, such as the spas and putting greens that Virgin had put in at some airport lounges.

One of the more far-fetched schemes they pondered was to lease a nineteen-seat Gulfstream jet and offer a super-first-class service to London

City Airport from Westchester County Airport in New York, which was conveniently close to Virgin's Connecticut redoubt. Wilcox dubbed it "Beat the Concorde" on the theory that you could make the trip door to door faster than by traveling to JFK to take the supersonic competition. Wilcox and Tait knew this would appeal to their boss for one simple reason: It had the power to annoy giant British Airways, which was to Virgin what the Texas airline establishment had been to Southwest— a big bully of an airline whose attempts to drive a challenger out of business had backfired spectacularly.

Virgin Atlantic started up in 1984 with a single flight between Newark Airport and Gatwick, England. The latter airport was more than thirty miles from London and was mainly used by leisure fliers. But later, when Virgin got valuable landing rights at British Airways' home base of Heathrow, the larger line decided to get even. In early 1991 vague reports began to bubble up about Virgin customers' getting phone calls at home from someone identified as a Virgin employee, explaining their flight had been canceled, when, in fact, it had not been. It soon emerged that a British Air worker had hacked into Virgin's computers, retrieved reservations records of premium passengers, and then called the unsuspecting customers offering to rebook them on British Air at no additional charge in first class or even on the Concorde, with the ultimate goal of winning them away from the upstart. This became a major scandal in the British press, and when BA denied the charges in a letter, Branson sued for libel. He ended up settling for $1.1 million, plus $2.5 million in damages, an unprecedented amount at the time. However, the senior management of BA got off unscathed, and Branson felt that the punishment was still far too lenient. And so, arguing that American courts had jurisdiction, Branson filed a lawsuit in the United States, asking for treble damages under antitrust laws.

Conveniently for Neeleman, then, Branson's battle with British Air required him to spend a lot of time in the United States. He was fighting them on another front as well: British Airways and American Airlines had teamed up to form a lofty-sounding "alliance," and combined, they would have fully two-thirds of the flights across the pond. Branson was not alone in criticizing this arrangement as giving the two airlines a virtual lock on the richest international market in the world, and he ran to Washington to join in the condemnation of the deal. As he made his rounds among members of Congress, Branson argued the alliance should be approved only in return for giving other airlines, namely Virgin, unprecedented rights to operate in the States, where U.S. law has long limited foreign ownership of a U.S. airline to less than 25 percent of voting control. This xenophobic restriction was, in part, based on the Pentagon's practice of requisitioning commercial aircraft during a war, which could get awkward if the plane belonged to someone fighting on the other side. But raising the quid pro quo was a sly move on Branson's part, because either way he stood to win. While many skeptics suspected that his real mission was to scuttle his rival's pact, if he gained a U.S. license, there was no telling what he could do.

One day in the fall of 1997, Alex Wilcox was sitting at his desk in Norwalk, when David Tait dropped a package on his desk. The cover page read simply: CONFIDENTIAL BUSINESS PLAN FOR "NEW AIR," the working name that Neeleman had slapped on it for want of something better. Neeleman's name and phone number were scrawled in the margin. Wilcox quickly scanned the manifesto, and "fell in love with it instantly,"

he said. With Southwest's low costs and the Virgin style, "it could not miss."

Tait, in fact, had been awaiting the plan; Branson and Neeleman had already met informally earlier in the year. Besides, the timing was good. Branson's penchant for slapping the Virgin name on anything that came his way was raising questions. He had taken his company public once already but had bought it back, and published reports suggested he had a tangled web of offshore corporations in the Bahamas and the Isle of Man, among other tax havens. Branson also had a taste for risky stunts and was contemplating another long-shot attempt to circumnavigate the globe in a hot-air balloon, even though he'd nearly been killed when an earlier try in January had ended in a crash landing over the Algerian desert. It was time, thought some of his aides, to reel him in with something that hewed closer to his core businesses.

Wilcox went in to talk to Tait. It was perfect: an airline that—with a relatively modest investment from Branson—would plaster the Virgin logo on planes traversing the richest consumer market in the world. "Let's not lose this one," said Tait. He told Wilcox to get on the phone immediately and invite Neeleman to New York.

A few days later, Neeleman hopped a flight to White Plains, New York. Wilcox remembers that he drove to the airport to pick up his guest with some apprehension. Here he was, a single guy who liked to party, about to meet a man about whom he knew very little except that he was a teetotaling Mormon from Utah with a lot of children. But he was immediately put at ease by Neeleman's low-key charm. He and Neeleman spent much of the next few days driving around the borough of Queens, obsessively navigating the eight miles that separate LaGuardia and Kennedy airports. Neeleman would later joke that that strip of asphalt is so reviled for its traffic bottlenecks that "people think it's eight hundred miles." Ironically, it was that very impression that Wilcox had been attempting to exploit with his Beat the Concorde scheme. But Neeleman was more interested in getting to the root of why it was that LaGuardia was seen as convenient while JFK was regarded as Siberia. It didn't make sense: LaGuardia was somewhat easier to get to, but had become so prone to delays that any time you saved on the road would be lost sitting on the tarmac. Neeleman's outsider viewpoint was working to his advantage. He didn't share the parochial view that everything emanates from Manhattan, and it also struck him that there were a large number of people, nearly five million, for whom Kennedy was actually the most convenient airfield. That was greater than the entire population base of Atlanta and alone was a huge catchment for any airport.

Neeleman later did his own study, with one of Dan Hersh's fellow practitioners of the "dark arts" of modeling and forecasting demand, a whiz named Dave Ulmer, who'd worked for Delta, ValuJet, and Frontier before striking out as a private consultant. Ulmer studied all the routes that had been pioneered by People Express back in the early 1980s—places like Newark to Buffalo or Burlington, Vermont. Those routes had racked up double-digit growth—not just from those flying People Express, but also from the bigger airlines that had selectively matched the discounter's fares. But after People imploded, fares shot back up, and some price-sensitive customers simply stayed away from the airlines; they drove, they took the bus, they wouldn't pay the going rate then charged by the few airlines that controlled this corridor. Ulmer's study showed for the first time how many, and the results were stunning. Fully eight million passengers had disappeared from these markets. "All you would have to do is to get those people back—nothing more. And it would be a success. It's a slam dunk," Ulmer said.

One day in early 1998, Kevin Murphy, then the senior airline analyst for Morgan Stanley, picked up the phone to hear a giddy voice demand: "Hey, guess who this is?" It was David Neeleman, whom Murphy hadn't heard from since 1993, when Morris had hired Morgan Stanley to handle the abortive IPO that was called off because of the Southwest merger.

Neeleman opened the conversation a bit sheepishly. "I bet you don't want to hear from me!" Murphy was amused that "he was still worried about my feelings" over the failed IPO. David continued: He was starting a new airline. He was already in discussions with the Port Authority of New York and New Jersey about basing the airline at Kennedy and the plan was moving along. He had, though, a more immediate request: Being a start-up company and all, he wanted to keep expenses down. Could Murphy give him a place to stay on his next trip to New York?

Murphy cracked up. Here's a typical entrepreneur, he thought: The guy made twenty-two million dollars from the sale of Morris Air and he can't cough up enough money to stay in a hotel? But sure, he said, he would be happy to host Neeleman at his home, which happened to be a large apartment in a luxurious building at Madison Avenue and Ninetieth Street. The two became fast friends: Murphy was in his mid-forties, about ten years older than Neeleman, but he was, despite his Morgan Stanley job and fancy address, as unpretentious as his houseguest.

Neeleman showed up on his doorstep with a revised version of his business plan, which now bore the name Virgin America. By the spring of 1998, Neeleman had already been to the United Kingdom to meet with Branson and other senior Virgin officials. Usually he'd fly into Gatwick, and drive to the Virgin offices at nearby Crawley, a drab suburb that was nicknamed "Creepy Crawley" by the Virgin crowd.

Branson and Neeleman got along well, despite their sharply different backgrounds. Like Neeleman, Branson suffered from learning disabilities, and his dyslexia had gone undiagnosed for years. When he had arrived at boarding school at the age of eight he was still unable to read, incurring numerous floggings from schoolmasters who'd assumed he was either lazy or stupid. He, too, left school without a degree and started up his first business venture as a teenager. Also similar to Neeleman, he claimed that he was able to profit from his disability. It has made him more "intuitive," he said, and "when someone sends me a written proposal, rather than dwelling on detailed facts and figures, I let my imagination grasp it and run."

Branson, ironically, had also been influenced by Don Burr's People Express, which in 1984 was the only U.S. airline flying the Newark to Gatwick run. After it took Branson two days to get through to the airline on the phone, he concluded that either People Express had far more business than it could handle or was extremely badly managed. Either way, he thought, here was a great business opportunity; as he had told his appalled associates, if nothing else it would be "fun" to have his own airline. He was right on both counts; within a year Virgin was airborne, and People Express had tanked.

Branson had grasped the timing was right for a similar opportunity with Virgin America. By the middle of 1998, the lack of low-fare competition within the United States was beginning to alarm consumer advocates and members of Congress, who were flooded with complaints from constituents about the lack of affordable air fares. The larger airlines had recovered from their losses of the early 1990s and were reaping annual profits in the range of one billion dollars. Regulators at the Transportation Department were drafting sweeping competition guidelines, which would punish big airlines for bad behavior toward their small-fry competition. Of course, part of the reason why large airlines could act with impunity was the dearth of new entrants. Following ValuJet, the number of new scheduled airline applicants in the United States plummeted from about ten per year to zero two years after the accident. Branson knew that Washington was eager to see a new airline succeed.

And so the talks progressed. Early in the spring of 1998, Neeleman was asked if he could bring someone to vouch for his character on his next trip to the United Kingdom. Neeleman asked if Murphy would act as his reference.

"I said, of course," Murphy recalled. "But we have to travel separately. I go first class; he's in coach. And I'm staying in an expense account hotel, and he's staying in some dump. The next morning I drop by to pick him up and he's there at the front desk, paying his bill, and he's insisting they add a charge for the extra orange juice he'd had at the breakfast buffet. They're saying it's okay, and he's actually arguing with them, saying he has to pay for it. And I'm telling him we've got to go, but he's still trying to give them that extra few cents.

"So I go into a private meeting with Branson and his lawyer, and they say, 'What do you think?'"

"And I say, 'You guys have *nothing* to worry about. This guy is so honest, he wouldn't even take an extra juice without paying for it.'"

Neeleman enjoyed these visits. On one occasion, Branson invited him to go to one of the Virgin company's theaters to see the movie *The Full Monty* and took him out to an Indian restaurant afterward with his wife and son. Neeleman was also struck by Branson's formidable fame, he told colleagues later; whenever they went out, gawkers would follow. After all, Branson was one of the few recognizable business executives in the world, a status he pretended to disdain but had actually cultivated all along. In fact, he later admitted that Freddie Laker had instructed him at the outset to "sell yourself along with the airline," since it was hard for an upstart to compete with the likes of Pan Am or British Air.

On one of these visits that spring, Neeleman and Branson signed a memorandum of understanding to go forward with Virgin America. They worked out a partnership that would lend the Virgin brand in exchange for Neeleman's raising the capital. Branson would have no more than 24.9 percent voting control, the maximum permitted by law, and thus he would need to chip in around twenty million dollars. It was generally understood, however, that his team would supply much of the branding know-how and would therefore have a substantial influence over strategy. It would start out like Southwest, with short flights and one class of service, but with classy touches like individual seat-back TV monitors; it would be sort of a Virgin Atlantic Lite.

Back at the Gatwick Hilton, Tom Kelly and Neeleman were almost pixilated at the thought that this "country boy from Utah" (as Neeleman sometimes referred to himself) might soon be working for Virgin, which, now that Pan Am had expired, was one of the few airlines that could summon some of the glamour that once attached to the airlines. Still, the cautious Kelly knew that the Virgin team had reservations about giving over so much authority to these two unknowns. "Branson got what David was trying to do," said Kelly. "But my gut feeling was it was the wrong time and wrong place . . . the sense was that Branson himself was warm to the idea but his team had more reservations."

Among the more outspoken critics on that team was Frances Farrow, Branson's general counsel. She was also among those concerned about Branson's promiscuous lending out of his brand name. Several of these ventures had turned out to be duds, and the airline franchises hadn't gone well. Virgin Express, which had started out as Eurobelgian Airlines, had developed a reputation for such unreliable service that it had proved a major embarrassment to Virgin Atlantic. Farrow pointed out how difficult it is to ensure quality control in the airlines, where the "product," unlike something static like a dress or a bottle of soda, was subject to myriad forces beyond their control. "Do we want another Virgin Express on our hands?" she reportedly asked.

Then Virgin's main U.S. banker, Merrill Lynch, ran the concept past their airline analyst at the time, Candace Browning. Unlike Morgan Stanley's Kevin Murphy, Browning was not impressed, saying in so many words that it was unlikely a low-fare domestic airline could succeed out of Kennedy Airport. At the same time, Branson was getting encouragement from the Washington lawyers he'd hired that the United States might change the laws on airline ownership; he'd been meeting with members of Congress, like Senator John McCain of Arizona, who were worried about rising air fares, given the dearth of new entrants in the post–ValuJet world. If the law changed, Branson could have full control and wouldn't have to worry about ceding decision-making power to Neeleman.

Meanwhile, the countdown was starting. Neeleman was now six months away from the time he'd be free to announce his new airline plan. In addition to his lead investor banker Michael Lazarus, Neeleman had lately reeled in some impressive backers. Kevin Murphy had run into former Morgan Stanley banker Frank Sica sitting in first class on the flight back from London and Sica's new boss, legendary billionaire George Soros, had subsequently signed on. Chase Capital Partners was another early backer. To be sure, Branson provided some name recognition, but Neeleman had more than enough money.

Then the relationship between Branson and Neeleman began to show strain. Branson had wanted to go slow, to see whether the U.S. law might change, he later admitted. He had failed to appreciate that the five years Neeleman had waited to get back into the business was, for him, an eternity. Neeleman had long promised to himself that the moment Kelleher's spell was lifted in 1999, he would be ready, and if Branson wasn't going with him, so be it.

Then one day in June, the news came from London: Branson and Neeleman would go their separate ways. David Tait called Alex Wilcox into his office and abruptly announced the deal was off. Wilcox was shocked. He'd spoken to Neeleman a few days before and everything seemed to be going forward.

A short time later, Wilcox got a call from Neeleman, who, far from being dejected, seemed strangely elated.

"Screw Virgin," Neeleman told Wilcox. "We'll come up with our own name."

Wilcox was impressed by the "we" presumption: Neeleman seemed to lack any doubt that Wilcox would leave an airline that flew around the world for a no-name start-up that might be closer to an airborne Greyhound. But Neeleman knew Wilcox well enough to know he was restless. He offered to guarantee him a year's salary and gave him a substantial stake in the corporation, which, if it ever went public, would be worth millions.

Wilcox soon resigned from Virgin, and other Branson executives would eventually follow him. Later, Branson admitted that letting Neeleman's start-up slip through his grasp was one of the bigger blunders of his career. "I really effed up on that one," he said.

When the Virgin deal fell apart, another hitch arose: Even if they succeeded in building a brand from scratch, neither Neeleman nor Kelly could visualize himself playing the outrageous extrovert, the way Branson and Kelleher had. Dressing in Elvis jumpsuits or even, as Branson sometimes did, in drag would be unthinkable. That raised the question of who would fuel the buzz, the strong identity that would erase the unsavory image of a low-fare upstart.

Wilcox knew it would be someone from the Virgin side; Southwest's cornpone humor would definitely not go over in their new hometown. His first thought was to call Amy Curtis-McIntyre, a friend in marketing who'd left Virgin a few weeks earlier after a falling-out with David Tait. She was a native New Yorker and had an impressive track record for attention-grabbing campaigns in a tough market: In two years, she had risen to a position of influence in Virgin.

Curtis-McIntyre, however, was thinking of leaving the airline business altogether; she was, as she put it, "sick of being the chick in a guy's world." She had worked for Celebrity Cruise Lines after cutting her teeth at the Hill & Knowlton public relations firm and imagined she'd return to one of these less testosterone-driven pursuits. Wilcox convinced her that she should at least meet David Neeleman in person.

One evening in early July 1998, Curtis-McIntyre arrived at Remi, the mid-Manhattan restaurant she'd chosen for her first encounter with Neeleman, who brought along Tom Kelly from Utah, Michael Lazarus, and his partner, Tom Patterson, from San Francisco. She was nervous and had met with a friend for a few drinks before arriving for dinner, but Neeleman immediately put her at ease.

"I just remember thinking, 'God, this guy is so handsome, but he is so unassuming.' There was nothing slick about him at all." The men, in turn, were equally taken by Curtis-McIntyre, who, with her husky voice and caustic sense of humor, was the quintessence of the single career girl. "David would later say he'd never met anyone like me before," she laughed. They spent most of the dinner talking about New York, a topic of fascination because none of the men had ever lived in the city.

Then the conversation turned to Neeleman's airline. The men took turns throwing lobs at Curtis-McIntyre, asking her how she'd handle various scenarios, all basic Marketing 101, and Curtis-McIntyre acquitted herself admirably. But as the dinner was winding down, Neeleman suddenly threw a curveball. "He looked at me straight in the eye and said, 'Name it!' And I thought . . . whoa . . . this could be dangerous. But by then, I was pretty relaxed. I was feeling no real pressure, no pain."

Curtis-McIntyre hardly hesitated. "Taxi," she said. There was a dead silence. Then Neeleman started laughing. "That was so funny," she said later. "I just blurted it out. And then we went crazy, we just couldn't stop talking about all the possibilities: We'd paint the planes yellow, put checkerboard patterns on the tails, it would be great."

The following morning she got a call from Alex Wilcox. "What happened?" he demanded. "Now he's telling everyone the airline is named 'Taxi.'" Wilcox went on: "He thinks it's really funny."

Curtis-McIntyre was ready to sign on, although first she had to convince friends that she hadn't lost her mind by giving up a glamour career for a no-name start-up. Neeleman had, however, won her over. "David used the term 'clean white paper' a lot," she said, "the idea of starting fresh. He would say, 'You've taken care of a company . . . wouldn't it be more fun to build one?'"

Neeleman was going to have a much tougher time assembling the rest of the "dream team" he had sold investors on. His plan for New Air was not just to make money. It was to find like-minded individuals who wanted to shake up the airline establishment, who shared his vision for how to change the status quo. While the "v" word doesn't appear much in Neeleman's first business plan, which, after all, was a sober-minded pitch to potential investors, clearly Neeleman wouldn't be content to be remembered simply as the founder of the airline with the lowest costs. But to create that "better Southwest" he envisioned, the offspring of the schools of Kelleher and Branson, he'd need a very experienced team with proven track records elsewhere, to attract the capital he needed. His experience at Morris was all well and good, but that on its own wasn't going to get Wall Street excited.

But he would have to summon all his persuasive powers as he set about luring some of the best minds to sign on. He knew he would have to persuade them to give up secure, well-paying posts to confront the risks of an airline start-up. Any overt attempts he made to recruit former colleagues at Southwest would violate his noncompete agreement.

Early on, Neeleman knew he had to persuade his old friend John Owen to come on board. Owen, after all, was the treasurer of the only airline in the country that had made money consistently for more than twenty-five years. His familiarity with all aspects of Southwest's operation—from how it paid its employees to its financing arrangements with the Boeing Corporation—would be a huge advantage. Owen's credentials were impeccable: He had an MBA from the Wharton School and had apprenticed with American Airlines' formidable CEO, Robert Crandall, so he understood well the kinds of responses a new airline would incite. So Neeleman pulled an end run around Kelleher. He flew to Dallas, invited Owen out to dinner, and yakked incessantly for six hours about his new plan, without once mentioning the possibility of Owen's coming aboard. Predictably, that bothered Owen enough that the next day he went searching for Neeleman's file and learned that, indeed, only if a Southwest employee made an overture could discussions proceed. So Owen sat down and wrote Neeleman a letter expressing his willingness to enter into talks about joining the new venture.

Owen had some misgivings. He was forty-two, with a young family to support, and as a Texas native was reluctant to pull up stakes completely. However, he also knew he had probably advanced as far as he could at Southwest. Neeleman was persistent: He needed a sober-minded financial presence who would balance his untamed exuberance.

Finally, after Neeleman promised him a large enough stake to quell his anxiety, Owen finally agreed to leave Southwest and uproot his family from Dallas, and he wanted to settle his family in a peaceful setting, far from the horrors of the Van Wyck Expressway and Kennedy Airport. As it happened, Neeleman was house hunting in the tranquil, and very affluent, suburb of New Canaan, Connecticut, where there is a large Mormon church, one of the biggest in the East. Vicki Neeleman had made David promise that he would find an office no more than twenty minutes from home. So Neeleman made another concession to Owen by agreeing to establish a small satellite office in nearby Darien, which would house Owen's finance department and some back-office tasks like payroll. Owen, however, was still nervous about jumping to an unknown quantity after Southwest, and he subsequently changed his mind and told Neeleman he wouldn't be coming after all. Finally he was reeled back in, but "for a long time we didn't really believe he was coming. That was the hardest one, getting him to believe that we were for real," said Neeleman. Owen later admitted he'd gotten cold feet more than once, and only when the venture capital money was, literally, in the bank, did he overcome his qualms.

Neeleman also wanted someone to help him clone the warrior culture of Southwest. Ann Rhoades, who had been "vice president of people" at Southwest during Neeleman's short tenure, was an obvious choice to reprise the role at New Air. She had moved on and established her own firm that helped businesses recruit and vet new employees, however, and was reluctant to leave her home in Albuquerque, so Neeleman agreed to allow her to commute to New York, spending two weeks a month living out of a Manhattan hotel. Tom Kelly also balked at the idea of moving across the country; he had two teenage children and did not want to uproot them, and, besides, New York held no appeal for him. Neeleman couldn't imagine starting up his airline without him, however, so they agreed that Kelly would discharge his duties as general counsel and executive vice president from the same Salt Lake City office at 6322 South 3000 East Street that he'd shared with David Neeleman since the early 1990s.

The biggest job to fill, though, was that of the number-two spot of president and chief operating officer. By the summer of 1998, one name kept coming up frequently: Dave Barger, a Continental Airlines executive. His success in turning around one of the industry's most undependable operations—Continental's delay-prone hub at Newark—had been noticed by many in the industry. Barger was in charge of the day-to-day operations at Newark, which, with more than three hundred flights a day and ten thousand employees, was equal to running a mid-size airline. He was close in age to Neeleman, but had far more experience in the airlines, having spent his entire life steeped in the business of flying. His father was a United Airlines captain, and his mother had been a flight attendant. Barger and his siblings enjoyed the perks that this allowed, flying first class all over the world on free passes, staying at five-star hotels (where flight crews bunk practically free), and generally living a privileged life that would have been impossible on a middle-class income. Unsurprisingly, Dave and his younger brother Mike both decided early on that being a pilot was perhaps the best job anyone could have. But only Mike made it to flight training; Dave was wearing glasses by the time he reached adolescence and was told, bluntly, that his poor eyesight had effectively banned him from the ranks of commercial pilots. He persisted—taking private flying lessons while in college—and was so determined to get into the business that soon after he graduated from the University of Michigan he was on his way to Detroit to look for a job at the airport.

He started as a minimum-wage gate agent for New York Air, one of the first start-up airlines to be formed as a result of the deregulation law.

It was also the brainchild of Frank Lorenzo, who was soon to become known as the most hated boss in America for his public battles with unions at Continental and Eastern airlines. But New York Air, with its low fares, wines of the month, and "nosh bags," was, Barger said, "young and cool and a great place to start out. Little did I know at that point that it was really a plot to get at the unions."

New York Air eventually was merged along with People Express into Lorenzo's larger airline, Continental, where Barger rose in rank, putting in time in some unusual postings. He worked for a year in Guam as the head of customer service for the airline's Air Micronesia unit, a job that among other things entailed making sure the pigs and chickens were swept off the runways before a plane came in for a landing. By the mid-1990s, he had landed at Newark Airport.

Barger had met Neeleman four years before on a visit to Salt Lake with his old friend Larry Twill, a prosperous New York investor who had briefly been president of New York Air, joining a long list of executives who had clashed with Lorenzo. Twill, a rumpled, heavyset man who favored suspenders and loud ties, could be a bit rough around the edges. Barger recalled that when they first met, Twill screamed obscenities at him over a missing airport sign and then introduced himself as Barger's new boss. But Twill also spotted Barger's talent and had kept in close contact. The two were always on the lookout for unusual investment opportunities and went to visit Neeleman to see if his Open Skies system could be adapted for other, nonairline uses, such as selling theater tickets. As he recalled years later, Barger was unimpressed by his first encounter with his future partner. Apparently, Neeleman's ADD was on display more than usual that day. "It was bizarre," Barger recalled. "He was like this waterbug," he said. "His eyes kept on darting around the room." Barger didn't give Neeleman much thought after that, and their ticket-selling venture went nowhere.

Barger was part of the airline establishment now, and Continental, with its huge hub, was, by some measures, the largest airline serving New York City. Barger had not seriously considered leaving the more prestigious world of international aviation for another surely short-term gig in an upstart. Delta Air Lines was courting him for a highly paid job to take charge of its giant operation at Atlanta's Hartsfield Airport, which has a somewhat dubious reputation as the biggest single airport operation in the world. For Barger, however, nothing he would face could equal the disaster he'd witnessed in February of 1987, when Frank Lorenzo decided to mash together, overnight, Continental and People Express, New York Air, and Frontier, and other airlines he'd acquired in a feverish buying binge. It was an event so cataclysmic that industry insiders still refer to it as the "big bang." The combined company had thirty-two different aircraft types and thousands of workers who'd received no training in routine procedures. People Express's ground crews didn't know the city codes of their new destinations and most of them had never handled checked baggage because the airline had charged passengers luggage fees to discourage them from bringing any. The resulting service disruptions reached epic proportions. For most of that year, Continental was losing anywhere from five hundred to one thousand bags a day, about ten times the number any airline can handle, and lost luggage warehouses were so full that airport workers would simply load any stray bags onto a flight to somewhere else, where the same scenario would repeat itself. There was apparently a vast number of errant bags circulating around in the air, Flying Dutchman style, never landing in one place for long. Airports were jammed with so many fliers stranded by delays and cancellations that members of Congress pressed the FAA to punish Continental by levying a particularly harsh fine.

Barger was appalled, not just by the chaos but by the attitude of top management. Lorenzo and his top lieutenants refused to communicate directly with front-line workers, and that implicit lack of trust became self-fulfilling. "Working with Frank [Lorenzo] taught me a great lesson," Barger said. "It's that you don't build an airline on the backs of labor. Whenever we heard Frank would be coming through the terminal, everyone would run and hide. And he'd hide too, in first class, arriving in the black limo, never talking to the employees . . . and I thought, man, have you really got it wrong."

However, the post–Lorenzo Continental was a far happier place—Lorenzo was forced out in 1991. Barger had done well financially; he was living in a hotel in Midtown Manhattan while building a country home in a rural corner of western New Jersey. He was even thinking of retiring early and indulging in one of his escape fantasies—to buy a sloop and sail it across the ocean.

It was Dan Hersh, David Neeleman's old pal and sounding board from his Morris Air days, who acted as matchmaker. Hersh had also worked with Barger at New York Air and he felt that Neeleman needed someone who was temperamentally his opposite, so that he wouldn't spend all his time kicking the tires at the airport. He tracked down Barger traveling in France at the end of July and told him just enough about Neeleman's venture to get him intrigued. "How fast can you get out to Denver?" he asked Barger—who responded that if he took the Concorde he'd be there in time for dinner the next day. The following evening Barger found himself sitting with Hersh and Neeleman in Hersh's box at a baseball game.

Barger was expert at managing the sorts of complex hub operations that are the hallmark of the big airlines, and so it was surprising that he'd be at all attracted to the prospect of running what would start as a tiny point-to-point operation. Part of his interest, however, was that he, like

Neeleman, had seen what happens when people get crushed by large institutions. Barger had, in fact, clashed with his superior in Guam, a rigid taskmaster, and once had even quit to take a lesser job back in the States for a time.

"And I thought, 'Man, this place sucks. Why am I giving critical years of my life to this organization?' And I learned another lesson. There are a lot of great people at these airlines but the management structure just pummels them. There is so much brain dead management in this industry it is unreal."

Barger was, it seemed, the perfect foil to Neeleman and all his quirks. Michael Lazarus was also brought in to meet Barger on a visit to New York. They hooked up in a bar in Midtown Manhattan late one night and, as Lazarus recalled, "He had two pagers and two cell phones and they were going off at eleven o'clock at night. And he was saying he had to get out to the airport to find out what's going on. And I thought here is the guy we need to catch all the details and have them seamlessly executed." Lazarus told Neeleman he had to hire him. "They were yin and yang," he said.

Barger had already accepted an offer from Delta by phone; he was set to fly to Atlanta in a week to close the deal. Neeleman and Lazarus persuaded him to come up to Boston for a meeting with all the key investors, where they had intended to unveil the management team. It was the usual bane of a start-up: The venture capital funds would not begin flowing until the money men could see the management they were betting on. But much of the putative management team was holding off until they could see the money was really there.

So on August 18, 1998, a dozen would-be airline moguls met with an equal number of finance men at the Hilton Hotel at Logan Airport in Boston. Amy Curtis-McIntyre and Alex Wilcox, who had already left Virgin, were joined by Dave Barger and John Owen. The money men were suitably impressed. Kevin Murphy of Morgan Stanley later commented, "I was reminded of what Warren Buffett says about not investing in companies, but in management . . . these guys were amazing for a start-up budget airline."

A few days later, the investors signaled their approval and Barger called Delta to turn down the job. John Owen soon made his defection official, and Neeleman would soon close the largest round of private financing in airline history—$130 million, with initial investors Weston Presidio, Chase Capital, and George Soros's Quantum Fund. New Air incorporated later that month.

One thing, however, did not survive the Boston powwow. "Taxi" as a name had failed to catch fire. "The suits at the meeting just didn't like it," Curtis-McIntyre recalled. Many of the investors associated "taxi" not with the Checker cabs of yore but with their own, less salubrious experiences in the backseat of an unclean and unsafe contraption. They were also dissuaded by the possible confusion to air traffic controllers, for whom the verb "to taxi" has a different and quite specific meaning.

Curtis-McIntyre was unfazed. She called a friend at Virgin's public relations department in Connecticut, Gareth Edmondson-Jones, an Australian ex-pat who had a knack for clever plays on words, and persuaded him to quit Virgin and join her. Together they thought they would come up with something equally edgy that wouldn't offend the sober-minded finance types. By then the half dozen or so full-time New Air employees were ensconced in the investor Larry Twill's offices at Fifth Avenue at Fifty-third Street, and "we got all caught up in what a cool New York thing this was going to be," Curtis-McIntyre said. Neeleman, Tom Kelly, John Owen all made sporadic appearances, but the Virgin gang had the run of the place. The two colleagues with the hyphenated names would often repair to the rooftop bar at the Peninsula Hotel across the street and rattle off ideas over martinis. The borough of Queens, their ultimate destination, seemed far away indeed.

Everyone assumed they would buy their planes from Boeing, and so, actually, did Boeing. John Owen was a frequent visitor to Boeing's humongous plant and headquarters outside of Seattle; he'd negotiated scores of deals for the efficient 737 series that Southwest used. He'd also signed on as the first customer for the most advanced version, the 737-700. "I'd been the guy who was driving that, and it was certainly my expectation that that's what we were going to do here." Neeleman was concerned, though, that it was one thing for a Southwest to negotiate with the giant jetmaker, and another for a virtual unknown with no track record. "We want a fair level playing field," he told Owen.

In 1999, that meant dealing with Airbus Industrie, the European airframe maker that was jointly owned by manufacturers in Great Britain, Germany, France, and Spain. Most of its planes were assembled in Toulouse in southern France, which was now a booming company town for the jetmaker as the consortium had been gradually catching up to Boeing in sales to commercial airlines. It had come down to that—just two main rivals, after Boeing had acquired McDonnell Douglas and Lockheed had gotten out of the commercial side of the aircraft business.

In early January, John Owen and Dave Barger went to Boeing to give them the initial pitch. That same week, Neeleman picked up the phone and called Airbus's American headquarters in northern Virginia.

"David just cold-called them; it was amazing. Because they (Airbus) assumed that we would just do the usual thing and go to Boeing," said Owen.

The Airbus people were skeptical; they had heard this before.

"Aren't you just using us to get a better deal out of Boeing?" they asked Neeleman.

Neeleman was prepared. "Has anyone ever used you to get a better deal, but ended up going with Airbus?" he asked. Yes, they responded. "All right," he shot back. "So convince me.'"

The week after their visit to Boeing, Neeleman, Barger, and a team of pilots who had just come on board went to Herndon, Virginia, to meet with the Airbus brass.

The plane they were considering was the Airbus A320, which was very similar to the best-selling 737; a narrow-body, single-aisle plane, it could hold anywhere from 150 to 180 passengers. Airbus already had a few U.S. customers, such as Northwest Airlines, for the model, but it had yet to make a dent in the 737's dominance of the domestic American market.

"In all my years at Southwest, I'd never seen anything from Airbus," said Owen. "But we were blown away by their presentation; it was amazing."

Airbus made a strong case that its plane was more technically advanced than Boeing's, would use less fuel, and—and this really got Neeleman's attention—was more spacious. The fuselage of the A320 was seven inches wider than the 737's. That may seem a trivial distinction, except when translated into personal terms: Each seat can be one inch wider; even the overhead bins could be larger. As anyone who has ever been shoehorned into the typical coach airline seat can attest, one inch can just about spell the difference between comfort and misery.

Owen, Neeleman, and Barger laid down the rules: They'd set up a "bake-off" between the two manufacturers, giving them deadlines to come up with successively more attractive proposals. The list price for the planes was about fifty million dollars apiece but, as in most businesses, no one actually pays full retail. Here again was an area where a start-up was at a distinct disadvantage. "A lot of it was convincing Boeing and Airbus we were a real business," said Owen. "And when David Neeleman is in salesman mode, it is something to behold."

In February, Neeleman met with Airbus executive John Leahy (an American, as it turned out) in a New York City hotel room. Leahy was nicknamed the "Boeing Killer" for his zeal in going after the U.S. rival, and "he is one hard-driving salesman who doesn't want to lose," Owen said. At the time, Airbus had a big problem with Boeing: All the low-fare airlines flew the 737, and "Leahy wanted his own Southwest."

Neeleman arrived for the meeting well prepared to overcome any doubts Leahy might have had about his ability to start up a new airline in New York City. He brought along detailed maps of the city and spoke intelligently about how many people lived in which borough and where all his customers would be coming from, even getting into detail on the road traffic to JFK. "Neeleman was what he had been waiting for . . . he saw that he could be another Kelleher," Owen said.

Meanwhile, Boeing was operating on the assumption that they had the deal sewn up, and Tom Anderson, a top Boeing engineer, left to join Neeleman. It was taken as a sign that Neeleman was serious; after all, his aircraft expertise was all coming from the Boeing camp.

Neeleman, though, wanted to get the best plane at the best price. And in his opinion, the A320 was the better product. On March 4, 1999, he signed a memorandum of understanding for eighty-two of the A320 jets in what was referred to as a four-billion-dollar order. Word quickly got out that the price per plane was well below fifty million dollars and, in fact, might have been closer to forty million dollars. Airbus had gotten what it wanted, and so had Neeleman.

four
building blue

On the morning of June 16, 1999, Amy Curtis-McIntyre arrived on the nineteenth floor of 90 Park Avenue, out of breath for she was rushing to what promised to be one of the more critical meetings of her career. It was unseasonably warm outside, and the office air-conditioning was barely functioning. The dozen people sitting around the table in the cramped conference room had long stopped caring about such matters; the shorts and T-shirts they wore looked like they'd been lived in for days. On the floor, a pile of crumpled coffee cups and empty pizza cartons attested to the hours they had been logging.

"So we're going to do it," she began. "We are going to name this airline. But I'm going to tell you now, not all of you are going to be happy. In fact, you may hate the name we choose."

But as she had told David Neeleman himself not long before, "It is *so* not important that you like this name." She had long ago claimed the role of provocateur as her own.

Neeleman had moved his skeletal staff into these offices a few months before, in April, fully expecting that they would have an official name to put on the front door by then. Nearly a year had passed since Curtis-McIntyre and Neeleman had met over dinner, and New Air as a working title was getting, well, old. Unlike Morris Air, Southwest, and countless other airlines whose names seemed self-evident, Neeleman's team had set their sights high. In part, it was a reflection of the syndrome that the aviation buffs among them could appreciate when gazing out of their windows toward the hulking skyscraper towering over Grand Central Terminal. It had once borne the distinctive globe of Pan American World Airways, once the second best known corporate name in the world after Coca-Cola. The "blue meatball," as Pan Am's corporate symbol was known, had vanished from the skyscraper soon after the airline had ceased flying in 1991 and the building was owned by the MetLife Insurance company. Some people still referred to the landmark as the Pan Am Building, however, and a wealthy investor from New England had bought the name and logo at auction and was planning to use them to launch a new airline of his own. Pan Am was that rarity in the airlines—a brand that rose above the ordinary to suggest a seductiveness about the service, regardless of its connection to reality.

Judging from the names and mock-up logos pasted on the walls, Pan Am was one of the few names that had not been considered for Neeleman's new airline. One poster leaning against the table listed some of the sillier rejects: Yeeeeeees!; Dairy Air ("Oh yes, David loved that one," Amy snorted), Air Hop, egg, Scout Air. There were The Competition and Home (apparently so one could say "I'm flying Home"). These were not plucked wildly from the air but had actually emanated from reputable sources, from Manhattan advertising agencies to one of the premier image consulting firms in the country. Clearly, creative thinking had degenerated at times into a shared lunacy, evidenced by clinkers such as Air Spray, Whistle, and Fresh Air.

One name, Civilization Airways, had advanced to the point where a crisp logo had been commissioned for it. Neeleman, however, thought it sounded too highbrow and might commit the cardinal sin of over-promising what his airline could deliver. That was the crux of the problem: what name to choose that would express not only what they were, but also what they were not, and that wouldn't send the wrong message, which is what had doomed Taxi, with its unfortunate connotations.

The naming process had been so drawn out and agonizing that it was to become a sort of company fable that would later be repeated and embellished with the varying recollections of those who were there. In fact, a presentation on how the airline got its name became part of the first day's orientation for new hires, perhaps because in its messy details it expresses the communal spirit in a more genuine way than, say, a mere mission statement. But the tale has another meaning for those who were there at the beginning, because the debate over the name became a vehicle for a large battle being waged among the various factions that had emerged and that fell loosely into two groups, the Texans and the Virgins.

The Texans, led by John Owen and Ann Rhoades, and, at times, Neeleman himself, could argue persuasively that Southwest's plain-Jane formula for success had worked for nearly thirty years. "For them it was just 'price and destination, price and destination,'" Curtis-McIntyre would say, mockingly. For the Virgin gang, the favored buzzword was "innovation," and the goal was nothing less than to forge another cult brand. Gareth Edmondson-Jones was stoking the media's interest with sound bites such as "We're a low-fare airline with high-quality service." Now, that juxtaposition was giving them agita.

They were in a bind. The news conference they had scheduled long before to tell the world about their plans was only two weeks away. At Airbus's manufacturing plant in Toulouse, workers were toiling to get the jets rolling off the assembly line in November, and even they were asking pointed questions about when they'd have a name to paint on the tail fin. Newspapers were starting to remove the quotes from around the words "New Air." If they didn't act soon, the decision would be made for them.

So it was against this background that Curtis-McIntyre continued her hyperventilating introduction, spewing out an unedited account of the past few weeks, a blur of all-nighters, fueled by illicit cigarette breaks and white wine. Dave Barger interrupted to tease her gently: "Hey, Amy, can you open up a bit and reveal a little of yourself?"

There was some muffled snickering, and then Edmondson-Jones spoke up: "Until benefits kick in, this is therapy."

On the wall, a handwritten time line showed their planned progress from paper airline to their first flight. The first planes were to arrive Stateside in early December, in time to launch the airline soon after the New Year. Everything else was progressing: They'd hired their first pilots; they were trying out seats to put in their planes. Stan Herman, a well-known fashion designer a few blocks away, was sketching uniforms and poring over fabric samples. But David Neeleman's "clean sheet of paper" still had a big empty space.

Amy flashed a slide on the screen, showing all the logos and names of the world's best-known airlines. Most airline monikers are either literal—Southwest, Northwest, Eastern, Air Florida—or platitudinous piffle—Presidential or Spirit. Then the slides switched to reveal the insipid advertising slogans that are so similar as to be virtually indistinguishable. "Do some people really know how to fly?" "Is United Rising?" Everyone laughed because United was at the time so beset with labor strife that employees were privately joking that the ad campaign should be called "United Uprising."

This sentiment seemed to rile Dave Barger, who, though normally cool and unemotional, suddenly let loose with a string of epithets about the airline that had been such a dominant part of his upbringing.

"It's unbelievable. They're saying: 'We know we suck, and we just want to let you know that we know we suck.'" Besides, he said, United's fuzzy message and George Gershwin soundtrack was all wrong. "These promises are so outrageous, when they are not even delivering on basic needs. That's the travel experience, all right: It's twenty to thirty opportunities to piss you off, from phone call to baggage delivery."

A slide flashed on the screen. "Promise underdelivery occurs frequently in airlines," it read, in bold letters. "Most airlines try to differentiate their messages while ignoring product differentiation. The result is commodity market masked by misleading communications." After that bit of consultant speak, it was refreshing to see the simple statement: "No wonder travelers distrust us."

It all went back to Neeleman's original thesis that a strong brand would surmount the handicap of being a new airline. Curtis-McIntyre called it a super brand. Few airlines had a brand identity, much less a strong one. "Starbucks, Heineken, GAP . . ." flashed across the screen. That was the star power they hankered after, to rise above the blandness and mediocrity that have defined the image of the airlines since the beginning.

Brian Coulter, a pilot Barger had recruited from New Zealand, helped bring everyone back to earth. "Uh, what you're saying is that we're not going to be your average loser airline, right?"

The quest had begun soon after Curtis-McIntyre signed on with New Air in the fall of 1998. One of her first decisions was to hire the Manhattan advertising agency of Merkley Newman Harty, an advertising and branding operation that had made its name with hip campaigns for corporate icons such as Citigroup and American Express. Taxi was still the working name when Merkley vied for the account, but when the agency submitted it to focus groups the confused reaction they got delivered the final coup de grâce.

Douglas Atkin, director of strategy, recalled that the process of trying to package an airline as an appealing product was far more arduous than they had imagined. "We did some research, and we concluded that the airlines were a 'poisoned' category. On the 'hate index,' it came up somewhere near the Internal Revenue Service and HMOs," he said. "And so I told David, "You are entering a category which is absolutely loathed and detested. If you call yourself an airline, you will be lumped in with all those others. Remove yourself from the category altogether . . . call yourself a customer advocate."

In preparation for its pitch to Neeleman, the Merkley team covered the walls of a conference room with paper airlines on which various agency employees had scribbled names or words that had strong evocative qualities: "mother," "chocolate," "superfly." Not that any would be serious contenders as a name for Neeleman's airline, but it was a way to trigger the associations that everyone hoped would lead them there.

The next step was to hand Neeleman and company a batch of blank planes and invite them to write whatever popped into their heads. "They were really into it," Atkin recalled. "We had literally hundreds of names up there."

Amy Curtis-McIntyre, he said, "was continually reminding us what this was all about; that it's not the planes, it's the people. . . . And one of the reasons why people hated the airlines was that they were being abused, but no one told them that they were being abused. And so that's where we first started talking about bringing the humanity back to air travel."

The other maxim that came out of these early sessions with Merkley was the "radical application of common sense," which, to the participants, meant reaching a simple goal through questioning the accepted way of doing things. An early example came when Neeleman decided to use leather upholstery, rather than fabric, to cover his seats. Leather was much more expensive, but it was easier, and thus cheaper, to clean. But the ultimate commonsense aspect was that customers preferred it, and therefore might look more favorably on flying a new airline, and that would translate into more business, and hence, profits. "It made perfect sense, but it was unthinkable for a new airline to do that."

It was no surprise when Merkley in early 1999 came up with three names and accompanying design mock-ups to present to their client, none of which bore any resemblance to the airline labels of yore: Egg, It, and Blue. It was the first mention of Blue that anyone can remember. "David loved it," Curtis-McIntyre recalled, if only because he thought the first two were so unsuitable. "He definitely loved the feel of 'Blue' but we knew it would be impossible to trademark."

Then another problem arose. When the first bills started coming in for Merkley's creative efforts, Neeleman was aghast; he just wasn't used to what these things cost in New York City. But it was also his cautious side coming out. He was keenly aware of how fast he could burn through the money he'd raised. He had allotted no more than nine million dollars to ten million dollars to promote the launch of the airline. That was chump change to the companies that his marketing team had worked for in the past, and so they put the brakes on any more branding brainstorms.

Everyone connected with the airline, it seemed, had his own ideas. By early April, hundreds of suggestions had poured in, many unbidden and utterly baffling, like Now! or The Big One. Airbus Industrie decided on its own to consult a French advertising firm for advice, which came up with a name, Fair Air, and a proposal to plaster blown-up photos of actual employees on the tail fins. Curtis-McIntyre exploded. "Yeah, right, we're going to put someone's picture on a fifty-million-dollar plane and . . . then he gets fired!"

The process, though, was bringing Curtis-McIntyre and Neeleman closer. "We would chat on the phone for hours, and we'd get punchy. One night, we went on the Internet to get ideas, and I said, 'Let's look up the top one hundred winners of the Kentucky Derby,' and he laughed because there were things like Polly's Knees, really crazy names in there. And then there were days where it was just annoying because somebody would call me on a Saturday night, or Sunday morning, with their wives' ideas or had run into somebody they went to high school with who had another brilliant suggestion . . ."

On another occasion, John Owen inadvertently set off a brouhaha when he had lunch with Holly Hegeman, a Dallas-based airline analyst whose PlaneBusiness Web site is a sort of an industry tip sheet for the airlines. When Hegeman subsequently ran an item jokingly suggesting a contest to name the airline for the new company, Neeleman, typically, responded "Why not?," infuriating his New York staff, who had to field a flood of calls from people wanting to know if it was true.

The debate was getting out of hand, so Neeleman decided to apply some pressure. One day that April, he called all the major investors to a meeting. "He taped the door shut, and said, 'No one is leaving until we've named this product,'" Curtis-McIntyre recalled. All the names that had been bubbling up got a second chance. Then one from the original list produced by Merkley, It, suddenly rose to the top. It was partly because of the visuals, Curtis said. "We'd be the It airline." "You could say 'Fly It,' we'd have baggage tags reading 'Shlep It,' you'd buy a tick-It and our snacks would say 'Eat It.' It would be so cool." Not everyone in the room quite got the New York sensibility of the concept, but the presence of the Merkley team and the power of their track record was enough. "It was a stretch for some of them, but everybody felt pretty good about it."

The good feeling quickly evaporated when Neeleman went back to Utah. "He freaked out," said Curtis-McIntyre. "He couldn't explain it to anybody without all the visuals and without the big ideas. . . . And people started saying to him, 'It's a big airline and 'It' is a very small name and it just started to eat away at him." When Vicki Neeleman told her husband that "it's not a name that makes you feel safe," that seemed to settle it.

It was getting near the end of April, and now everyone was starting to panic. They decided that It could work if it was positioned as an acronymn for something more imposing. What if they could tap into the rich history of JFK Airport, whose iconic TWA terminal still stirred nostalgia for the days it was the premier gateway to the country? The airport had entered the jet age as Idlewild Airport, they recalled, so they hit on the notion of calling the airline Idlewild Transport, which, although a bit of a mouthful, possessed the right measure of gravitas. They also picked Home as an alternative, not only for its punning possibilities but also for its vast cobranding possibilities. They had already approached Restoration Hardware about decorating their boarding lounges so they'd look more like a living room than the typical sterile airport waiting areas. All these ideas soon tanked as just too off the wall.

Curtis-McIntyre was increasingly losing patience, and one day she blew up at Neeleman. "I got furious," she said. "I told him, 'We can't get it right, because we're in a fish bowl. Every time we have an idea, you tell all the investors at once and you get nine different opinions and nine different reactions. Then you tell your wife and your kids, instead of what you should be doing—taking time to bring an idea to life, or sitting there alone to consider that it's just a label against this great thing that we're building.'"

After one of these dustups, "We'd sort of calm each other down and then it would get all emotional the next day again. . . . To some degree, we were both caricatures of ourselves at that point. I was so afraid to let down the New York thing, and I had to make sure that this didn't shake out as some alternative Southwest. And he was just all over the place. . . . He would say things like 'Why don't we just keep it simple?' He didn't get the marketing process at all.

"We laugh about it today because nothing we've done since has ever been as hard as that. I would say to him, 'You cannot have this many cooks in the kitchen. Someone has got to be cast with making the decisions, and if it is the CEO, fine, and if it's the creative officer, fine, but you will never find consensus.'"

At the urging of Michael Lazarus, Neeleman turned for help to Landor Associates in San Francisco, although Merkley would continue as the lead advertising agency. Landor, which styles itself a "branding consultancy and design firm," had executed image makeovers for companies as diverse as Microsoft and Frito-Lay. Curtis-McIntyre acknowledged she was stung by the implication that she'd struck out, but resigned herself that it was time to get help. "We needed some parents to break up the fights," she said.

Again, Neeleman couldn't believe how much it would cost—the tab would come to around one hundred thousand dollars—and the elaborate methodology Landor employed. The company sits down with everyone it can, interviews them, researches the competition, and concocts a series of fancy-looking matrices. Then it short-lists some candidates and runs them through the focus group grinder. The process normally takes around thirty weeks. Neeleman told Landor he couldn't wait that long—it had to get back to him in eight weeks.

They gave Landor the list of all the names that had been considered, which by then had swelled to more than two hundred. As Landor bore down, Neeleman got "obsessed . . . it was all we could think about. Sometimes David and I would ride in cabs together. I remember taking a long walk around the block, we just wanted to sort out how we're doing," Curtis-McIntyre said.

Landor refused to leak any of the final list of nominees to Neeleman or anyone else, and it insisted that it be allowed to present the ideas to a small group of the founders at a meeting that was set for June 14. As the date approached, Neeleman became increasingly disturbed that a consultant he'd grudgingly agreed to hire had important information about his company that he couldn't share. "It made him psychotic. . . . He couldn't stand to know that they had the list," Curtis-McIntyre recalled. "He started stalking me! He would not leave me alone." So she went to Landor privately and persuaded it that it needed her as an advocate. "I'm on your side," she told Landor. "I can't be caught off guard. If you give me the list in advance, I'll help build a case with one of the names."

So it divulged the list on the phone. As they went down the list, her heart sank. Air Hop was one limp contender, followed by Avenues (not Neeleman's style, she thought), then Lift, Highway (spelled Hi! Way), and Scout. The last one was True Blue. She didn't need much time to think it over. True Blue was the only one that wasn't objectionable. The word "blue," after all, had been an early favorite of Neeleman's. "Of all the crazy ideas, blue was clearly something that had not offended him," Curtis-McIntyre said. "He didn't seem to realize that it meant porn to some people."

On June 13, the night before the meeting, Curtis-McIntyre told

Neeleman the name she'd selected over the phone. The phone went silent. "I just kept telling him we can make True Blue work. There was an authenticity to it, and it was a little audacious . . . like who would ever have the guts to say you're true in the airline business?

"And then I had to get off my high horse and I sold True Blue to Michael Lazarus and the other investors. And to Dave Barger. I sold my heart out. It was hard work. But I did it."

Two days later, she was back at 90 Park, selling her heart out all over again to the rest of the team: John Owen, Brian Coulter, and the other flyboys. But in the intervening two days, a serious problem had arisen. True Blue, it appeared, was already owned by someone else. Thrifty Car Rental had registered the name for a loyalty program it had never activated. It was Landor's responsibility to vet any names for possible trademark violations, but the law firm it usually relied on hadn't been available. In fact, it was only through the efforts of Tom Kelly, who ran his own check, that the glitch had been discovered at all.

So as Curtis-McIntyre flashed the slide with True Blue in big letters, her ambivalence was palpable. There was a strange letdown; after all the angst, they didn't have something that would truly blow people away. But Rhoades had connections at Thrifty, and the thought was that they'd try to work out something amicably. Neeleman was livid at Landor's blunder and delayed paying the remainder of the six-figure fee he'd agreed to; the firm ultimately agreed to halve the bill.

A few days later, Neeleman abruptly changed course. "I don't care if we can get it," he told Curtis-McIntyre over the phone. "I hate the name." This was on a Friday evening, and she was about to leave the office for the weekend. The press conference was ten days away.

"Why can't we just call it Blue?" Neeleman said.

Curtis-McIntyre reminded him they'd gone through that months ago: You can't trademark a commodity, and with the dot-com craze, most phrases incorporating the word were taken.

"So let's make up a word," she said. "What if we call it Flyblue, one word? Then nobody would say, 'I'm going to "fly flyblue."' They'll say, 'I'm going to "fly blue"' and that way you get your name blue in it."

"Okay, that's cool," said Neeleman. "I just kept babbling," she said, "and I said, you can call it 'fly blue' or you could call it 'jet blue' or you could . . ."

They both paused. "Jet Blue," conjured seemingly from nowhere, was, clearly, what they'd been groping for. It got David's "blue" in there, it was a subtle play on words, and adding the "jet" would get across the notion that this wasn't some puddle-jumping turboprop operator. But Curtis-McIntyre was so strung out that she could not believe it was over. At dinner that night she test-drove it for her family and got enough encouragement that she quickly sketched out a logo on a cocktail napkin, since lost, with a distinctive small jet and large "Blue." Then she called Edmondson-Jones, who loved it, too. But they knew once it got out to the Utahans, to the investors, someone would hate it and they'd be back to the drawing board. So they staked out a claim on www.jetblue.com as well as any name that could be used to ridicule it: jetbluesucks.com, jetblew.com, and the like. (The backlash against the airlines had produced a rash of sites like Northworstair.com and Untied.com.) Neeleman didn't seem to mind; he'd taken the precaution of dialing 1-800-JetBlue, which reached a tractor distributor in the Midwest, who indicated he would part with the number for a modest sum.

Their worries had been prescient. That Monday, Neeleman phoned Curtis-McIntyre to tell her that one very important investor—Michael Lazarus—had a major problem with the moniker. "Michael thinks it sounds like ValuJet," Neeleman said.

She started to cry. "It does not!" she shouted into the phone. "We're not canceling the press conference. We will prove to him that it will work."

Another debate was taking place inside the offices at 90 Park at that time. It all boiled down to what they would do about those "twenty to thirty opportunities to piss you off" that had so riled Barger during the meeting. It was destined to be a tumultuous process, when you consider that it involved more than a dozen people, all of whom had spent years contemplating just what they would do if they had a chance to build an airline from scratch.

Landor had referred to "touch points" in its presentation; these are the interactions where subtle signals can get crossed. Airlines have more of a problem living up to their promises because the total experience involves so many separate components, any one of which can go awry and taint the whole experience. "Each touch point provides an opportunity to test the promise" of the brand, it said. "Many are outside of an airline's direct or indirect control."

Neeleman and Barger, however, knew that while indeed there are many things out of their control, how an airline chose to deal with them was very much its call. Barger recalled that one of their first decisions was to set basic parameters on how often to communicate with customers and crew: In delays, for example, no more than ten to fifteen minutes should elapse between updates.

In fact, Neeleman was flying often then, between Salt Lake City and New York, usually on a major airline like Delta or United. And he frequently burst into a staff meeting with the latest horror tale from the road. One day he'd shown up at the airport in the morning to find out his flight, which he had just confirmed an hour earlier, had been scrubbed because the crew had "timed out" by arriving too late the night before. "They knew at midnight that they had this problem. Do you think they could have told me?" It was this sort of glitch that makes people wonder, said Neeleman, "if they can't get something like this right, then are they screwing the bolts on the plane?"

Alex Wilcox, as the original Virgin refugee, had taken to heart Merkley's idea that they should shun the airline category altogether. "We're a people delivery system!" he would say. "If we don't make it look different from any other airline, then we've totally failed." Wilcox, of course, was accustomed to having a Branson-sized budget to play with. Since the airport terminal is where most customers have their first direct contact with their airline company, Wilcox proposed ridding the complex of check-in counters, which he regarded as a dehumanizing barrier. Instead, he imagined a lobby furnished with kiosks and bar stools, where the customer would sit side by side with a check-in agent, who could swivel the computer display so that both could "share the experience" and see exactly the same information. Wilcox also wanted to jettison the standard-issue banks of ugly and uncomfortable seats and replace them with sectional sofas. "It's airports by Ikea," one observer joked, but John Owen was skeptical. "It's all well and good to think 'out of the box,'" he would say, "but you have to be able to *see* the box." The Port Authority of New York and New Jersey, as firmly inside the box as anything could be, finally nixed most of Wilcox's fanciful ideas, pointing out that they would violate the airport's building code (which, unsurprisingly, is far stricter than your average shopping mall's).

Dave Barger recalled one early showdown over, of all things, the number of lavatories to put on the planes, which would be laid out to seat 162 people. John Owen, ever the cautious number cruncher, argued that they needed only two restrooms: Southwest did it that way, after all, and they were anticipating that most of their flights would be under two and a half hours. With the space they would save, they could put in a few revenue-producing seats. Barger strongly disagreed. "And I said you can't just have two, not with all the families, and little kids, and the old people going to Florida," he remembered. Neeleman agreed; this was the quintessential example of where the trade-off between comfort and revenue would be too great.

Early on they had decided that one aspect of Southwest's service they would gladly duplicate would be its Spartan cuisine. That had many advantages; not only did it save money—most large airlines spent anywhere from five dollars to ten dollars per passenger—but it would free up space on the plane by dispensing with full-size galleys. Neeleman had been revolted by many of the repasts he had eaten on planes and was convinced that most passengers would readily forgo the average airline mystery meal in exchange for getting a break on the fare. Here again, it would not be too hard to make a modest improvement over Southwest—instead of just a bag of peanuts, they came up with the idea of having a big basket of various snacks, including the odd-looking blue (actually purple) Terra Chips they would soon make famous. And anyone could go back for seconds or thirds of these caloric infusions.

The culinary value of the airline meal was really beside the point. Most airlines view the ritual of "Will you have chicken or beef?" as a welcome distraction from the monotony of the flight, a sort of alternative form of entertainment. When major airlines like American and Delta had tried to cut back sharply on their meal service in the mid-1990s, it provoked such outrage from consumers that they soon restored some of it. But Wilcox and Curtis-McIntyre, along with Tom Anderson, were already working on the category killer: the idea that had caught their imagination. It was to give everyone in every seat his or her own entertainment, something that had never been done before on a domestic budget airline. Some sort of in-flight entertainment had always been on the table; indeed, it was in Neeleman's first business plan. But no airline had ever offered more than an individual set and canned programming; real-time television was unheard of.

By coincidence, LiveTV, a small company in Georgia, had just begun to pitch the idea of satellite TV to the airlines. A joint venture of the Harris Corporation and the Sextant Corporation, LiveTV had tested the idea of putting an antenna on a plane that could pull off cable programming from a satellite. While this premise had been successfully proven aboard corporate jets, scheduled airlines were put off by the cost of rewiring their entire fleets, not to mention the additional expense of taking planes out of service for several days at a time.

So Neeleman had a clear field. And that, strangely, was the biggest argument against it. "No one expects it on a domestic flight, so why bother?" was how John Owen put it. "I thought it was an unnecessary expense." They proceeded on the assumption that they would charge a fee for the use of the sets, so the system would pay for itself. But how much to charge? And what about the extra work for flight attendants, and the passengers who didn't have a credit card? It started getting complicated and one thing JetBlue had to be was simple.

Ultimately, Owen was swayed by the argument that they couldn't launch the biggest start-up airline in history without a "holy sh—" news flash, said Edmondson-Jones. "For God's sake, we were in New York, the toughest market in the country. We needed to surprise people," and a tarted-up People Express wasn't what they had in mind. They did a comparison: a dreary snack in a cardboard box they'd priced out early in their catering discussions was $1.25 a passenger. They priced the TV service on a per-person basis and it came in at around $1.00. They signed a letter of agreement with LiveTV so they could announce that on day one, they'd have it "at every seat on every plane," of which they would have exactly two. That would give them breathing room to put off the difficult decisions on pricing; it would be free while they tested reaction and figured out what to do.

There was another bottom-line benefit to the decision to go with TV—it would be one aspect of JetBlue's service that rivals couldn't quickly match. Neeleman was fully expecting the big guys to greet the newcomer with their usual hostile reception and indeed every version of his business plan had raised this possibility. But American, Delta, and all the other big airlines couldn't possibly buy and install TVs, even if they were inclined; each had more than five hundred planes in their fleets and taking them out of service to be refitted would be a nightmare. JetBlue, it seemed, had already won round one.

The press conference was now set for July 14. The night before, Curtis-McIntyre got a call from Edmondson-Jones, who was down at the place they had chosen for the debut, an aviation theme bar called Idlewild on the Lower East Side. Brian Glazer, the satellite television producer in charge of the press event the next day, was in a snit, it seemed, because the place was tiny—far too small to accommodate the requests they'd gotten from television crews. When Curtis-McIntyre arrived, however, what she saw alarmed her further: "God, it was this horrible bar. It stank of cigarettes and booze. And all I could think was that David was going to kill us."

Meanwhile, a technician from LiveTV was climbing over roofs trying to hook up the satellite TV feed that would be their coup de grâce—proof to a skeptical public and press that this newcomer was not the latest flaky upstart. Curtis-McIntyre was so obsessed with eradicating the stench that might permeate the reception that she ran to a local convenience store and "bought up every Casablanca lily in sight," she joked later, spending hundreds of dollars during what her colleagues later kidded was her rather shortlived transformation into domestic doyenne. Still, the place was as foul smelling as ever. "I was sweating bullets . . . because I was so afraid of what David would think."

Exhausted, Curtis-McIntyre went home for a few hours of fitful sleep. She and Edmondson-Jones had figured out a way to finesse the location: The press release referred to it as "The Idlewild Bar and Grill," although, as they recounted later, "no one had eaten a meal there in their lives." The next morning, she arrived on Houston Street, still nervously anticipating Neeleman's reaction when he realized that he, of all people, would be announcing his new airline from a bar. Neeleman's only reaction was to laugh. "That was the day we found out how cool he really was. He even kidded us about how bad it smelled," said Curtis-McIntyre.

A few days before, Edmondson-Jones had sat down with Neeleman for the expected prep session to get him ready to face the television cameras. From the outset Gareth knew this would be very different from working with Branson. "David always said he was not comfortable in the limelight. He told me at our first meeting, 'I don't want to be the spokesman. . . . I'm no Branson.'

"That threw me for a second, but I said, as gently as possible, to launch this kind of carrier, you need to be the face of the company. You don't need to grow a beard or fly a balloon, but you need to get out there.

"So in advance of the conference, we got to talking about what message he would convey, what he needed to be saying, but he drew the line. He said he could talk only from his heart about what he wanted to it be. We couldn't put that cheap chic verbiage in his mouth, and all that other stuff that we were doing with our advertising. Instead, he wanted to talk about taking care of people, treating them with respect.

So that's where he decided that his message was, simply, that he was 'bringing humanity back to air travel'" (that phrase had resonated in the early brainstorming sessions with Merkely).

That line was to become his most favored sound bite, the sort of "morning in America line" Ronald Reagan deployed to such effect. And it worked: The only negative question from the press came when someone asked Neeleman, "Isn't 'blue' sort of suggestive of being down?" Neeleman threw out something about "blue skies and happy flying" and, as Curtis-McIntyre put it, "if it had come from anyone else we would have puked."

The press conference was packed: More than one hundred people were jammed into a tiny space. There was an amusing footnote to the coverage the next day; a number of networks reported with a straight face that JetBlue would have cappuccino machines aboard its planes, an industry first. They'd picked up on a teaser that Brian Glazer, the producer of the JetBlue satellite feeds, had slipped into the promo he'd sent out to excite interest.

Amy Curtis-McIntyre had investigated whether it was possible to brew fresh cappuccino aboard a moving aircraft and found out that there was a good reason why no other airline had ever considered it: It would be impossible to pull off in a pressurized cabin. However, even the erroneous mention got the desired message across to the discerning downtown crowd. A couple of days later Dave Barger wrote the first edition of "Blue Notes," a sort of chatty e-mail missive that would become the vehicle for regular communications to JetBlue employees.

"It's amazing how fast New Air disappeared in light of events over the past week, and the name has already started to take hold throughout the city," he gushed. More than four hundred separate TV news reports were aired across the United States, which, in televison-ad speak, translated into fifty million "impressions." In fact, for the hundred thousand dollars they'd spent on a satellite hookup to network affiliates around the country, they'd gotten the equivalent of five million dollars' worth of advertising.

Barger threw in a subtle dig at the location, asking "How did you find that bar, or nightclub or whatever it's called . . . when it didn't even have a sign outside?" Among the worthies who were wondering the same thing, he wrote, were the FAA's chief of the JFK air traffic control, George Dodeline, as well as the airport directors for Buffalo and Burlington, Vermont, all of whom had found their way to the nether reaches of lower Manhattan to witness JetBlue's public debut. If they were unmoved by the hipness factor that day, so be it. For Barger, the launch was just beginning.

five
paper airline

In November 1998, David Neeleman spotted a story in the *New York Times* about the state's newly elected senator, former congressman Chuck Schumer of Brooklyn. Schumer would soon succeed Senator Al D'Amato, the Long Island Republican who'd earned the sobriquet Senator Pothole for his attention to the parochial needs of his constituents. The campaign had been ugly—D'Amato had memorably ridiculed Schumer as a "putzhead"—and Schumer's unseating of the eighteen-year veteran was seen as one of the more dramatic upset victories in the midterm congressional elections.

Schumer had made the lack of affordable air service in New York State one of his main talking points in the campaign. And he had pledged that if elected, he would work to bring low-fare air service to upstate burgs like Buffalo and Rochester that had never recovered from the loss of People Express and, indeed, now enjoyed the dubious distinction of having among the highest air fares, on a per-mile basis, in the entire country.

When the two met at the Waldorf Hotel in Manhattan for breakfast soon afterward, as Neeleman recounted later, he laughingly asked, "So, how do you think you are going to make good on that pledge?" He made Schumer a simple proposition: "You help me in Washington, and I will help you make good on your promise." New York City to Buffalo hardly excited the arbiters of cool that the Virgin ex-pats had in their sights. But if that is what it would take to grab Schumer's attention, then Buffalo it would be.

At Neeleman's side was Rob Land, a young Washington attorney he'd just hired to help him navigate the politics of starting up an airline. Despite all the money, brainpower, and buzz it had accumulated, Neeleman's company in early 1999 was little more than a paper airline. It had no planes, no place to land, and, most crucially, no permission from the government to do so. It had been much harder to get a new entrant past the safety-minded regime in Washington ever since 1997, when the FAA had imposed far tougher standards in the wake of the ValuJet crash.

Enter Usto Schulz, a white-haired septuagenarian who had spent nearly his entire life flying and inspecting airplanes. He had helped Neeleman through the Federal Aviation Administration bureaucracy at Morris Air, and now, Neeleman had persuaded him to join JetBlue as the airline's safety czar, a position that was now mandatory at all new entrant airlines. Most airlines, even the largest ones, had lacked such a post, reasoning that it would be superfluous since safety controls are, by definition, integral to maintaining and flying planes.

Schulz, a former military test pilot and federal aviation inspector, quickly evolved into the resident kindly curmudgeon, his W. C. Fields-like mien and gruff voice the perfect foil to the more agreeable styles of David and Dave (as they were often referred to, as if they were a single individual). It fell to Schulz to call the meetings, check where everyone was, and scold those who fell behind. If someone arrived more than a minute late for his daily 8:45 A.M. briefing, they would be fined one dollar.

Neeleman was racking up an impressive backlog of these levies; he often sauntered in after 9:00, and when he did attend a meeting, he would spend much of it on his feet, wandering off to a corner to take calls on his cell phone. He would sometimes bring his children, and after one such visit, a caricature of a beefy bodybuilder with the label DAVID NEELEMAN, JETBLUE MAN had appeared on the wall. Thirteen-year-old Hilary had snuck into the room to post this cartoon portrait of her father while no one was looking. It fit well with the eclectic decor one would expect of a start-up in the middle of its gestation: Seat samples were strewn around the halls, mock-up logos were pasted on corridor walls—while the plane and the name were chosen, what it would actually look like was far from certain.

Neeleman refused to claim an office of his own in the cramped suite they'd rented, jokingly saying that his apparent self-denial was intended to save expenses. However, his aversion to meetings, and even just to sitting still for any length of time, was well known. Yet little escaped his attention; he still displayed, as Dan Hersh had noticed years earlier, the spongelike ability for absorbing vast amounts of data.

And there was a lot to absorb: Operating manuals had to be written, documents processed. In the old days, an aspiring airline would simply buy a manual from an existing airline that had the same plane type, slap its name on it, and it'd be in business. Federal regulators tolerated this sort of short cut in the past, but in the post–ValuJet world, nothing would be taken for granted. Neeleman and Barger would have to pass a final exam; federal inspectors would interrogate them for up to six hours to see if they knew what was in their manuals, and more, if they fully understood them—a test most airline chief executives would have had trouble passing if this requirement had been imposed retroactively.

In 1998, two years after the Valujet crash, the FAA created a new division whose sole mission is to oversee the whole certification process for new entrants. Called Certification Standardization Evaluation Team, or CSET, the program added a new layer on top of the existing one—a corps of seasoned aviation professionals breathing down the necks of their counterparts in the field. The FAA assigns at least three people full time to each applicant, and at certain intense periods there could be as many as one hundred government watchdogs assigned to a specific contender. The process doesn't end when it gets off the ground, either; the minders are supposed to remain attached to the new airline for its first five years—if they make it that far, that is.

If the FAA was arguably underregulating before, this new level of oversight was having the unintended effect of throwing up a new barrier to entry, making it much more expensive and time consuming for a newcomer to break in. The Transportation Department, which rules on the economic fitness of airlines while the FAA checks them for safety, was also tightening the requirements. The department now demanded that applicants prove they had at least four months' operating expenses in the bank before they could start up, on top of the millions in expenses they'd run through before opening their doors. A new airline was not allowed to collect a penny from a single customer until all these tests were met.

So Neeleman was spending a lot of time shuttling back and forth to Washington, he was regularly meeting with Schumer, and courting people like Bob Francis, vice chairman of the National Transportation Safety Board. Francis was one of the few aviation safety regulators in the capital who was widely known to the public for he was the human face the government put forward during the ValuJet and TWA Flight 800 tragedies in the deadly summer of 1996. Francis had been startled when Neeleman first called on him; for a nascent airline to reach out to the federal agency that investigates air crashes was rather like asking the IRS for an audit before you had earned a single cent to pay tax on. Neeleman had specifically wanted Francis's guidance in drafting a family assistance plan that would be used in the event of an accident, so that everyone could avoid the sort of ugly recriminations that follow when victims' families are kept out of the loop.

But sometimes the hovering presence of the CSET team could have almost comical overtones. At one point, Tom Anderson had set up a showroom with the airline seats he was considering and was pulling in various company employees and even, occasionally, people from other floors of the building, to sample the wares. In industry parlance, this was a "fanny test," a blind testing of seat models, and the reactions would be critical for the average coach seat can cost up to two thousand dollars—three hundred thousand dollars per aircraft. During one of these sessions, a man who had slipped in unnoticed suddenly began pulling the seat apart, examining the cushion, tapping the aluminum pan underneath, scrutinizing the undercarriage. When Anderson finally asked him who he was, the man revealed himself to be an inspector from the FAA. His interest, he explained, was in whether the seats were "9G"; that is, did they meet the government requirement that they withstand 9Gs of impact? Again, this rule was a response to several air crashes in which some seats had torn loose, adding to the casualties. It was, as someone recalled, as if a team of chefs at a new restaurant had suddenly found a health inspector in their midst.

Ultimately, JetBlue installed seats that were at the higher end of the comfort, and price, range, and went with the 16G seats that would be even more resistant to gravitational forces, should they ever encounter a situation where such distinctions would matter.

The safety angle was arising in other unexpected ways. In the spring of 1999, the founding team met in a conference room at the Doubletree

Hotel in Times Square to hash out a mission statement of sorts, only they wouldn't call it that; as John Owen put it, "No one reads mission statements; they just sit there and gather dust." Instead, Ann Rhoades called everyone together to concoct a list of values that would if nothing else be easy to remember. She handed everyone markers and paper and ordered them to start writing—words, not phrases—that evoked what was most important to them.

It became another revealing clash between the styles. "Honesty," of course, everyone could agree on, although it became "integrity" after a semantic debate. Naturally, the Southwest alumni insisted "fun" had to be in there. "Caring," as in taking care of one's employees, also got the nod. Devotion to one's job was important, so they came up with "passion," which amused some of those present. "Hey, John, do you know any passionate accountants?" Alex Wilcox teased Owen. "I'm passionate about getting it right," Owen shot back. Some of the pilots and others who were involved in the safety side were unsure about adding that to the value roster; after all, isn't that understood? Putting it on a pithy list of feel-good sentiments might trivialize it.

In the end, safety became their number-one value, creating an appropriate distance between it and the other four principles that followed. "Without it, nothing else matters," Ann Rhoades wrote later in the company's first flight attendant manual. JetBlue would "never compromise safety for business decisions" and would not only comply with all regulations, but strive for "consistently high standards." To a layman, all this might seem obvious. Many of the airline veterans in the room knew firsthand that it was not.

When Rob Land first met David Neeleman, he was toiling inside the sprawling Transportation Department. Neeleman had refused to do the usual thing of hiring a highly paid squadron of lawyers and lobbyists to speed his airline's progress. Land was impressed when Neeleman showed up with only his pal Tom Kelly at his side. Here, too, Neeleman had been favored by a confluence of events. Land's boss, Deputy Assistant Transportation Secretary for Aviation Patrick Murphy, was in the uncomfortable position of trying to encourage new airlines to wade in while at the same time showing the public that the government would make it tougher than ever to succeed. He kept on his coffee table a volume, *Deregulation Knockouts: Round One,* a glossy guide to dead airlines, some as short-lived as a straight-to-video movie flop. The Lord's Airline, for instance, was designed to appeal to Born Again Christians (whose faith, apparently, didn't keep it in the air); there were an all-smokers' carrier and airlines with names like Best or Majestic that were anything but. In all, it was a testament to the power of the ego to trump common sense, which called to mind economist Alfred Kahn's crack: "There is something about an airplane that drives otherwise sensible persons out of their minds."

When Neeleman walked through Murphy's door, it was clear to everyone present that he wasn't just another crackpot destined for inclusion in volume two of this pitiful history. It was not just his well-thought-out plan—he had timing on his side. The Clinton administration was prosecuting the first antitrust lawsuit against a major airline in twenty-five years, charging American Airlines with using illegal tactics to drive several small-fry competitors out of its Dallas redoubt. Two of these obscure targets were already out of business, but a third, Vanguard Airlines, was still alive and the government's case was aimed, in part, at keeping it that way. According to the charges, American had attacked its competition by simultaneously undercutting them on price and overwhelming them with lots of additional flights, usually timed to depart just before and after those offered by the target prey. These "flood the zone" tactics had been used by large airlines to great effect ever since the government had gotten out of regulating airline prices, but they were hardly new; giant chain stores had attacked small independent retailers this way for years. And while such predatory practices were technically against the law, it was maddeningly difficult to prove it in court. Often the evidence, such as it was, vanished along with the victim.

American had vehemently denied the charges and it was likely the case would drag on for years; even lawyers sympathetic to the government's case doubted it could win. Murphy also had been working on his competition guidelines that had attracted Richard Branson's attention as an opening wedge for changing the foreign ownership law. Like the Justice Department's antitrust lawsuit, however, these guidelines were far from the stage where they could bring results. In fact, they struck skeptics as the first step to reimposing price controls on the airlines, for the government would be in the position of determining what a "reasonable" response was to a competitor.

Murphy was facing a long fight if he continued to threaten the big lines. Now, however, he had a far better, and infinitely more appealing, alternative. The charismatic and ambitious Neeleman would be his weapon—he'd be able to bludgeon the big lines with the impending arrival of a new Southwest.

Then in his fifties, Patrick Murphy was a soft-spoken, thoughtful public servant who had worked for decades behind the scenes in one of the more obscure functions of the federal government: the economic regulation of the airlines. He had started out in the early 1960s as an analyst in the bowels of the Civil Aeronautics Board, then a corrupt handmaiden to the established airlines that essentially functioned as public utilities, with little risk they'd be exposed to real competition.

Then came Alfred Kahn, the Cornell professor and wise-cracking "stand-up economist" whom President Jimmy Carter tapped to head the

CAB and upend an industry. The biggest airlines, many of which had been around in some form since the 1920s, were ill prepared for the sudden transition from a public utility protected from competition to a free market free-for-all. They were flying dinosaurs, their inefficient route systems and high costs making them easy prey for any low-cost challenger that cared to come in. And that's exactly what happened, at first. From 1979 through the early 1980s, nearly sixty maverick airlines sprang up, and with their low costs and high attitude, they cleaned the clock of the entrenched airlines. Several pundits confidently predicted these lumbering "legacy" airlines would soon waddle into aviation history.

They were wrong. The real story behind airline deregulation "knockouts" was, in effect, evolution in reverse. Led by Bob Crandall, then CEO at American, the big lines found ways to exploit their sheer size. Although Crandall later earned notoriety for a clumsy attempt to fix prices, he was also regarded by his peers as a brilliant innovator, and many of his ideas helped transform the industry. It was Crandall's airline that came up with the first frequent-flier program in 1981, which grew into a potent marketing tool, giving more than seventy million members an incentive to stick with the giants. "It was hardly Einsteinian thinking," he used to crack. "It's just an exploitation of that basic human emotion: greed."

Crandall was also an early advocate of the hub-and-spoke model that sprouted across the airline landscape, giving the reigning carriers a tight grip on their markets. A large airline with about three thousand flights a day could actually serve thirty thousand city pairs by collecting customers at hubs and then shuffling them out to the spokes, sort of like a postal sorting center. That fed into another obsession of the big airline chiefs: to attain critical mass. They believed that if they cornered a large enough share of the market, their dominance would be ensured; it would just be too tough for a newcomer to break in. This credo manifested itself in all sorts of ways. At certain airports, for example, the biggest airlines would corner much of the space with long-term leases on gates and rights to landing and takeoff slots. A start-up often could enter the scene only by subletting space from the very companies that wanted them to go away.

The airlines' most fearsome weapon was the pricing technique known as yield management, another one of Crandall's innovations. Alfred Kahn defined it this way: "The airlines manage—you yield." Using some of the most powerful computer networks outside the Pentagon, by the mid-1980s the major airlines were able to juggle one hundred million fares at a single time. It is this system—perhaps the most complex pricing structure of any service industry in the world—that resulted in a passenger's paying two hundred dollars being seated next to one paying ten times that amount. It works using complicated algorithms that study the history of each flight and determine the likely pace at which seats will fill up; that allows airlines to divvy up blocks of seats (or "buckets" in industry lingo) on each flight according to the fare. Typically, as the day of departure approaches, fewer seats are set aside for discount customers, and the remaining places are sold for increasingly higher prices. The aim is to make sure no one ever gets on a flight for less than he was willing to pay. It is, of course, logical that a business traveler flying at the last minute will place more value on being able to fly at a specific time than a leisure customer planning months in advance. As the airlines got really good at the game, the gap between the lowest and highest fares widened to breathtaking proportions: A business traveler could end up paying a premium of as much as one thousand dollars over the lowest discount fare.

By the mid-1990s, the major airlines had succeeded in crushing most of the early discounters spawned by deregulation—most disappeared in a wave of bankruptcies and mergers. The next generation of upstarts wasn't faring much better. It now cost nearly two thousand dollars to fly across the country and back with no restrictions. The big airlines had effectively created a web of minimonopolies around the country: Prior to deregulation, the top five carriers controlled a combined 54.3 percent of the domestic market; by 1994, that figure had grown to around 75 percent. The majors simply had some airports locked up: No fewer than twenty large hub airports were controlled by one or two companies.

But the story was strikingly different when Southwest was present. Murphy had come up with firm proof of another syndrome, the so-called Southwest effect. For cities a thousand miles apart, the average one-way fare ranged from $200 to $250; if Southwest or another discount competitor was present, however, the average fare fell to a range of $65 to $165. This could sometimes stimulate demand powerful enough to spark an economic boomlet akin to what the building of a new railroad line had done a century before. For example, when Southwest began flying to Columbus, Ohio, its arrival prompted Spiegel catalog to open an enormous mail-order processing center with fifteen hundred employees.

The fact that consumers were so dependent on one airline for their salvation was worrisome, however; Southwest carried 90 percent of all discount air travel in the country. Since the big expansion that began during Neeleman's brief tenure in Dallas, Southwest had been steadily spreading eastward to secondary cities like Providence, Baltimore, and Tampa. Then Kelleher put on the brakes. In 1997, no fewer than 167 airports had tried to woo Southwest, but just 1 got the nod: Manchester, New Hampshire. Kelleher dubbed all those cities clamoring for his services "pockets of pain," where the big airlines were free to gouge their captive customers. There were limits to what Kelleher would do to palliate them. "I'm not going anywhere where I'll have to sit on the tarmac for forty-five minutes," he'd declared many times, effectively eliminating New York City from his radar screen. Neeleman was relieved; it was another validation of his designs on Kennedy. For he was determined to avoid competing head to head with Southwest.

Rob Land had grown up on Long Island, New York, within a few miles of Kennedy Airport, and was an avowed airline junkie from childhood, a frequent visitor to the fringes of the airfield to watch the jets lifting off the runways. Even after he had outgrown this pastime, he still had some affection for the place; he didn't readily join in the bashing that was so fashionable among frequent travelers. In fact, as a student at Lawrence High School, Land had been so drawn to Kennedy's potential that he'd drawn up a mock business plan as part of a school project that, he joked later, was the real antecedent for JetBlue. His Land Air would fly out of JFK all over the country; Land came up with detailed route maps and schedules for his fanciful company. "I wasn't part of that whole Manhattan-centric thing," he said. "We hated going to LaGuardia—that for us was the inconvenient airport. And I thought if there were an airline at Kennedy that could take me everywhere, that would be perfect."

Neeleman quickly adopted Land as his cicerone through the regulatory thicket as well as through the murky world of local Queens politics. In one of their early meetings, Land recalled, the talk turned to the mob's role at Kennedy. While mobster Henry Hill's heist of nearly six million dollars in loot from the Lufthansa hangar had been immortalized by the Nick Pileggi book *Wiseguy* and the movie *GoodFellas,* the crooks basically stuck to petty thievery and rackets like shaking down the cab concessions. It's not organized crime you're facing; it's the organized airlines, Land told him. The airlines that were already in there could, and would, do a lot to stop him.

Their ability to do so hinged on another anomaly, which, though not as loopy as the Wright Amendment that had hobbled competition at Love Field, made little sense in a deregulated industry. Kennedy Airport was one of only four airports in the United States (along with LaGuardia, Washington Reagan, and Chicago O'Hare) that had been designated by the government as "slot-controlled." That means that the right to take off or land at a specific time—the slots, in airline vernacular—is limited during the busiest hours of the day. These limits were adopted in the late 1960s, and back then it was sound public policy: Air traffic control simply didn't have the capacity to cope with demand in crowded urban areas. The government created a board of federal and local officials to sort things out, and it set limits on what flight operations would be allowed and decided who got the right to fly them.

By the late 1990s, nearly everyone involved in aviation safety had concluded that these slot constraints were no longer necessary with the new technology that helped the FAA manage air traffic. But local politicians fought any change, lest they get on the wrong side of the airport noise opponents, and Neeleman had to beg the Transportation Department to give him an exemption from the slot limits based on his status as a new entrant, an exception that Congress carved out in 1994 to encourage competition.

Land knew the minute that Neeleman formally filed for his exemption from the slot rule that his rivals would quickly gang up on the interloper. The three airlines that dominated Kennedy—American, Delta, and TWA—typically lined up in opposition anytime someone tried to grab new slots, always with the same arguments: Kennedy was too crowded already and would not be able to cope with any more traffic. Their case was usually supported by an odd alliance of noise opponents and their friends in the local legislature as well as union officials who could be counted on to object if the start-up was nonunion, as most are. As a result, most airlines trying to get in made very modest proposals for a handful of takeoff times. Neeleman thought that was self-defeating since it only seemed to embolden the existing airlines; besides, it would hardly do for a "megastart-up" to tiptoe in.

As Land became closer to Neeleman over the ensuing months, he began to think seriously about quitting the government. One day, he brought Neeleman to his office and opened his desk drawer. "See this?" he said, and pointed to a thick sheaf of rejection letters from every airline in the country. Land, it seemed, had longed to work inside the airlines rather than remain on the regulatory fringes. He had hankered after a post with an established line; he was so intimately familiar with the problems of airline start-ups that he'd long resisted any thoughts of joining one—until Neeleman came along. Land soon became JetBlue vice president for governmental affairs, employee number six, right before Chuck Schumer was elected senator.

Land and Neeleman, meanwhile, had come up with an audacious approach to the slot-control hurdle. Neeleman had originally thought he'd schedule most flights outside the restricted hours of 3:00 P.M. to 8:00 P.M., not only to sidestep the slot barrier but also to cut down on delays. But the reason the later hours are restricted is because that's when many people want to fly, and if Neeleman didn't get first dibs on these choice times now, he'd risk tempting someone else to come in and compete. Mindful of Kelleher's exploitation of his Love Field fief, Neeleman asked for an unprecedented seventy-five landing and takeoff spaces. They wouldn't have the fleet to use all of them at first, of course, so they also asked permission to phase in these rights over three years. It was a long shot, to be sure; the largest number of these slots that had ever been granted at one time was eleven.

Politics permeated every aspect of the airline's progress, it seemed, and Dave Barger also wasn't leaving anything to chance. He was courting New

York's mercurial mayor, Rudy Giuliani. Barger was careful to play down his former allegiance to Newark Airport when he was around the mayor, who had been so angered by a Continental ad campaign mocking Kennedy Airport that he had actually urged New Yorkers to boycott the airline. One of the early ads that apparently went too far, for it was spiked, had carried the impudent tagline: "What do you call a West Sider who flies out of Kennedy? An idiot."

Now that Barger was himself one of these idiots, he would need Giuliani's help in unblocking the clogged arteries that connected Manhattan to the airfield it loved to hate.

Neeleman and Barger spent a lot of the summer of 1999 inspecting real estate, finding a place to park their planes. There was no shortage of possibilities; Kennedy's general downward slide mirrored that of its former flagship tenants. Barger found himself poking through decrepit warehouses and offices that once housed thousands of Pan Am workers who managed everything from uniform stockrooms to the employee credit union from their facilities at Kennedy. The other longtime presence here, TWA, was still alive, but it was on the critical list, having been in and out of bankruptcy since the late 1980s. Since the tragedy of TWA Flight 800 in July 1996, it had been seeking a buyer to give it one more chance. TWA's Terminal Six was an unsettling reminder of the airline's uncertain fate: The building, designed by I. M. Pei, was obviously neglected. TWA had moved all of its flights to its more famous, and architecturally distinguished, Eero Saarinen-designed edifice next door, the "soaring, concrete poem" that had opened to great acclaim in 1962. Terminal Six was being used by United Airlines for a few flights and had enough space for JetBlue to start up modestly. But Barger was nonplussed: Here the decor had changed little since it had opened in 1970, all plastic benches and marble floors covered with thirty years of crud. He would have to negotiate with TWA for a lease, setting up another awkward scenario as TWA, of course, was on record as opposing Jet-Blue's slot request at the Department of Transportation. Even assuming that was merely a knee-jerk reaction by an established airline to a new competitor, Barger was struck by the obvious conflict of interest. He was also familiar with the tedious process of getting people to the airport; he typically would chat up every taxi driver and airport worker he met about getting to Kennedy, because after nailing down his precious slots and gates, he wanted to operate a shuttle bus and rail connection for his passengers to get them all the way to Midtown New York by public transportation.

Barger was convinced that the airport's forbidding image would change, just as he had seen Newark Airport transformed not long before with a train-to-plane link, the sort of conveyance travelers had come to expect all over the industrialized world, except in the city that most needed it. And while he, along with everyone else from Manhattan, had wasted hours sitting in traffic trying to get to Kennedy, he persisted in imagining that this, too, would be fixed. In late July, he got some encouraging news: New York's City Council had, after years of debate, voted to spend $1.5 billion on a long-awaited air train to carry riders from New York's Penn Station to JFK, with a stop at Jamaica, Queens. It was to be finished by 2003, a remarkably ambitious timetable for such a project. And yet, already, the skeptics were saying that no one would ride it.

Indeed, there was no shortage of skeptics when it came to JetBlue; many in the local aviation establishment were openly dismissive of the airline's odds of surviving. The negotiations with the Port Authority for Terminal Six were telling. When the JetBlue team proposed that it be given a lease on the entire building, figuring it'd need the space in a couple of years, "They basically laughed at us," Neeleman said. "They had this idea that so many other people had tried to start an airline.

And where were our slots, where were our planes? As they saw it, there were so many things that could doom us."

Merkley's Douglas Atkin recalled that he accompanied the JetBlue team one day to Kennedy with several other people from his agency, just to "bulk up" the presence of his client. "They didn't have that many full-time employees at that point, and we were asked to go along and sort of pretend we were part of the airline . . . just to impress the Port [Authority] that this was real."

Neeleman's hubris in angling for an oversized helping of airport slots at JFK got the expected reaction from his would-be competitors, who singled out for scorn the idea that JetBlue would get three years to use its slots, rather than the normal six months. Would JetBlue, at three years, really be considered a new entrant, deserving of special protection? they asked. But Neeleman and his inner circle knew they had to gain a stranglehold on the rights, and often in meetings they would worry aloud about the possibility that they might lose out at the transportation agency. If so, they said, they might have to go back to square one. "Our whole business plan depends on getting the slots," Neeleman admitted. Even the sympathetic officials at Transportation seemed to agree. When Patrick Murphy wrote a tentative decision in May 1999 granting Neeleman his certificate, he clearly made it subject to his getting the space he sought at Kennedy.

Neeleman and Land were also on the phone to some would-be supporters. Land contacted father of deregulation Alfred Kahn at his office in Ithaca, New York, asking him to lend his support in the slot bid. After all, Kahn had been vocal of late about the lack of competition in the airlines, and, conveniently, Neeleman's airline would rescue the professor from the outrageously high fares he personally had to pay to fly out

The Dream Team: The four senior executives who joined David Neeleman in New York City in 1999 to begin work on his as-yet-unnamed airline. Here, pictured on an East Village street, are (LEFT TO RIGHT): Dave Barger, president and chief operating officer; John Owen, executive vice president and chief financial officer; Ann Rhoades, executive vice president—people; Neeleman; and Tom Kelly, executive vice president and general counsel.

In December 1993, David Neeleman (LEFT), then president of Salt Lake City–based Morris Air, announced the sale of the airline to Southwest Airlines, chaired by Herb Kelleher, for $129 million in stock. Neeleman borrowed liberally from Southwest's quirky no-frills formula to make Morris a success.

David Neeleman (LEFT) and Richard Branson might have failed to agree on their proposed Virgin America in 1998, but the two remained on friendly terms. Here, at a reception hosted by Virgin Atlantic Airways at JFK International in 2000, Neeleman presents the Virgin chief with a mock logo for the airline that might have been—in reverse.

At Airbus Industrie's factory in Toulouse, France, David Neeleman (LEFT) and Airbus's North American director John Leahy stand inside the shell of a widebody aircraft jet.

Soon after it touched down at Kennedy Airport, the Neeleman family came to see the first JetBlue plane. LEFT TO RIGHT: Erica, Vanessa, Vicki Neeleman holding Isabel, Victoria, David Neeleman holding Seth, Daniel, and Ashley. Not pictured: Hannah and Hilary.

Bob Zimmerman (LEFT) of International Aero Engines, maker of engines that power JetBlue's Airbus A320s, sharing a toast with David Neeleman (MIDDLE) and John Leahy (RIGHT) in France.

JetBlue's opening festivities brought out the politicians. David Neeleman (RIGHT) accompanied the elected officials whom he courted in his bid to get takeoff space at Kennedy Airport. To his immediate right is Senator Chuck Schumer (Democrat, New York); to his far right is New York Mayor Rudy Giuliani.

First Flights: On February 11, 2000, JetBlue formally debuted in Buffalo, New York, where Gareth Edmondson-Jones (LEFT) and Rob Land, vice president for government affairs, showed it was front-page news in the local paper.

The "Virgin Gang" doesn't take themselves too seriously. Here are three of the original defectors from the Virgin side (LEFT TO RIGHT): Tracy Sandford, marketing director; Amy Curtis-McIntyre, vice president of marketing; and Gareth Edmondson-Jones, vice president for corporate communications.

The Flyboys: JetBlue's first pilots were charged with finding like-minded colleagues to take a chance on an airline start-up. LEFT TO RIGHT: Mike Barger, vice president of JetBlue University (and brother of JetBlue president Dave Barger); Al Spain, senior vice president for operations; and Brian Coulter, director of flight standards.

David Neeleman tries to fly at least once a week on JetBlue, doing double duty as a flight attendant.

On August 29, 2001, JetBlue launched low-fare flights to New York City out of Long Beach Airport, twenty miles south of Los Angeles, throwing down the gauntlet to the major airlines that had jacked up cross-country fares out of LAX.

JetBlue's first Airbus A320 plane was taken for a test spin over Manhattan soon after it arrived in the States in December 1999. The Federal Aviation Administration had to grant special clearance for the plane to fly at an altitude of only 2,000 feet. Less than two years later, this photo became a powerful reminder of how the world had been changed by the terrorist attacks.

Just seven months after the terror attacks of 9/11, JetBlue went public in what was the hottest offering of the year. Here, standing at the NASDAQ exchange in Times Square, are (LEFT TO RIGHT): Neal Moszkowski, managing director of Soros Fund private equity division and JetBlue board member; Michael Lazarus, managing director of Weston Presidio and then JetBlue chairman; David Neeleman; Brian Wilson of NASDAQ; Dave Barger; John Owen; and Natalie Wood of NASDAQ.

In February 2003, David Neeleman christened his newest Airbus A320, named Song Sung Blue in an unsubtle dig at his new rival, Delta's spin-off airline, Song. The names for JetBlue aircraft come from a semiannual Name the Plane contest open to all company employees. Those who submit the winning entries win a trip to France, with guests, to tour the Toulouse factory and "pick up" the plane.

The Competition: A view of the intense rivalry in the airlines, circa 2003, seen from the tarmac at Fort Lauderdale Airport.

JetBlue cabin crews must learn how to ditch an aircraft in the ocean. Here, I joined a group of flight attendants and pilots practicing their survival skills in a Miami swimming pool.

Graduation from JetBlue U is cause for celebration.

of his upstate home. But Kahn turned him down. He was, it seems, a purist, and the whole notion of hoarding scarce resources went against his principles. "I told him while I wished him the very best, and I truly did, I couldn't in good conscience endorse something that smacked of protectionism." To Kahn, it was not much different from Southwest's, the supposed underdog, profiting from an egregious distortion of the marketplace at Love Field. Neeleman, however, was a pragmatist and understood that success would come from discovering not just under-served airports but those where the limitations, if cleverly exploited, would tie the hands of his rivals more than his own.

In all, Neeleman and Land succeeded in getting 250 supporters to contact Transportation Secretary Rodney Slater. Many of them (including Chuck Schumer) played the political card, arguing that if JetBlue didn't get a strong start, then it would be chalked up as an embarrassing flop, on the administration's watch. As the months wore on, the picture worsened: One of the more successful start-ups of the 1990s, Newark-based Kiwi International Airlines, suddenly shut down amid charges that it had skimped on safety measures to save money. And industry pundits started to proclaim that the era of new airlines was over, it was just too difficult to break in. The authoritative airline analyst Julius Maldutis, of Salomon Brothers, put it bluntly: "There aren't going to be any more start-ups. What you see now is what you get."

In the middle of September, Slater personally presented David Neeleman with the entire allotment of seventy-five slots permissions that he wanted at Kennedy Airport. Slater also took the occasion to send a pointed message to the big airlines. "We are going to be watching what the (other) airlines do very closely," he warned. Senator Schumer was there to claim his share of the credit: "I stand here like a proud uncle to announce the triumph of an airline. The era of sky-high airfares is about to end."

six
air born

Late in the summer of 1999, a small classified advertisement appeared among the personals and help wanted ads of New York's *Village Voice*. This one proffered not romance, but nearly everything else one could desire: unlimited travel, an enlightened employer, decent pay, and, the clincher—a guaranteed interview to anyone who responded.

Ann Rhoades had come up with the original notion of luring recruits to JetBlue via notices in Manhattan's venerable alternative weekly. But she was unprepared for the concert-sized crowd that showed up on the appointed day for a promised shot at the allegedly glamorous job of flight attendant. Her associates had known better. "My staff was furious at me for doing that ad," she said. "And so they got even with me." Scanning the motley lineup, Rhoades's assistants selected the most bizarrely turned-out candidates and sent them to the front of the line. Rhoades looked up from her desk at the very first job seeker who would cross her door at JetBlue: a woman of indeterminate age with a shaved head, nose ring, and little covering her body except for a riot of elaborate tattoos.

"We saw maybe two people out of a couple hundred whom we might consider hiring," she said. "We laughed about it later, but I had no idea it was going to be so tough."

For a company that would peg a great deal on its knack for hiring the "right" people, JetBlue was getting off to a slow start. "Everyone told me, 'You'll never get anyone good in New York, they're so rude,'" Neeleman said. Not that he truly believed that, but he also knew that many of his recruits would come from all over the country. The only qualification that mattered, he said, was their ability to deliver that intangible quality, that "humanity" he had rashly pledged to restore to the airline business.

When he hired Rhoades, in fact, he told her she should interview as many people as it would take to find the right employees. "If you have to look at a thousand people to get the right one, then just do it," he said. The in-flight jobs were the most critical, he said; that's where the customers will have the most exposure to the human face of JetBlue.

Still, this was New York, not Dallas, where many of the flight attendants at Southwest had put "cheerleader" on the experience section of their job applications.

In the fall of 1999, JetBlue U opened its doors, figuratively at least. Recruiting and hiring would be done out of the New York office, but the pilots and flight attendants would get their hands-on training in a few rooms in the Airbus Industrie facility at Miami International Airport. Many airlines had tarted up their basic training drills with the trappings of something loftier: Southwest had its University for People at Love Field, and American Airlines famously once ran a Stewardess College, a distaff boot camp where conscripts had to spend six weeks abiding by curfews and other indignities in order to enter a decidedly short-term career. The changes here, of course, mirrored those in the industry at large. During the 1960s and 1970s, flight attendants were required to be female and single, and the average tenure in the job was about two years. An American Airlines recruiting brochure from that era shamelessly flogged the job as a sure path to matrimony. "This isn't surprising," the pamphlet pointed out, "when a girl who can smile for five hours is hard to find. Not to mention a wife who can remember what 124 people want for dinner."

Southwest had once been one of the main offenders; in the 1970s, applicants for the job were actually required to show up for their interviews in hot pants and clingy tops, since that was to be their uniform. The airline's "love airline" theme was behind some of the airline's more dubious pitches to its mostly male clientele, such as having flight attendants hawk cocktails with such unsubtle labels as "love potion" or "passion punch" to passengers as they boarded. "Our love service means having things around to make you happy . . . like me!" a shapely Southwest stew cooed in a typical television ad.

In 1971, the U.S. Supreme Court issued the first of several court rulings that were to radically change the makeup of the flight attendant corps, determining that men could no longer be automatically excluded and also tossing out limits that forced women out of the workforce when they married or turned thirty. The "appearance standards" that were enforced by humiliating weigh-ins and girdle checks weren't completely scrapped, however; appearance could still be a factor in hiring within certain legal boundaries. Herb Kelleher, among others, had fought the change, according to Ann Rhoades. "And he knew he'd lose, but he also knew (if he succeeded in delaying it), he'd get another year of hiring good-looking women." Just two years later, men made up fully 20 percent of the new flight attendant hires in the United States. And the age range gradually crept up as people lingered; after all, the pay rose steadily with seniority and there were all those travel benefits to consider.

The job of flight attendant, then, was no longer a lark; it was potentially a long-term career. However, many an airline manager joined Kelleher in mourning the passing of the politically incorrect days when rapid turnover in the cabin crew guaranteed a steady supply of fresh meat. Rhoades herself had witnessed the distress of burned-out veterans who stayed on for years at other airlines. "At other airlines, you have these 'flight attendants for life' who just sit around and bitch," she said. "It is not a fun job to have for twenty years."

Of course JetBlue, with its vaunted values and caring philosophy, wouldn't put crew members out to pasture because they were overweight or over the hill. It could, however, encourage people to move into other jobs. Don Burr had tried to keep up morale at People Express by requiring everyone to switch jobs periodically; gate agents would try their hand at sales; pilots would moonlight as reservations agents. Eventually a fitting example arrived at JetBlue in the person of Doreen Lawrence. If anyone personified the contradictions that came with the job, it was Lawrence, a cheerleader from the Midwest who'd also played on the high school football team. Lawrence started out in the airlines as a Pucci-clad stewardess for Braniff Airways in the late 1970s, when false eyelashes and big hair were still required accessories. Braniff's training included practicing a provocative number known as the dime walk, a trick accomplished by holding a dime between one's buttocks as you sashayed down the aisle. After Braniff tanked in 1982, Lawrence had succeeded in moving into management jobs and became head of in-flight service for Eastern's entire Latin American network. She would hold a similar title at JetBlue, but little else was the same, and Lawrence would use her past as a shapely stew mainly as amusing fodder for training classes.

Neeleman had imagined that he'd draw his flight attendants from the ranks of recent college graduates who might see it as a way to live in New York City for a few years before moving on to more serious pursuits. He hardly visualized someone eligible to collect Social Security showing up, but the final group of selectees was a diverse lot, ranging in age from their early twenties to mid-sixties; half were male, and many on second or third careers. The coveted spot of flight attendant number one went to Lenny Spivey, a sixty-year-old retired New York City fire-fighter who answered a JetBlue recruiting ad on a whim. Ann Rhoades immediately offered him the job after he answered one of her trade-mark trick questions—"Tell me about the time you broke a rule on the job." Those who insist they have never done such a thing are automatically disqualified.

Spivey's answer blew her away. He had worked at the fire station near the World Trade Center and was there when the towers were bombed in 1993. He'd been ordered by his captain not to enter the build-ings because of the smoke; however, when he heard noises coming from inside on the ground floor, he had found a way to enter the building through another door, guiding several of those trapped inside to safety.

For someone like Spivey, flying had enough appeal that he could live with the kidding he would inevitably get from his former colleagues at the fire house. It wasn't a bad way to supplement his pension, he thought, and a flight attendant could easily make more than thirty thousand dollars a year, more than forty thousand dollars if you worked really hard, and that wasn't including travel benefits (you could take family and friends, and the actual dollar value of this perk could be worth up to ten thousand dollars). Neeleman threw in a few other good-ies to make it more alluring, such as a job-sharing deal allowing two people to share a single position, for which they'd get benefits but only have to log thirty-five hours each per month, instead of the seventy-hour minimum for full-time crew members.

The job could also be difficult and tedious, even more so with the general lack of civility that had come to define airline travel. During 1999 and 2000, incidents of air rage were believed to have nearly dou-bled and had become something of a media phenomenon, enlivened by picaresque accounts of drunken rock stars or other celebrities behaving badly. But it was also serious stuff, and after an emotionally disturbed passenger died from blows administered by fellow fliers during a fracas on a Southwest flight in 2000, a number of airlines hired trainers in conflict resolution. One such practitioner of Verbal Judo would open a flight attendant training class at Southwest by telling his audience: "Face it—you take crap for a living."

There was something else on Ann Rhoades's mind: the prospect that workers might at some point be motivated to organize. A nonunion company in the airline business was a rarity, largely because of historic reasons, but also because the cyclical nature of the business had convinced airline workers they needed a union to add a layer of protection. But airlines had an uneven record where labor strife was concerned: Some airlines had withstood strikes but Southwest, which, ironically, was among the most unionized of all airlines—with all employee groups organized—was known for its relatively harmonious labor relations. Still, since deregulation, most start-up airlines had been nonunion and by rewarding workers with profit-sharing and company stock, they had managed to stay that way. People Express, for example, actually required that employees purchase one hundred shares of stock when they joined the airline.

Rhoades came up with several ways to lessen the likelihood of Jet-Blue's following Southwest into the union camp. For flight attendants, there would be three types of employment: In addition to the full-time and job-sharing options, there would be a one-year contract, with a stipend in lieu of full benefits, that was specifically aimed at luring those college students Neeleman had imagined were hungering for some adventure before heading off to law school or the like. Having three disparate groups would make it far more difficult to unify these workers into a single force, she knew. Other employee groups would be similarly hard to organize, such as the home-bound reservations agents that Jet-Blue was just beginning to recruit in Salt Lake.

That left the pilots, who have been among the most militant union activists at major airlines and were likely the greatest challenge facing Neeleman and company.

Dave Barger picked his younger brother Mike to head the airline's training program and especially to help on the pilots end. Mike's credentials were impressive enough to ward off any suggestion of nepotism: He was a decorated navy pilot and had been an instructor at the legendary Top Gun academy in Miramar, California. The typical career path for a military pilot like him was to migrate to a large commercial airline where, like his father, he could look forward to a generous paycheck and more appealing assignments as he rose in seniority. But Mike had no interest in joining a big airline like United. "Hell, I'd grown up in the industry and I didn't like what I was seeing. I just decided early on I didn't want to be an airline pilot."

The brothers had grown closer after Mike returned from a tour of duty in the Persian Gulf during Operation Desert Storm, and they began talking, idly, about going into business together. They thought about running a small airport for private operators (a favorite second career for commercial pilots) or, perhaps, a marina to indulge Dave's sailing hobby. Mike imagined that Dave, too, would become disenchanted with what the airlines had become.

In the summer of 1998, Mike was on duty on an aircraft carrier off Marseille, contemplating going back to school and earning an MBA, when his brother called to give him the news that he was quitting his big job at Continental to join a start-up airline. Mike was shocked, even more so when Dave told him he needed his help. It was not going to be easy to recruit experienced pilots for a start-up airline. Too many of them had been burned by all the failures, not to mention the rash of mergers in which pilots of the acquired airline would often see their hard-won seniority vanish, so that even the most seasoned pilots would be treated like rookies where pay and perks were concerned.

Besides, there were not that many pilots looking for work. "It was a tough time to be hiring," said Ann Rhoades. "The big airlines were all hiring, the unemployment rate was low, and here we are, 'Jet Who?'" Worse, she said, many pilots who had heard of Neeleman were wary of getting involved with him. "David was known as the guy who sold Morris, so pilots did not believe that JetBlue would be there for the long term . . . after all, their number-one thing is security."

But the Barger brothers knew well that pilots typically are their company's best recruiters. Dave had already reeled in one of his oldest friends, Al Spain, an experienced 727 captain at Continental. Spain had an unusual background that made him attractive to the JetBlue founders: He had an MBA and an entrepreneurial bent, honed by such experiences as working for a Dubai-based company that, among other things, had to arrange diplomatic clearances for VIPs and royal family members in the Middle East. He had started out with People Express and was a firm believer in the sort of employee-ownership, "everyone's a manager," philosophy espoused by Don Burr.

And so the flyboys sat down with Rhoades and worked out a way to overcome resistance from their more hidebound colleagues at other airlines. Each pilot would get an individual contract, which, as Rhoades put it, "would give them all the things they would get from a union contract, and more," the more being stock options, which at most companies are limited to those holding executive jobs. One of the most critical provisions in this pact was a severance agreement that promised the pilots would get paid for up to twelve months in the event of a merger, sale, or bankruptcy.

Still, there was only so much JetBlue could do to transform the pilot culture: Seniority rules in the cockpit, and the most seasoned pilots typically get first crack at their choice of routes and plane type. Experienced pilots can thus arrange their schedules to squeeze the most hours out of the fewest days, to the point where many supplement their incomes with second or even third jobs on the side. This practice became ever more entrenched by the mid-1990s, when American, Delta, United, and most of the other big lines were flush with cash. The airlines had become so profitable that unions started to demand steep wage increases to make up for the austerity of the early 1990s, when raises and benefits had been capped. So it was even less likely that someone with a secure job at a major airline would leave now and give up a shot at a larger share of the lucre.

Mike returned to the States in the fall of 1998, left the navy, and began putting feelers out to the pilot network, working his way down, in descending order of prestige, from the biggest carriers to the small commuter airlines, cargo carriers, and then to the ranks of charter jets and air taxis. Mike's Top Gun stint was his calling card; thanks to Hollywood, even those without a military background knew what it signified. It certainly had impressed the JetBlue backers, and Dave thought his brother might be able to smooth talk some of his compatriots into quitting the navy for a shot at what they were trying to sell as a "great opportunity" to get in on the ground floor at a growing airline. But most of Mike's buddies simply laughed at him. Pay wasn't necessarily the issue: JetBlue had decided to peg its starting salaries at 10 percent below what Southwest Airlines, whose pilots are unionized, was paying, leaving some room to grow, but far better than the typical starting wages at the average discount start-up.

Then the FAA informed the JetBlue team that they could not proceed with their application until they had a chief pilot in place, and only someone with years of commercial flying would do. Fortunately, they found a few geezers in their fifties, close to the mandatory retirement age of sixty set by the FAA, who seemed to regard a stint at an upstart as a fine way to wind down their careers.

If the pilots were going to break from the past, it would have to be in subtle ways. One was sartorial: The military-style jacket and pilot's cap and the pilot's bars that hark back to the role of ship captain just wouldn't send the right message, Rhoades thought. JetBlue pilots would instead wear bright-blue short-sleeved shirts, which made them look more like bus drivers, but perhaps that was the point. Anyone who objected to the casual Friday look presumably lacked the "right" personality for the resolutely unbureaucratic company they were building. The principle behind this had been stretched to comic effect at Southwest, where applicants for pilots' jobs—as for all other positions—are required to demonstrate a sense of humor. Pilots who show up for interviews clad in a suit and tie are often ordered to change into shorts and a T-shirt before they can proceed—and are sent down the hall to a closet to pick out their size. Those who huffily refuse, and many do, will never take a seat in the cockpit of a Southwest plane.

But it would be in the cockpit where one of JetBlue's most radical changes to the status quo would take place. Al Spain had long wanted to test the idea that a laptop computer could substitute for a pilot's massive ten-volume manual. In business school he had written a paper outlining a case for a paperless cockpit that would rid the flight deck of the reams of paper that were required to do the job. The idea was that each pilot would be given a notebook computer, loaded with all the required operating manuals and also with the software to do load and flight planning that was often managed by someone else sitting in an office.

Pilots could then do the preflight weight and balance checks, in which they estimate the weight of their payload based on the number of passengers, in four minutes. When Spain discussed this idea with colleagues in the industry, however, one senior pilot had a fit. "Do you know how many people this will put out of work?" was the refrain. Yes, Spain said, they might need fewer people to update information manually—a chore for which most airlines have sizable clerical departments. But going digital would not reduce the number of pilots they would need to fly their planes. This had never been tried before in the airlines and Spain and Usto Schulz were not sure how the FAA would react. But now seemed as good a moment as any to try it.

They first experimented upon the FAA itself. When the time came to submit the papers necessary to win formal flight certification with the agency, the JetBlue team arrived not with the usual truckload of boxes of files and paperwork, but with a single CD-ROM that contained the airline's entire submission. The FAA did, as Spain hoped, come around.

By late 1999, the first of JetBlue's aircraft had arrived in the States, beginning the most grueling part of the FAA revved-up review of new entrant airlines. Mike Barger had flown the plane from Toulouse and had had to put the craft down on an icy runway in Keflavik, Iceland, as the plane couldn't make it across the ocean nonstop. Now he would have to prove himself all over again amid a crew of FAA enforcers breathing down his neck—flying his plane through all manner of simulated emergencies: engine loss, gale force winds, even a hijacking. Upon that everything depended because JetBlue could not sell a single ticket or advertise a single flight until it passed muster with the FAA and got its certificate from the Transportation Department.

That meant JetBlue would have to make good on its proconsumer manifesto. For inspiration they had to look no further than room 4107 of the Transportation Department at 700th Street in Southwest Washington, the Consumer Protection Bureau, where the file cabinets were filling with a record number of tales of bumped passengers, canceled flights, insane fare regulations, and punitive charges for making a schedule change. Many of the complaints involved perverse fare rules: It actually cost more money to fly one way than round-trip on many routes. But if one did the logical thing and bought the cheaper—i.e., round-trip—ticket and threw away the return coupon, he'd risk getting the airlines' price police all over him. Airlines did enforce their illogical rules by charging fliers who transgressed the full, undiscounted fare.

Neeleman huddled with his sales team to draft the details. This was an aspect of the airline business that he always loved, because it all goes back to the concept that what an airline is really selling is not a tangible item, like a seat on a plane, but, rather, a promise that it will take you where you want to go at a given time.

They began with the reservations process: They'd have a Web site so simple a child could use it, and customers would be rewarded for going there with an additional discount. All fares would be one way; there wouldn't be any Saturday stays or other restrictions. All ticketing would be done electronically, similar to what Neeleman had done at Morris Air, and fares would be nonrefundable. If you couldn't make your flight, you could change your dates, for a twenty-five-dollar fee, and use the ticket for up to one year. (Many airlines had similar policies on the validity of the ticket, but most charged up to one hundred dollars for ticket changes.)

At the airport there would be other subtle differences. Passengers who checked in but failed to appear at the gate would be tracked down by JetBlue agents; most airlines wash their hands of these absentees (whose numbers are higher than one would assume). If a flight was delayed, not only would fliers get frequent updates but if the wait exceeded an hour, they would start to earn compensation, such as a fifty-dollar voucher against a future trip.

Next, they tackled the boarding process, at many airlines an exceedingly painful experience. Neeleman decided that even though his computers would be sophisticated enough to manage it, JetBlue would never oversell a flight.

At the other end of the journey, they would try to use both ends of the jet for deplaning; both Neeleman and Barger shared an obsession with the typically glacial progression on and off the plane. They came up with what is now a widely imitated arrival announcement, in effect giving passengers an economic incentive to tidy up. "JetBlue is committed to keeping airfares as low as possible," it goes. "One significant way we are able to do this is by getting the cabin ready for the next departure while still in the air." JetBlue would have cleaning crews to help the flight attendants, of course, so this would help speed the next flight on its way.

Then there was the final piece—the wait at the baggage carousel. Barger was a self-confessed bear on the subject, mindful of the lasting damage that the lost luggage debacle had had on Continental's reputation in the late 1980s. Besides, it was the last aspect of your trip where the airline could screw up, and "no matter how good the flight was, what they'll remember is that it took forty-five minutes to get their bag," Barger said. At JetBlue, the first bag would be expected to arrive on the carousel within ten minutes of arrival at the gate; the last one, twenty minutes.

It was hardly altruism that fueled these ideas. In many of these cases there would be a clear bottom-line benefit. Giving customers money off to use your Web site was a no-brainer. A reservation taken over the phone costs the airline, on average, four dollars; the same itinerary booked on its Web site costs twenty-five cents. Simplifying the airlines' byzantine fare structure would not just be easier on the consumer, but on the airline, too. It would be cheaper to manage, cutting down on training and booking time. Electronic tickets, as Neeleman knew, saved an enormous amount of money in travel agency commissions and distribution costs.

And then there was the promise not to overbook flights. Anyone who bought a ticket would be sure of getting on. To a layman, the notion that you would sell tickets only for the number of seats you could offer on a particular flight hardly seems radical. But here, JetBlue was truly breaking ranks. For years, airlines have had large staffs to manage the delicate dance of supply and demand, gauging how many people will fly at any given time, using historical patterns. Airlines know, however, that a certain number of passengers holding confirmed reservations simply don't show up—a pattern established in the days when airline tickets were like cash and fully refundable. This encouraged people to make multiple reservations so they could fly when they wanted. On some flights, this no-show factor could be substantial. At People Express, it famously reached 80 percent at one point, but that was because the airline's overtaxed phone lines made it so hard for customers to cancel. So most airlines, if a flight is selling out, will oversell the availability by a certain percentage, a closely guarded number that is the product of years of experience. Of course, they'll often miscalculate, and more fliers will show up than they'll be able to accommodate.

That led to the often vexing "auction" system that was adopted in the 1970s, after consumer advocate and future presidential contender Ralph Nader was denied boarding by Allegheny Airlines, a precursor to US Airways, and missed an important speaking engagement. He sued the airline for a quarter of a million dollars, charging that it deliberately misled passengers by selling more seats than it could offer. The government eventually crafted a compromise allowing airlines to overbook but requiring them to first seek volunteers to give up their seats in return for a payment, to be determined by a bidding process, and to compensate generously any passengers who were still involuntarily denied boarding. But as anyone who travels frequently has observed, the system is far from perfect.

Neeleman was disgusted with the resulting histrionics he'd witnessed at the boarding gate. He thought airlines should treat their sales more like theaters or sports arenas did: If you bought a ticket to a Knicks game, there were no refunds, and barring some unforeseen happenstance, you would likely show up (for security reasons, air travelers cannot sell their tickets privately to someone else, as can sports fans or theatergoers). Passengers would have a strong incentive to appear at the appointed time, Neeleman reasoned, because all JetBlue tickets were nonrefundable and payment was made at the time of purchase (most airlines allow travel agencies and corporate accounts to pay later). The only reason someone would not show up, Neeleman cracked, was "if they got hit by a bus or got stuck on the Van Wyck [Expressway]." A couple of old airline hands, however, couldn't quite get used to the idea of not overbooking at all, so ingrained was it in the airline DNA. "Can't we just sell a few more seats?" they would ask. Neeleman responded that he would rather give up the money the company would get from overselling by even one or two seats than risk inflicting that abuse on paying customers.

"You know, he was right," said his old friend and airline colleague Dan Hersh, who was always concerned that Neeleman got too emotionally involved with passengers' tribulations. Not only did JetBlue avoid angry scenes of bumped customers and the delays that inevitably result when trying to coax people off the plane, it would not have to compensate bumping victims and would get an undetermined amount of value in added goodwill. Besides, there were the DOT complaint tallies to consider. Every month, the transportation agency's consumer division issued a closely watched report card, showing how each airline treated its customers in a variety of categories, detailing how may flights were late and how many bags were lost. No matter how well it did in other ways, JetBlue would always be sure of grabbing the number-one spot in the denied boarding department.

JetBlue's first scheduled flight was set to depart JFK on the morning of February 11, 2000, for Fort Lauderdale. But the airline's real debut would take place earlier that day in Buffalo, using a plane ferried up at dawn, technically honoring Neeleman's pledge to Chuck Schumer, although regularly scheduled service wouldn't begin for a few weeks. Tickets had gone on sale at $49 to $79 one way from New York to these first two cities, and Merkley had produced a humorous ad campaign featuring smart-alecky lines from cynical New Yorkers who apparently did not believe JetBlue was for real.

"A comfortable seat for $49? Well, I'm the Queen of Sheba!" one spot read.

Launching an airline in mid-February from a city famed for its brutal winters was a dicey proposition. By the morning of the eleventh a heavy fog had settled over the region, and the flight to New York was delayed by two hours, an inauspicious start for an airline that had made punctuality one of its rallying cries. Mayor Rudy Giuliani, who was considering running for higher office, had secured a seat, and Governor George Pataki, a fellow Republican with whom Giuliani had an uneasy relationship, had arrived by car from Albany. Schumer, who had flown up from New York, had his sound bite ready; reprising his "proud uncle" line, taking sweeping credit for JetBlue's arrival, a subtle one-upping of the Republican contingent that had been less evident in JetBlue's journey through the regulatory thicket. But now that Neeleman had gotten the slots he needed from DOT in Washington, Governor

Pataki was likely the most important elected official for JetBlue's future. He, along with the governor of New Jersey, appointed members of the Port Authority, and the authority would have vast sway over vital matters such as gate space and airport facilities.

Meanwhile, Amy Curtis-McIntyre and Gareth Edmondson-Jones were recovering from a celebration the night before. The pair had reprised the "satellite tour" they had done in July and had beamed out images of Neeleman's intoning his by now standard promise to "bring humanity back to air travel" to hundreds of stations, even landing on NBC's *Today* show. At Terminal Six, amid blue balloons and cake, New York City politicos and civil servants mingled with the media throng as they awaited the landing of the first flight. But this fete was different from the others that had preceded it; among all the partiers were actual paying passengers who'd bought $79 tickets to Florida. Several were getting their proverbial fifteen minutes of fame as television cameramen roamed the concourse. "It sort of hit me at that moment, we actually could pull this off," Edmondson-Jones said.

Congressman Gregory Meeks, the U.S. representative for the district that includes Kennedy Airport, was there to gloat: "I'm really glad I stuck my neck out" and fought for the upstart. Queens Borough President Claire Shulman, who had been less than friendly at first about the prospect of more jet noise rattling her constituents, had come around. A few of the Port Authority officials present weren't quite so ebullient; a budget domestic airline operating out of Kennedy was such a long shot that they seemed ready to deliver the inevitable eulogy. One Port Authority manager even began his remarks by admitting "Frankly, a year ago I thought your idea could never be a reality."

It took only ten weeks before it became clear that JetBlue would not heed the warnings of myriad well-wishers to quietly "stick to its knitting," in the words of management guru Tom Peters. Most onlookers still regarded the airline as the Northeast equivalent of Southwest—offering flights of under three hours up and down the Eastern seaboard, avoiding the sorts of airports popular with business travelers (LaGuardia, Reagan, O'Hare, Logan) that were perpetually backed up. As such it was hardly an imminent threat to American, then the largest airline at JFK, where it used its massive two-terminal complex mainly for international and long-distance flights to places like California and the Caribbean. JetBlue instead had staked out People Express territory, places like Burlington, Vermont, Syracuse, and Rochester, and the usual sun spots of Tampa and Fort Myers. JetBlue was seen as an airline whose main competition, on a sizable number of flights, was the bus or automobile.

But up in Darien, Connecticut, John Owen and scheduling wizard Dave Ulmer were running scenarios using all that data on their competitors that the federal government so helpfully supplied. One of the ploys they were looking at was adding red-eyes to the mix. For a good reason; the incremental costs are lowered by extending the number of hours per day a plane is airborne. By taking a plane that would otherwise just be sitting on the ground, they could charge under a hundred dollars for a coast-to-coast flight and still make money.

Long flights, however, were not supposed to be in the picture at that point. By the end of March, they were still working out the kinks. JetBlue had only two planes and the televisions it had publicized so heavily weren't working yet, so on each entertainment-free flight, passengers had to be mollified with five-dollar vouchers. Launching the airline without one of its prime selling points struck some as risky but JetBlue couldn't wait—it had already accepted the first two planes Airbus had rushed over, on lease, to get it going. The novelty of the new airline's leather seats and low fares, however, seemed to distract from the absence of this feature.

TV would make more of a difference in the coast-to-coast market, the busiest in the country and so lucrative for the big airlines that they would go to great lengths to keep a low-cost challenger out. American Airlines had gone after Pan Am 2 when it had the temerity to challenge AA from New York to Los Angeles, flooding the market with extra flights and cut-rate fares. The only low-fare line that had been tolerated by the club was Tower Air, a fringe airline known mainly for rude and unreliable service. Packing in crowds on its fleet of geriatric 747s to Europe, Israel, and California, Tower recalled the days when student charters were the only way to travel cheaply by air. The airline was privately held by an Israeli businessman who kept a low profile, in part because he was frequently fined by the FAA for safety violations.

For all these reasons, any thoughts of heading West were kept firmly under wraps. But then, on May 3, 2000, Tower Air suddenly closed its doors. That meant there would be no dependable low-fare alternative from New York to the West Coast. Cheap fares on the majors were getting increasingly hard to find, and if JetBlue didn't seize the opportunity now, it would cede the discount slice of the market to someone else.

So the decision was made to plunge in with a single overnight flight between JFK and Ontario, California. Ontario was a fairly obscure airfield, at least for New Yorkers. It was about thirty miles east of downtown Los Angeles, hardly a serious rival to LAX. But JetBlue was nonetheless seen as throwing down the gauntlet in the nation's most heavily traveled airline route.

Within a few weeks of announcing cross-country fares of $99, Jet-

Blue knew it had made the right call. The flights were selling out; a second red-eye, between Oakland and JFK, was quickly rustled up.

It must have hit American and United that this new airline could well end up being more than a minor nuisance. American's planners in Dallas scrambled for ways to respond. Curiously, they would eventually choose not just to match JetBlue on price, but also to launch its own flights from Kennedy to Ontario, an airport that it previously had expressed no interest in serving. (It later abandoned the plan.) To call attention to JetBlue's lack of a frequent flier program, it would hand out triple miles to anyone who chose American.

There was a curious aspect to the airlines that Herb Kelleher had adeptly exploited. While American, United, and Delta were beating up on the low-fare upstarts, they were capable of coexisting with them as well. This harks back to the days before deregulation when the airlines were run like a club, and members would tacitly agree to stay out of one another's way. Typical of this paradox was the relationship between Kelleher and American Airlines chief Bob Crandall, who, despite the supposedly bitter rivalry they displayed in public, were in private good friends; they went on vacations together with their wives, they socialized frequently in Dallas. And every year, right after Labor Day, they would quietly slip off to a remote mountain retreat in Wyoming to join dozens of their rival executives in one of the more bizarre rituals that exists in American business: the annual gathering of the Conquistadores del Cielo ("conquerors of the sky"), a mysterious society of aviation executives founded in 1937 by then-TWA chief Jack Frye. While it began as a purely social club, over the years it evolved into an exclusive and increasingly secretive fraternity, which is open only to chief executives and presidents of airlines and aerospace companies. Every September they meet at the

A-Bar-A Ranch owned by Lear Gates Chairman Charlie Gates, for five days of horseback riding, hunting, knife-throwing competitions, and other macho rituals in an unintentional parody of the bellicosity they display in public.

On the rare occasion when a woman has reached the top, as in the case of June Morris, she has been politely discouraged from attempting to crash the gender barrier. (When Colleen Barrett became president of Southwest in 2001, she quickly let it be known that she "couldn't imagine anything more boring" than joining Kelleher and his compatriots at the A-Bar-A.) Insiders know otherwise: the Conquistadores is one of the remaining relics of the all-boys club that ruled the airlines for years, and admission into this elite fellowship is a much-sought honor, conferred only after inductees are tapped in a torchlight ceremony on the final night of their retreat—a ritual that requires them to dress in tattered costumes and tights acquired from a Spanish opera company.

Getting JetBlue into the air meant that David Neeleman was now eligible to join this society, and he could now look forward to a few spirited games with Kelleher and the gang at the A-Bar-A. His status as an upstart wouldn't hurt him; Kelleher had shown you could play both sides and thrive.

Now that they were in the air there was a more pressing question: Would JetBlue be able to sustain its buzz, to live up to the press notices? Gareth Edmondson-Jones had gotten the airline an unheard-of amount of press for a budget start-up. But many a phenomenon that had ridden high expectations had collapsed into the gap between hype and reality.

It appeared that Neeleman wasn't as averse to performing for the press as he had once seemed. Edmondson-Jones soon began arranging for journalists to accompany Neeleman on one of his weekly flights. Neeleman would spend the flight walking down the aisle and chatting up passengers, and soon he was handing out snacks, just like his crew members.

It was an irresistible hook, especially in a business where most CEOs went out of their way to avoid face-to-face interactions with their customers. (American's Bob Crandall was known to bark at anyone who dared approach him while confined in one of his first-class seats; he claimed he was too busy working to mingle with the hoi polloi.) Even so, there was potential for embarrassment in these benign forays. Once when at JFK, Neeleman got word that one of his planes had indeed been overbooked, by one passenger, apparently to accommodate someone who was traveling at the last minute due to an emergency. Neeleman bounded over to the gate, made sure that someone willingly relinquished a seat, and then, as the volunteer got off, handed her a twenty-dollar bill—in addition to the free ticket her gesture had already earned her. "Here, go get yourself something to eat," he told the startled woman.

In the first six months there were indeed ample opportunities to test JetBlue's mettle; this was, after all, an airline operating in the unforgiving territory of the Northeast. A couple of early snafus had been resolved so successfully as to create a grassroots buzz. Al Spain recalled an early mishap, when a flight in Buffalo was delayed due to a bomb scare. Spain, who was the captain on the flight, made frequent appearances in the cabin to reassure passengers personally, and even offered the use of his cell phone to those who wished to call home.

Stories of small, but nonetheless heroic gestures also made the rounds: There was the tale of an eighty-two-year-old woman who had flown Jet-Blue from Buffalo to connect to an overseas flight at Kennedy, only to realize that she'd left her passport back home. A JetBlue customer service agent managed to track down the woman's son, who retrieved her passport from her apartment and put it on the next JetBlue flight to New York. The agent received a bottle of Jameson's as thanks upon the woman's return. "And you know that's what we have to keep going here; we can't let that die," Al Spain told the troops.

There were also some moments when the JetBlue spirit would be put to a severe test. The reservationists in Utah, many of whom had never set foot in New York, would get an early taste of the city's fabled attitude. At first, it was the customers who were a bit taken aback by these almost frighteningly perky types, at an airline, of all things. The dissonance worked both ways. The Salt Lake natives weren't prepared for the edgy impatience of the New Yorkers and Florida retirees who made up much of their clientele. "They were really shocked at first when they started dealing with some of these people," Ann Rhoades said. "We had a few in tears. . . . They would say, 'Is everyone there so impatient?'" They soon adjusted.

On January 21, 2001, JetBlue had its first test of how it would handle an emergency. A plane arriving at JFK from Ontario, California, early that Sunday morning skidded off an icy runway in the middle of a storm. The jet came to a halt immediately, however, and the passengers reportedly were not even aware that they weren't at the terminal until they were told they would be deplaned via a bus.

Chris Collins, JetBlue vice president of systems operations, wanted to get the word out fast, so he phoned Edmondson-Jones at home at 7:00 A.M. Within a half hour a bulletin had gone out to the media and the local television crews were shuttled to the scene by the Port Authority. The passengers were taken to the terminal—by then the airport had closed to all flights—and given breakfast and vouchers good for a future trip on JetBlue. Cell phones were handed out to anyone who wanted to make a call (this was by now a standard response to a delay) and preparations were made to deliver people's bags later in the day. As mishaps go, this was a minor one and was handled so adeptly that the incident later got favorably mentioned in a *Business Week* article about how companies manage problems (although sometime later a passenger sued Jet-Blue for emotional distress). While the public quickly forgot about it,

Usto Schulz bore down, interviewing not just pilots involved in that incident but all who flew for the airline because he wanted to see if there were any patterns of difficulty in landing at the airport. For JetBlue, the fact that this incident had ended up on the evening news was early warning that the high profile they had cultivated had a negative side.

Meanwhile, Dave Barger began pulling together the results for the anniversary letter he would soon send out. He and Neeleman had spent much of their first year in the air; between them, they had flown more than 250 flights on JetBlue. Barger would not have to work hard to spin the results positively; the first thousand flights, he wrote, had been completed without a single cancellation; their on-time performance was more than 79 percent.

But one detail revealed, if anyone needed reminding, the vagaries of trying to make money in the airlines. Neeleman's business plan had never predicted a profit for the first year. Any start-up has extraordinary expenses at the outset, and JetBlue was no exception, posting what it characterized as a "significant" loss in the first quarter, followed by a smaller loss in the second. By the end of the year, however, things were looking up and it appeared that JetBlue might post a profit for the second half of 2000. If so, JetBlue suggested, it might be in a position to make a profit-sharing distribution. But a sudden spike in fuel costs threw off its projections, costing it five million dollars more than it had originally budgeted to gas up its growing fleet.

No one had really expected the profit sharing this first year, but it still rankled.

In February 2001, a few weeks after the airline's first birthday, Neeleman took his family to California on vacation. Southern California was almost a second home to him; his grandparents had lived there, and at

Morris one of the first regular routes, Salt Lake to LA, had developed into a sort of shuttle connecting the large Mormon populations of both cities. It was on this trip that he decided to take a closer look at Long Beach Airport, a place that had long intrigued him. It was a curiosity, to be sure, a single Art Deco terminal, framed by the requisite swaying palm trees, seemingly removed from the realities of the contemporaneous airline business. However, far from escaping the upheaval, it had instead earned a reputation as an airline graveyard. Draconian noise limits imposed in the 1980s had discouraged many airlines from coming in; and those that did—minor players like Jet America and Win Air— quickly flamed out. American and America West operated a small number of flights there, but American recently had cut back, in what was seen as a snub to the local chamber of commerce types who'd persuaded them to come in.

Yet Long Beach had two very strong assets: One, it was only twenty miles south of central Los Angeles, and thus was convenient for a huge population base that included not only its home city of Long Beach and much of Orange Country but also LA proper. Its other advantage was simply that it wasn't LAX. One of the busiest jetports in the country, Los Angeles International Airport was to its hometown what JFK had long been to New Yorkers—a tangled mess of terminals to be endured only because there were no good alternatives. But at Long Beach, not only the terminal but the experience harked back to the 1930s; passengers boarded planes by walking out onto the tarmac and climbing up a set of stairs. It looked so much like a movie set that it was said—erroneously— that the famous airport scene in *Casablanca* had been filmed there. Airport officials did nothing to discourage this misperception.

But the limits imposed by the local noise activists were tight. In early 2002 there were only twenty-seven unused takeoff slots at Long Beach. It was the same dilemma Neeleman had faced at Kennedy; if he started up modestly, he'd risk waving a flag at American, which would likely swoop in with new flights. But he did not have the planes to launch a more ambitious schedule.

Still, Neeleman was attracted to Long Beach. It was the sort of neglected airport he could resuscitate with his low fares, the way Kelleher had always done. And conveniently, Southwest had avoided Long Beach in favor of building up a sizable presence at LAX. Neeleman could have the place practically to himself.

Or so it seemed. First, he would be forced to dabble in the unfamiliar realm of local politics. This wasn't like JFK, where, even if politics did intrude, the process of handing out landing rights was conducted mostly in the open, with an opportunity for public comment. Here, the permission to land was controlled by the local city council and the airport authority.

Rob Land recalled the day in early April when Neeleman called him with a proposal so ridiculous Land was sure he was kidding. In fact, it was so far-fetched that total secrecy was required. He *had* to get all the slots at once—even if he couldn't use them; the risk that American would retaliate was just too great. And they had to convince the local pols that it was in their own self-interest to nurture this new airline rather than let the typical scenario unfold, which could be reduced to this shorthand script: Small discount line enters, big airline strikes back, small airline goes under, big airline decamps. It was that cycle, Neeleman believed, that had led to the present predicament at Long Beach. "Give us time to build and we'll stick with you," was the line they would use on the city council members.

In May they met privately with council members. Land recalled that they furiously worked all the angles; anticipating some objections from the aircraft noise activists in nearby Huntington Beach, they reworked some of the environmental impact charts they had drawn up for the

New York audience, showing the Airbus's A320 was much quieter than the jets of the competition, such as the older MD-80s and 737s American favored in the region. They promised to charge $99 fares to New York for starters, and to the politicians who would likely be seeking reelection in the coming year that sounded like a compelling sound bite. But mostly Neeleman played the loyalty card, cagily exploiting the airport's disappointment over American's fickle behavior.

Long Beach also had something of a local aviation aristocracy; the city had long ties to the industry—McDonnell Douglas, Lockheed, and Boeing at one time all had a strong presence there—and it evinced the insularity one would expect in a company town. Lest he come across as just another parvenu, Neeleman sought out a contact who could open doors. Soon he was introduced to Kristy Ardizzone, the daughter of a famous aviatrix and an accomplished private pilot herself. A somewhat intimidating presence—she was about six feet tall, slim, and blond—she was also acquainted with everyone who could deal out the slots.

"We hired her as a consultant to help navigate the political waters," said Land. "We had to show why we weren't like all the other airlines that came in here and were driven out."

Ardizzone had an office at the headquarters of the aptly named MillionAir, which performed ground services for private jet operators at the airport. She arranged a series of catered lunches and soon, as Land, put it, "we had the mayor and half of the city council in private in these hourlong meetings." Neeleman and Land eventually emerged with an agreement that locked up all the remaining spots at the airport for the next two years.

Later that day, Land and Neeleman raced back to LAX; they were on different flights—Land to DC, Neeleman to JFK—and Land recalled that they were furiously sending messages to each other via their pagers. Both got to their respective flights minutes before departure. "And we're e-mailing each other, like 'Can you believe we did it!' It hadn't really sunk in."

A day later, it did. American, as they could have expected, was outraged and immediately vowed to fight JetBlue in court. JetBlue had arrived.

seven
9/11

On the morning of Monday, September 10, 2001, David Neeleman arrived in his office in Queens, where the airline had moved shortly after launching, to await a letter from his auditor, the final item needed before he could file to take his year-and-a-half-old company public. This had been part of the plan all along; even the first proposal he had scratched out with Tom Kelly five years before had set a goal of taking the company public within two years, not only to raise additional capital but also to reward the investors for their early confidence. Yet Neeleman had at first resisted the idea. He was not looking forward to the constant focus on quarterly results and short-term performance that comes with running a public company. The directors and other founders had wanted to move sooner, however, and the timing now seemed perfect. JetBlue had racked up its best monthly performance in August and had set what was believed to be an airline industry record for the number of seats filled, 88 percent, and the money they would raise in the market would be used to get those planes out there faster, to slake the demand. Neeleman also saw that going public would have a benefit for JetBlue's workers, who would be given a chance to buy shares at a discounted price. Neeleman hoped that a majority of his employees would become owners; a stock purchase plan would allow them to do so with payroll deductions.

The prospectus, by necessity, had to touch on all the risks to investing in an airline. It was the standard parade of horribles: the cyclical nature of the business, its vulnerability to fuel price swings, the possibility of union organization. These were all theoretical, of course, and terrorism, which was considered a threat mainly to airlines flying abroad, was not even mentioned. That day, there was only one tangible threat to JetBlue. Just two weeks before, Neeleman had opened the morning paper to see a full-page advertisement by American Airlines promoting steep discounts off its cross-country fares that bore a startling similarity to the prices JetBlue was charging out of its brand-new Long Beach hub. Industry wags quickly labeled the American move the "Kill JetBlue" fare, and as Don Burr and countless other victims of this treatment could attest, this was no minor mugging. Neeleman even had gotten a little testy when asked about it at a press briefing the day he launched his first flight to Long Beach from Kennedy in late August. The Long Beach debut had gone well; Alex Wilcox had been brought in to manage what was being described as JetBlue's "West Coast hub," even though the sort of traditional hub-and-spoke operation would never work there. But he'd pulled it off, with plans to debut up to twenty flights across the country and up and down the West Coast. A billboard on the 405 freeway said it all: GOING TO LAX? it asked. WHY?

Since then, Neeleman had taken a short break with his family and had spent much of the first week of September in Wyoming for the annual retreat of the Conquistadores del Cielo. As Neeleman took a quick look at the forward bookings that morning, he detected no fallout from American's crude maneuver.

Gareth Edmondson-Jones was down the hall from Neeleman, preparing the news release that would go out the day after the public filing. One of his counterparts from the Port Authority press office, Greg Trevor, rang him up to alert him that a photo of Neeleman and Neil Levin, the director of the Port Authority, standing in front of a JetBlue plane, would go out on the news wires first thing Tuesday morning. The photo op was well timed, as tensions had reportedly flared between the authority and JetBlue, which wasn't getting the gates it wanted at Terminal Six fast enough. Levin, a one-time protégé of former Senator Al D'Amato, had been in the job for only six months, but was politically savvy enough to sense that Neeleman's airline was just the sort of venture they should be supporting.

Edmondson-Jones was also on the phone to a photo editor at *Vanity Fair* to arrange a portrait of Neeleman, who had just been chosen for inclusion in the magazine's annual roster of movers and shakers that would appear in the December issue. Annie Leibovitz had been mentioned as a possible photographer. The magazine had declared JetBlue the "It airline" in a recent "what's in—what's out" tally, and the media coverage, far from slowing, was producing a reliable stream of tributes saccharine enough to induce sugar shock. Neeleman seemed both flattered and flummoxed by his incipient celebrity; he'd been in New York for nearly three years but in many ways was as resolutely unhip as on the day he'd first arrived from Utah. Once, told that Richard Avedon was interested in doing a photo shoot of him for an ad campaign, Neeleman reacted by asking "Uh . . . who's Richard Avedon?"

Late in the day, John Owen and Holly Nelson, a former Northwest Airlines executive who was his deputy, received the auditor's letter they'd been awaiting. But they decided to go over the S-1 prospectus one more time. It was too late to make it to the Securities and Exchange Commission that day, so they decided they would stay overnight in lower Manhattan. Everything was set to go forward at 10:00 o'clock Tuesday morning.

At 8:50 A.M. the next morning, Neeleman, Barger, and a few other senior managers were in their regular weekly strategy meeting at headquarters, when someone opened the door and told them that a small plane had hit one of the World Trade Center towers. Barger, who'd flown small planes himself, thought that was odd: The skies outside were so clear that it was inconceivable any pilot could blunder that badly. Barger and Neeleman turned on the television outside the office door just as United Airlines Flight 175 sliced into the south tower, at 9:03.

A few seconds of shocked silence elapsed before the obvious question came to everyone's minds: Could it be one of ours? JetBlue had eight aircraft in the air at that moment; several had taken off from Kennedy within the past twenty minutes. At that point, the aircraft involved in the attack had not been identified. Bobby Di Francesco, a former New York State trooper who was JetBlue's security chief, ran into the room. "How do we know it isn't one of ours?" he remembered thinking. The position of all the JetBlue planes was quickly confirmed. Flight 70 was en route to Ontario, California, and over Kansas when the news came in; Flight 93 was halfway to Oakland; Flight 205 had left JFK at 8:25 A.M. and was just passing over Pennsylvania when the towers were hit. Other JetBlue planes were heading for Orlando, Tampa, and West Palm Beach.

The emergency command center that they always had in their plans was quickly assembled in a spare office; it would be manned around the clock and everyone would take turns answering phones. Ann Rhoades was in her office for what was supposed to be one of her last days on the job as vice president of people; she had decided to retire from day-to-day responsibilities so she could spend more time in her home in the mountains outside Albuquerque. Her replacement, former retailing executive Vinny Stabile, had just reported that morning for his first day at JetBlue. Rhoades's office had an unimpeded view of lower Manhattan, and she was one of the few present who had seen the first plane, American Airlines Flight 11, slam into the north tower at 8:46 A.M. Soon she was joined by colleagues who watched as black smoke billowed from the towers ten miles away. Neeleman and Barger came by, and as Neeleman recalled later, "It sort of hit us that we'd worked so hard to be 'New York's hometown airline,' and now that hometown was under attack." Visual proof of that allegiance was on display all around the offices; many had on their walls an aerial photo taken of JetBlue's first plane flying low over the Trade Center, so close that it seemed to buzz the buildings. Tracy Sandford, another marketing whiz who had come over from Virgin, had arranged the shoot, hiring a photographer who'd worked on *Top Gun* to trail the Airbus from a Learjet, a stunt that had to be cleared by the FAA, for the planes were cruising at an altitude of only 2,000 feet above Manhattan. Now the FAA was ordering all planes out of the country's airspace; there was no telling when any of them would be airborne again.

The phone lines were jammed with calls coming in from JetBlue crews all over the country. JetBlue planes were alighting in unfamiliar places like Wichita, Kansas, and Raleigh, North Carolina. Some of the Jet-Blue headquarters staff got in their cars and drove for hours to help their stranded colleagues; in all, nearly five thousand commercial aircraft in the United States were grounded for more than forty-eight hours.

One detail that day did not get much outside attention: JetBlue passengers who happened to be airborne that morning were, uniquely, able to view live television coverage of the horror at the Trade Center and the Pentagon. This had the potential to set off a panic; one reason all the planes were being grounded was the fear that other hijackers might still be out there. Of course, there had always been concern that airing live TV might put fliers in the uncomfortable position of watching

24/7 coverage of an aviation disaster and commercial airlines had long censored in-flight movies to remove any references to aviation safety—once even deleting a critical scene in the middle of *Rain Man* where Dustin Hoffman's character recites statistics on airline crashes. But, as JetBlue flight attendants later reported, access to television, paradoxically, seemed to calm their customers that morning; they understood why their plane was making an unscheduled landing. JetBlue had always had the option of censoring newscasts, and there was a delay function it could have deployed, but it had chosen not to. Its decision was vindicated that day.

Doreen Lawrence, head of in-flight, was driving west on the Grand Central Parkway when the news came over the radio. She was heading toward Connecticut, with Brian Manubay, an in-flight manager, where she was to host a lunch for some of the crew at JetBlue's Darien offices. They were halfway across the Whitestone Bridge to the Bronx when they realized they had to get to JFK fast. Lawrence pulled a quick U-turn and sped back in the direction of Queens, moments before the bridge was closed to traffic. They got to the airport ten minutes later, again, just before all access to the airfield was closed off. They found Terminal Six packed with passengers, many of whom were not holding tickets on JetBlue flights but, rather, had been expelled from other terminals. Most airlines had shut the doors to their terminals soon after the attacks on the advice of the Port Authority, which was acting prudently—who knew if other attackers were still at large? Several strandees told Manubay that a rumor had circulated at the airport that "if you go to JetBlue, they'll help you." What had happened was this: Barger had sent out e-mails immediately to the entire JetBlue workforce, telling them what little he knew, without waiting for clarifications from the authorities. Although Barger's information wasn't much more detailed than what was being broadcast on television, his gesture was meant to reassure employees and keep the lines of communication open. Few airlines had done that, so JetBlue workers were forwarding Barger's bulletins to their news-starved colleagues at other airlines. Lawrence and Manubay set up an emergency booth and tried to help passengers get on their way, but virtually all transportation in and out of the city had been shut down. People continued to straggle in, including a group of young European students returning home, one of whom was in a panic: She needed to get access to a doctor as the medication she was taking to treat a serious condition was about to run out. There was a hospital located near the sprawling JFK campus and a few JetBlue people had had occasion to use it; Lawrence sent word that it might be needed.

An hour later, the Port Authority told JetBlue it, too, had to evacuate its terminal. Lawrence and Manubay made an announcement: All present, no matter whose customer they were, could go with them to a nearby airport hotel, where they could stay until they had someplace else to go. For the next three days, the JetBlue pair slept on cots in the ballroom of a nearby Best Western, with hundreds of displaced fliers; no one, it seemed, could get out.

Lawrence had not needed to check with her superiors to approve this act of charity; early in the day Neeleman and Barger had told anyone from the field who called in that they should just follow their conscience and no questions would ever be raised about the expense.

There were lighter moments as well. Al Spain, who was in Toronto at a meeting of airline safety directors the morning of the eleventh, had gotten back to New York by renting a car and driving nonstop for twenty hours. When he arrived in Queens, he'd gone to the airport to lend a hand. There were so many diverse passengers under JetBlue's wing at that point, he recalled, that they finally secured space in a motel some miles away for a tour group that was due to fly back to Europe on Delta as soon as service was restored. Their luggage was back at the airport, and so that they could have a change of clothes, Lawrence handed out JetBlue T-shirts to everyone. "So imagine how Delta feels when they see this huge group show up in JetBlue T-shirts, because we—not they—took care of their passengers," Spain recalled.

JetBlue not only had people dispersed all over the United States; a team was in France, at the Airbus facility, taking delivery of the eighteenth jet in its fleet. Jim Hnat, a specialist in aircraft transactions who had recently joined the company as assistant general counsel, was about to board the plane for its maiden flight when he heard what had happened. With U.S. airspace closed off, he made plans to spend a few more days in France, a fate that in other circumstances would have been welcome. Hnat was young and single and was fluent in French, having lived in Paris as a junior law firm associate. He was, though, desperate to get back home to get a sense of what the company was facing. He made a few calls and was told that perhaps the JetBlue jet would be permitted to enter U.S. airspace ahead of regular commercial flights; it was, after all, a delivery flight and there were few passengers to screen. "But then I thought, there must be lots of other people over here who can't get out, and we had all these empty seats." So Hnat put out the word through the expatriate grapevine: Anyone in the south of France who needed a lift to New York would be welcome to ride, gratis, aboard JetBlue. A couple dozen people gladly took him up on the offer, and on Friday, September 14, the newest JetBlue Airbus made its way down the runway at the manufacturer's private landing strip.

As it took off, a group of workers from the plant marched over to

the side of the tarmac, grasping a large American flag in a solemn tribute as the jet rolled past. The pilot of the plane choked up; many of the
passengers were in tears.

The next few weeks were a blur. Dave Barger, who seemed to know
everyone in the airlines and in New York politics, was attending several
funerals a day; one of his close friends, chief inspector of the Port Authority Police, Tony Infante, had perished rushing into the Trade Center
just minutes before the South Tower collapsed. Neil Levin was having
breakfast at Windows on the World on the 107th floor of the North
Tower when the first plane hit; he never made it out.

A few weeks later, on yet another clear September day, Gareth
Edmondson-Jones boarded a nearly empty JetBlue plane for Buffalo,
and sat there and waited for the rest of the customers to show up. And
waited and waited. "It hit me that, God, this is going to be bad. I didn't
know if we're going to get through this." Airline traffic had plummeted
sharply across the country, and for the first month after the attacks, fearful travelers were allowed to cancel without penalty. Many thousands did
just that. Most airlines had shaved their schedules by 20 percent and
were sending surplus jets to an airplane parking lot in the Mojave Desert.
Whatever JetBlue's leaders privately felt about their odds of survival,
however, their public utterances were optimistic. They promised no layoffs. They promised to maintain service to every city on its route map,
although they made a few minor cuts in the number of daily flights. But
new cities were another story; in a few weeks, Neeleman was supposed
to open the airline's much-anticipated service at Washington's Dulles
Airport, but now it seemed especially inappropriate to stage a celebration so close to the capital, and the inaugural was put off.

By mid-October, things started, slowly, to improve, and Barger and

Neeleman wrote a measured note to employees, with their usual upbeat message tempered with some sobering observations.

"We are not out of the woods yet," they wrote.

While bookings were stronger, they said, the war in Afghanistan and the anthrax scare were taking a toll. "We need to keep a realistic sense of the challenges . . . that JetBlue continues to face."

JetBlue had, they noted, put fares on sale, and load factors—the number of seats filled—were climbing, steadily, to more than 70 percent. "Keep in mind, though, what $29 fares to Buffalo . . . and $99 fares to California do. . . . We've got a long way to go to break even."

The letter went on to detail the "efficiency measures" it had adopted. Short of laying off staff, it had asked pilots and in-flight crews to fly reduced hours until the schedule returned to its pre-September 11 levels. Since crew members got paid per hour, that amounted to a cut in pay.

A few JetBlue crew members decided they just couldn't fly anymore; at other airlines the number was much higher. But many airline workers departed involuntarily. Within weeks of the hijackings, more than one hundred thousand airline employees in the United States had been furloughed.

Although it was doing better than most other airlines, JetBlue still had to figure out how to stay in business, to "get the butts back in the seats," as Edmondson-Jones's associate Fiona Morrison put it. For most of the summer, JetBlue had been racking up sales of nearly two million dollars a day, and for the first few weeks after the attacks, that was cut in half. While JetBlue's small size was an advantage—it didn't have much fat to cut—it was also a drawback: The public might logically assume that if big airlines were slashing the equivalent of several JetBlues from their companies, then a start-up line like JetBlue might just disappear.

They needed to find a tasteful way to get the message out. "We were all stumbling, trying to find things to say that didn't seem commercial or callous," Edmondson-Jones recalled. "And how to sell an airline when, naturally, everyone's focus was on safety and security, which were the two subjects that an airline could never come close to broaching in advertising."

It had long been an unwritten rule in the airlines that individual companies did not talk publicly about safety (or, worse, attempt to gain a competitive edge by claiming they were safer than their rivals). Not only would this sort of public dialogue stoke more general fears of flying, the thinking went, but airline people also knew well that while fatal accidents were rare, what are euphemistically described as "incidents"— landing gear collapsing, an engine fire—occur on a regular basis, and most go nearly unnoticed by the public. No airline could say with certainty that a more serious accident couldn't happen to it. Thus, when one airline experiences a fatal crash, all airlines pull their advertising for a respectful period of time. It is an acknowledgment that in aviation, one tragedy reflects on the entire business. The attacks of September 11, however, were so outside the pale that airlines found themselves in uncharted territory.

As airline service began, slowly, to return, little else in the business could be considered normal. The national guard was stationed at more than 150 large airports to create the impression that security had been stepped up, but this was widely derided as window dressing and did little to calm the flying public. As debate began over more permanent steps that could prevent a reprise of the hijackings, Neeleman was already working at one solution. On the day after the hijackings he had phoned executives at Airbus Industrie in Toulouse and asked for help in reinforcing the doors that separated the cockpit from the cabin. Airbus had already developed and produced a series of attackproof Kevlar cockpit doors for Swissair and had some surplus samples sitting in its factory. Airbus hadn't expected there would ever be much demand. Neeleman went ahead with his plan to immediately fortify all the doors on the eighteen planes in his fleet, for a cost of about thirty thousand dollars.

On October 15, Edmondson-Jones alerted the media that if they came out to Kennedy, they'd get their first look at the first attackproof cockpit doors in the American airline business. Again, JetBlue had been able to use its diminutive size to its advantage. "It is hard to remember how big that was," he said later. "In twenty-four hours it was a huge, national story and that took us a long way to getting back to business . . . because once you could broach that topic, what came across is that we're a forward-thinking and safety-conscious company." Neeleman had even scooped Transportation Secretary Norman Mineta, who had wanted to come out first pushing for a requirement that all airlines replace the flimsy barriers that had failed to protect the flight deck from intruders. Money was going to be a problem; given the devastating losses facing the industry, the government would have a hard time ordering airlines to pay for all the improvements themselves. But while the larger airlines tussled with Congress over how much of a bailout was forthcoming, JetBlue tapped into its cash on hand to cover the security upgrade. JetBlue, however, was feeling the pinch; its cash fund was draining fast.

On November 12, New York City was paralyzed by another aviation disaster. Shortly after takeoff from JFK Airport, American Airlines Flight 587, bound for Santo Domingo in the Dominican Republic, crashed into a Queens neighborhood, killing all aboard. A JetBlue plane was so close to the crash that the pilot reported watching it roll and suddenly nosedive, then burst into flames as it hit the ground. For the second time in two months, all air traffic in the skies over New York was ordered to a halt. In a few hours, however, the flight ban was suddenly lifted; the FAA declared, a bit too fast for some people, that it had all but ruled out terrorism as the cause. It was now deemed to be either a mechanical flaw or a pilot error in manipulating the rudder of the Airbus A300. This did not do much to quell anyone's anxiety over getting on a plane.

As Thanksgiving approached it appeared that what was usually the busiest travel week of the year would be a financial debacle for the airlines. And there was a limit to how much discounting they could do to get customers to come back. "If you're not flying, you've probably got some very good reasons, and bribing customers isn't going to work," said John Owen. As it happened, JetBlue at that time was between ad agencies. Amy Curtis-McIntyre had been planning to shop the twenty-million-dollar account around New York, and the attacks had left everything in limbo.

"After September 11, every advertising message that we had produced suddenly seemed uncomfortable, weird, and just insensitive," she recalled. Like other airlines, JetBlue had pulled all of its spots for a few weeks. Then one day, Neeleman walked into her office to tell her they couldn't continue to sit by passively as their business evaporated. "We're going to have to get back out there," Neeleman said.

They were still uncertain how to proceed until Curtis-McIntyre got a call one day from Paul Capelli, founder of the Ad Store, which had done stylish work for Alitalia and other European companies in the United States. "He was heartbroken for us and for the city, and he was so genuine and completely empathetic," she remembered. "And he said, 'We will help you with anything you want to do in the market.'" She decided to give him a try, but first she sat down and wrote out the copy for the first post–9/11 ad. The ad showed a photo of an American flag flapping in the breeze with the headline STILL FLYING. She gave it to Capelli and together they produced some tasteful black-and-white print ads.

"They never talked about money, they never talked about contract, they just got on board and helped us," she recalled. Next followed a TV campaign called "Reasons to Fly," an understated litany of all the reasons why people might want to travel that had not changed. The whole bill came in for under twenty-five thousand dollars.

The Ad Store got the account, and still had it three years later.

In early December, JetBlue began training a new class of flight attendants. It was a bigger than average group, and, one could say, a more hardened one. They were people like Tim Frawley who had just retired after twenty years on the New York City police force and, after so many years in law enforcement, was looking for a pursuit that would not seem dull. Or Boris Millan, an émigré from Cuba who had been working as a flight attendant on American the day of the attacks, only to find himself out of a job a few weeks later.

The three-week training course could not proceed unless it was updated. Here, JetBlue would be ahead of other airlines by default; most airlines were not in a position to hire at all. Nearly thirty years had elapsed since the airlines had made a self-defense training video. Back then, crews were instructed to cooperate with their attackers in order to minimize loss of life; and, in fact, most hijackers were in a sense holding the plane and passengers as hostages to win some objective: release of prisoners, escape to another country. The industry simply had never prepared for the prospect that hijackers would be able to fly a plane. So JetBlue hired a film crew and a West Coast special effects team to produce a new lesson: a graphic video teaching the recruits how to fend off a violent attack, just like the ones that had felled fifty of their colleagues in September. It was titled "JetBlue Fighting Back."

For those who saw it early on, it was a profoundly disturbing glimpse into the new world of the in-flight cabin crew. The documentary-style tape, a mere five minutes in length, opened with some warm and fuzzy shots: the usual motley collection of passengers' boarding the plane to effusive greetings of "Welcome!" from a smiling flight crew. Actually, the crew and their customers were ringers: They were JetBlue executives or supervisors moonlighting as actors. Brian Manubay, tall, dark, and wearing sunglasses, was cast in the role of the villain.

The film jumped ahead to a quarter hour after takeoff. Passengers stared trancelike at the TV screens on the seat backs in front of them. All except Manubay, who appeared in ominous close-up, sliding an orange box cutter from its hiding place inside his pant leg. In seconds, he rose from his seat, bounding toward the front galley.

Screams filled the air: "Help me, oh my God, help me." Brian seized a slim, attractive attendant, played by Val Jenkins, head of the JFK in-flight base, who wrapped her arms around herself to fend off the blows. And then a close-up of Jenkins's face appeared, horribly slashed, blood oozing from dozens of tiny wounds. Then the crew grabbed its makeshift weapons from the galley—scalding hot coffee, fire extinguishers—along with a few well-placed kicks. The scene faded as Brian collapsed on the cabin floor under a pile of squishy foam. "I need to declare an emergency," the pilot intoned from the other side of the cockpit door, and a scene followed showing attendants communicating with the flight crew with a series of coded knocks. The film's final scene showed the captain as he is granted permission to make an emergency landing at the nearest airport.

The point of this explicit re-creation of what likely transpired aboard the hijacked airliners was to make flight attendants "feel empowered," said Manubay, so they could repel an attack, if necessary, with street smarts and a few common items. But it was also an unnerving reminder of the shift that had taken place in in-flight protocol. Up until September 11, a pilot could leave his post to help with a disturbance in the cabin; indeed, many a flare-up had been tamped down with help from the cockpit. Post–9/11, the pilots would remain behind locked doors. The tape made it clear flight attendants were now on their own, and while the likelihood of another hijacking was remote, other emergencies were not. Many crew members, in fact, started to feel the strain, as passengers began coming back. JetBlue even had an in-house shrink, Dr. Matt, who was available to counsel crew members. There were new rules on how many passengers could mingle near the forward galley; if they got close to the cockpit, flight attendants were expected to shoo them away—not exactly the type of reaction for which JetBlue was known. Federal sky marshals would occasionally ride on their flights, and while their job was to protect the flight deck, their presence could cause uneasiness.

A few months later, JetBlue announced another first, but it was one that the managements of other airlines likely couldn't duplicate, even if they had wanted to. To help cabin crews overcome the loss of support from the flight deck, the airline would install hidden surveillance cameras in the plane. That way, pilots could see what was happening in back and respond. This would not just help to prevent a 9/11-style takeover, but also help pilots handle medical emergencies: They could decide whether a crisis merited diverting the flight to the nearest airport. Other airlines' workers wouldn't consider allowing cameras in the back cabin for fear that they would be used to monitor their job performance. Pilots, in fact, had long fought surveillance cameras in the cockpit, which had been pushed by some safety experts as a tool in investigating accidents, again, because they feared airline managements would use them against them.

JetBlue was, however, approached by some of its competitors who were interested in getting copies of its new antihijacking video. And it responded that it was happy to share it with any airline that asked; after all, they were fighting a common enemy. For a brief period after the attacks, it seemed as if a moratorium had been declared on cutthroat competition in the industry. Taking the high road, then, most airline chiefs remained silent as Congress rammed through a fifteen-billion-dollar rescue package that would not only compensate airlines for the business they had lost during the two-day grounding in September, but also set up a bailout fund that would allow ailing airlines to apply for loan guarantees, similar to a program that was set up to rescue Chrysler in the late 1970s.

Few dared to point out the obvious: that a number of these giant airline companies had been in trouble well before 9/11 and that the industry—dominated as it was by a half dozen high-cost, high-fare behemoths—was likely overdue for yet another shakeout.

On April 11, 2002, JetBlue went ahead with the IPO that had been aborted exactly seven months before. The company issued 5.8 million common shares at an initial offering price of $27 under the symbol JBLU. Outside the NASDAQ exchange at 4 Times Square, a pro-Palestinian demonstration swelled to thousands, and police barricaded nearby streets. But JetBlue went ahead with its planned celebration, setting up a mock boarding lounge on the sidewalk. Neeleman's oldest child, twenty-year-old Ashley, joined flight attendants in handing out blue chips and bottled water to passersby. By the time the trading ended at 4:00 P.M., JetBlue's share price had gone up to $47, making it the most successful IPO of the year so far.

By the summer of 2002, airport security was settling into something resembling a routine, if a clumsy one, and the flying public was no longer getting a daily stream of alarmist stories about another "incident" (most often, a dozing screener) that would force a terminal somewhere to be evacuated. While air travel was still down from the last "normal" year, 2000, and many of the largest airlines were still in deep financial trouble, JetBlue was now reliably pumping out quarterly profits and more than adequately justifying its decision to go public.

JetBlue's success, on the surface, could be explained by basic economics. The airline's lean cost structure was better able to withstand a shock than most of its competitors, and Neeleman's decision to go into the sorts of long-distance routes where the automobile was not an alternative now seemed prescient. But JetBlue had done more than survive; it was thriving beyond even the most fevered expectations and, thus, there was something else at work here, a curious sort of cult following that had nothing to do with prosaic gambits such as its new frequent flier program (which it introduced that fall, finally giving it a place to put the True Blue moniker it had gotten from Landor Associates).

This impression had been borne out by some actual consumer research. In late 2001, 54 percent of a sampling of some fifteen thousand of JetBlue's customers said they had heard of the airline through word of mouth, advertising accounted for some 24 percent, and 13 percent learned of the airline through a media report. A year later, the word-of-mouth factor was now being cited by nearly 60 percent of those polled;

advertising had sunk to less than 20 percent as an influence. JetBlue, it seemed, had become a prime example of the "tipping point," the phenomenon so ably described in Malcolm Gladwell's book of the same name, a study of how consumer trends can spread like epidemics. Neeleman had read the book and had been so taken with its message that he bought copies for all of his managers. "It proves you don't need to spend a jillion dollars on advertising to get your word out," he said.

As the first anniversary of the attacks approached, JetBlue quietly made another gesture to mark the date. During the first few weeks after 9/11, people who had canceled because they were afraid to fly were given a credit, which was valid for one year, for future travel on JetBlue. By early summer, many of these vouchers had still not been used. So JetBlue assigned a team of reservations agents to track down every one of these customers and remind them that the vouchers expired in three months, recalled John Owen.

"And they were blown away," he said. "Because they probably wouldn't have remembered. There was no debate over whether to do this because the right thing to do was to call them."

On the day after Labor Day, 2002, it appeared there was one aspect of the airline business that had not changed. That was the annual migration of chief executives to the A-Bar-A Ranch in Encampment, Wyoming, where the Conquistadores gathered that year as if nothing had happened. Nearly a year had passed since the World Trade Center and Pentagon attacks, so there was no reason to forgo this hoary tradition, especially since many in attendance could undoubtedly use a break from bad news; the airlines, in all, had lost nearly ten billion dollars in the last twelve months. For Neeleman, there was a more pressing reason to attend. Although he had run an airline for only two and a half years, he had been chosen for induction as a life member of this society, an honor that in the past had required recipients to parade awkwardly in a velvet cape and tights as other costumed "conquistadores" circled on horseback, brandishing swords and flaming torches.

Neeleman's airline was one of two that had eked out a profit the past year, Kelleher's Southwest being the other. JetBlue stock was soaring and his fledgling company, with just thirty-two planes and 3,000 workers, had a market capitalization greater than United and US Airways combined, which between them flew one thousand planes and employed 150,000 workers. Given the general devastation in the industry, it is not hard to imagine that some of Neeleman's fellow conquistadores were privately hoping that he'd be a flash in the pan.

At the ranch, all was temporarily forgotten. But as the gap widened between the major airlines and their low-fare brethren, that would change. In fact, many airline chiefs were starting to display impatience with JetBlue's growing prominence. Not long before the airline retreat, Continental Airlines' famously pugilistic chief, Gordon Bethune, had apparently let down his guard when speaking to a reporter for *Time* magazine, resulting in this choice quote being published in a national magazine:

"I don't think JetBlue has a better chance of being profitable than one hundred other predecessors with new airplanes, new employees, low fares, all touchy feely . . . all of them are losers. Most of these guys are smoking rag weed."

Neeleman thought it was funny. So funny, in fact, that he ordered up a raft of posters displaying Bethune's words in bold type, and they were soon emblazoned on office walls around headquarters. Neeleman would later credit Bethune for giving him "great chalkboard material" to whip up the troops. In the coming year, he would need it.

eight
blue envy

"Is JetBlue the next Southwest or another People Express?" If that question was on many people's minds in the autumn of 2002, it was thanks to a cover story in *Forbes* magazine that effectively answered it with its flattering portrayal of David Neeleman as the wunderkind heir to Kelleher—the very destiny some had foreseen for him a decade before. That, and an exceptionally cordial interview with Dan Rather on *60 Minutes 2* that aired around the same time, had vaulted Neeleman into the ranks of the semifamous, and he would sometimes get stopped in airport lobbies or on street corners by people who wanted an autograph or, sometimes, a job. But the very mention of People Express was unnerving. Don Burr, after all, had garnered adulatory coverage at the same point Neeleman was at now, and his career had imploded shortly thereafter.

But the question had a broader point: JetBlue was moving from the heady start-up phase to the uncertainty of the long term; the next period would either validate Neeleman's original plan or prove its undoing. "Everybody's asking, is JetBlue for real?" he said. Neeleman started telling his colleagues and employees that his company was at a critical phase, a turning point, and that the coming year would "make us or break us." And while the comparisons with Burr continued to grate—JetBlue was nothing like the anarchic organization that became known as People's

Distress, Neeleman would point out—he was sensing that the big lines had finally decided it was time to teach him a lesson. "You know, the bull's-eye is on us, and they are going after us" . . . he would say.

If it was to be a critical year, then Neeleman would leave nothing to chance. If anything, he would devote more time to meeting his employees face-to-face. He started holding town meetings for any workers who cared to attend once a month at Kennedy Airport and at the company headquarters. Neeleman would typically begin these confabulations, known as pocket sessions, with a twenty-minute stream-of-consciousness ramble through his mind. And on October 21, when he stood up in a pilots' lounge at Terminal Six to give that month's spiel, what was on his mind was an unsettling rumor that had been circulating around the airline community. Delta Airlines—his perennial nemesis—had decided to strike back at JetBlue, and not just with the traditional assault-and-battery in the form of below-cost pricing. No, the word was that Delta would start up a brand-new airline within the larger airline that would try to replicate JetBlue's unique mix of low fares and high style.

It was, of course, similar to United Airlines' strategy to punish Southwest for invading its California turf. But "Shuttle by United" had ultimately failed for it was unable to mimic the discounter's fast turn-arounds and low costs. That had been followed by US Airways' Metrojet, Delta Express, and even a short-lived Continental Lite, and all flopped for the same reason: They couldn't quite shed the baggage of the parent company.

Neeleman had assumed all along that his success would spawn another generation of these clones. But he knew it would be several years before any airline could even get close to duplicating JetBlue's TV-at-every-seat service advantage.

What Neeleman had heard, he told the audience, was that Delta would nonetheless attempt to upstage JetBlue in some way. Maybe it'll take some bigger single-aisle planes, the 757, he said, and give everybody a little more room than on the cramped cattle-car flights of Delta Express. There was something else afoot. The previous month, Neeleman had convinced the JetBlue board that it should make an offer for the company that supplied the satellite TV service, to keep it out of the hands of rivals. Although LiveTV had signed a few other airline clients, such as Denver-based Frontier Airlines, it had yet to sign a major airline client. The deal made sense, and JetBlue snapped up the company for eighty-two million dollars and the assumption of some thirty million dollars in debt. In the due diligence process, Neeleman's fears had been confirmed: JetBlue had learned that United and Delta had indeed been sniffing around. Neeleman's preemptive strike should have taken care of that, but still the speculation continued. And he knew well that other tech companies were looking to get into this side of the business. Worse: He knew that Delta was getting desperate. Delta's chief executive officer, former banker Leo Mullin, in September had said publicly that the rise of the low-fare lines was the biggest single threat to Delta's long-term prosperity.

So, yes, Neeleman said, he was worried that American, Delta, Continental, and all the other big airlines, while still feeling the aftershocks of September 11, were hardly going to sit by idly and watch JetBlue encroach on their turf. The most recent financial results were starting to cause panic in airline boardrooms. American Airlines had lost nine hundred million dollars in the previous quarter, and it had the highest costs of any airline in the business. But, strangely, American had not long before decided to plunge into the routes between JFK and Long Beach and Oakland, two of JetBlue's most successful markets. It's that crazy, destructive competition again, Neeleman said, the idea that you should defend market share at all cost.

"How long can they keep this up?" a pilot asked.

"Well, we kind of prefer they don't file for bankruptcy," Neeleman said, with a laugh. "Better for us that they just stay crippled."

But Neeleman's sardonic line had a more serious point. It is true that the airlines' woes would ultimately force their costs down, either through bankruptcy or the threat of one. And if they succeeded in lowering their costs substantially, then JetBlue's future would be more in peril than if the airlines had continued their profligate ways.

Two months later, the situation had deteriorated even further than anyone had predicted: US Airways and United Airlines had declared bankruptcy; several smaller airlines, including National Airlines and Vanguard—low-cost upstarts like JetBlue—had ceased flying altogether. JetBlue was quick to capitalize on the carnage: It had accelerated its plans to start flying to Las Vegas to fill the void left by the flame-out of National, which had styled itself the gaming capital's hometown airline. So it was with more than a bit of irony that Neeleman opened his monthly meeting by opining: "It's a pretty nasty business out there . . ." The latest revenue estimates for the industry were, in fact, "horrible," he said. The talk was that the airlines collectively would lose nine billion dollars in 2002, on top of the six billion dollars they had hemorrhaged the year before. American's losses were now expected to top more than one billion dollars. And amid all this, JetBlue had beaten even the rosiest of forecasts with a 16 percent profit margin. Double-digit profit margins have always been scarce in the airline business, even in the best of times. "I hear from analysts who see these numbers and they say, 'Are you sure you're an airline?'" Neeleman joked.

There's more news on Delta's plans for the JetBlue wannabe, he said. He's heard it'll put in individual seat-back screens and show first-run movies and offer other amusements. After all, nothing could prevent it from putting in the hardware, which was so common on international flights. But it still couldn't offer live television anytime soon, and "that's so important to us," he said.

But there was something else Neeleman wanted to share: All this emphasis on gadgetry obscured what JetBlue did well, he said, something the demoralized workers at Delta, American, and all the other wounded competitors would never be able to match. "It's not just the TVs and the leather seats, it's our service. . . . And you can't just stand up and say you are going to have great service," he went on. "It is not that simple. And that's the question: How can we continue to inspire and motivate all of you? We don't sit still at JetBlue . . . it's all about improvement, getting better, every day. Our survival depends on it in this industry."

But, Neeleman added, it is a continual struggle. "The worst sort of e-mail I get is not, 'You screwed up,' but the one that says, 'Well, you were okay but I thought you were letting your guard down a little there.'" If it's bad we can make things right, "get a customer for life," he said, and if you hit it out of the park, that's great, too . . . but it's that middle ground, where you are nothing more than unexceptional, that is the danger zone.

And so that's it: What is bugging him is the fear of falling into a complacent mediocrity. "What is keeping me awake at night?" he would ask. "It's figuring out how do we grow this culture? How do we bottle this and keep it going?" These were no idle musings. A few months earlier, Neeleman's antennae had picked up on some incipient rebellions out in the field. The growing company was promoting quickly up the ranks those who showed promise. It all went back to their faith in their ability to "pick the right people," and to Neeleman's maxim that "if you treat them right, they'll do the right thing." However, it stood to reason that some of these people might not be ready to be thrown into a management role without preparation.

From the outset, Barger and Neeleman had conducted an annual "speak-up" survey of their growing workforce; employees were invited to air any gripes they had about their jobs anonymously. During the first two years, the results had been gratifyingly positive, so the duo were startled when in the middle of 2002, the marks in the category of teamwork had taken a dive. They did a little digging and got a disturbing earful about autocratic supervisors run amok. "We were hearing about these 'little dictators,'" said Neeleman; in one incident, an airport supervisor had ordered ground crews to work overtime, threatening that anyone who refused could "turn in your badge on your way out." David and Dave quickly got to work snuffing out any disquiet that might wave a flag to union organizers. Mike Barger was instructed to come up with an intensive five-day leadership training course that would be required for anyone in a supervisory role. To complement the quintet of values that had been drummed into them since the beginning, they came up with a new "soft skills" curriculum and another set of five "principles"— essentially, variations on the Golden Rule:

1) Treat your people right
2) Do the right thing
3) Communicate with your team
4) Encourage initiative and innovation
5) Inspire greatness in others

Everyone who took the course was expected to broadcast this fact by displaying a laminated card listing the principles in their plastic ID holder.

Many of those who'd been around the airlines for years were familiar with another list, known by the memorable acronym TIPS, or "four things managers must avoid during a union organization scenario":

T—Threaten

I—Interrogate

P—Promise

S—Spy

If the first list worked, of course, the second one wouldn't be necessary.

On February 3, 2003, Neeleman arose in the predawn darkness at his house in New Canaan and, as he did the first Monday of every month, got in his SUV to speed toward Kennedy to catch the 7:00 A.M. flight to Fort Lauderdale to deliver his habitual talk to the new crew members on their first day of class.

It would be his first opportunity to talk to the troops since Delta had gone public with the details of its new airline. The name, the totally baffling Song, had already been held up for ridicule after it was leaked to the press. But Delta had still managed a rude surprise: It would, it said, have live satellite television on its planes by October, shattering Neeleman's confidence that he'd successfully fended off the move by buying the LiveTV company. Delta had instead gone to Matsushita, and Neeleman had already started muttering about possible patent infringements. But it seemed the frightening might of Delta was about to come down on him: It was planning to swamp all the markets where JetBlue was whipping its tail, with lots of extra flights at lower fares.

All this would make good fodder for that morning's lesson. He would be traveling with Gareth Edmondson-Jones and a film crew from the Discovery Channel, which was interested in doing a segment on the competition between JetBlue and its new imitator.

By 6:40 A.M., Neeleman hadn't showed, and his traveling companions were getting unnerved about the possibility he'd miss the flight. Suddenly Neeleman materialized—emerging without warning from the metal detector, minus a coat, jacket, or any other gear one would expect an upright corporate executive to be toting in the middle of February. Seemingly oblivious to the presence of television cameras, he muttered something inaudible, and then, seeing someone he knew, broke off in midsentence and bounded off.

The flight was full and Neeleman leaped aboard minutes before the cabin door was due to close. After introducing himself on the intercom, he remained on his feet for the next two and a half hours, performing his trademark snack-and-schmooze drill, which had apparently not lost its appeal, for by now he had acquired an apron embroidered with his name and the nickname "Snack Boy." By the end of the flight he had harvested a crop of business cards and a dozen suggestions for new places for his planes to alight.

Arriving at 9:45 A.M., he hopped into a rental car idling by the curb and raced down I-95 to crew training in Miami. There he would give a forty-five-minute talk, and then head back to the airport for the 1:55 P.M. flight to New York. Why do I do this month after month? he wondered aloud. It's the palpable fear, he said, that "we'll lose our edge and then we'll be just like any other airline."

As he sped down the highway, Edmondson-Jones checked the day's headlines on his pager. "Hey, David, get a load of this," he said, reading the headline of the *Journal*'s "Heard on the Street" column: WILL AMR JOIN UAL, USAIR IN BANKRUPTCY? David perked up. "What are they saying?" Edmondson-Jones obliged with a dramatic rendition of a litany of woes, which the article recited in mind-numbing detail. American, it seemed, was continuing to hemorrhage cash and was faced with the unpalatable choice of squeezing more pay concessions out of a recalcitrant workforce or of joining its compatriots in the purgatory of Chapter XI protection from creditors. Neeleman looked interested, but was careful to avoid any unseemly gloating; however, the prospect of nearly a third of the U.S. airline capacity being under the control of the bankruptcy courts was a development that no one could have predicted three years before.

The training class that day was larger than average, nearly one hundred new flight attendants and pilots, and Neeleman plunged into his self-styled Airline Economics 101. The idea was to explain to the uninitiated the basics of costs and revenues and to deconstruct that all-important metric in the airlines, the CASM—pronounced "kazm"—which stands for costs per available seat mile. Everything flows from that; it's what drives the decisions. The Holy Grail is to have the lowest CASM in the business—and JetBlue had beaten the longtime champ, Southwest, with its 7.3 CASM, by coming in at just over six cents a mile. By contrast, major airlines' CASMs are often in the nine- to ten-cent range. Purists could point out that if adjusted for the length of the flight, Southwest still has the lowest costs (JetBlue's average flight is about 1,200 miles; Southwest's about 500 miles). But Neeleman likes to keep it simple, to make everyone feel good for having joined the best company on the planet, as he put it. And it also would allow him to lay out the company's financial benefits and to give his pitch on the wisdom of buying stock in JetBlue.

He's given the talk so many times that his extemporaneous performance came naturally. But that day Song provided the hook: He could use it to illustrate the perversities of the airline business, the lengths to which airlines will go to squash a good company like his.

"You probably want to hear what I think about this new airline out of Kennedy . . ." he began. "Well, you know, I hear United's also talking about starting up a low-cost airline, and they're going to call it 'Dance.' So it's the same old song and dance." The audience was primed; even this awkward attempt at a one-liner drew a big laugh. (Actually, it was not entirely in jest. Rumors as well were swirling that the bankrupt United might shift 30 percent of its seating capacity to a new low-fare imitation.)

"And it's really funny," he went on, "because in all their press announcements, they talk about their planes, their entertainment, their food . . . they never say anything about their people."

People, of course, had little to do with it. Delta had always claimed a sizable portion of the dependable migration southward from New York City and it was just trying to hold on to what it regarded as rightfully its. But the heart of the problem was that Delta's first response to JetBlue's incursion into its turf at Kennedy had been to beef up service on the bare-bones Delta Express out of Kennedy, inadvertently showcasing what was in reality a bus with wings. This sideline had sort of limped along, and after September 11, the airline was trying to find a way to phase it out.

"Frankly, their product stinks," said Neeleman. "Their planes are old, cramped, and noisy. So it's no wonder that they are trying to do something with this Song thing, because their product really is bad." JetBlue was now carrying the most passengers of any airline between New York and Fort Lauderdale, operating sixteen times a day, a near shuttle operation between the city and what has been referred to as the sixth borough. In deference to this relationship, Neeleman had even met with a local rabbi and put kosher snacks on board.

So, yes, Neeleman said, Delta could tart up its unit—substituting the larger, and newer, 757s for its geriatric 737s, putting in satellite TV. "But," he teased, "here is a little known fact: Did you know that we're a low-fare airline but on most routes we have the highest average fare?" As everyone pondered this mystery, he whipped out a marker and went to work on a poster board, writing $108 in large letters.

That, he explains, is JetBlue's average fare for a flight of three hours. In other words, all the flights from JFK to Florida.

Next to it, he wrote $82, Delta's average fare on the same flight. Customers are paying, then, a premium of $26 to fly on JetBlue instead of a major. This had never happened before in the entire history of the budget airlines, whose primary selling point, after all, was a better price. And why is that, he asked? The bigger airlines just keep shooting themselves in the foot. Some anecdotal evidence is in order: a letter he had received from a customer who had just learned that his mother was dying and was rushing to be at her bedside. "So this guy calls Delta, and they tell him the fare is going to be $800, and he asks, 'Don't I get a bereavement fare?' And they say 'Well, that depends . . . has she died yet?'"

That drew an audible gasp for there it is, in just one choice image, the reason why airlines are such poison to consumers: that abject lack of humanity, that twisted logic behind those irritating rules.

"And so he came to us, and we gave him our lowest fare. And now he flies with us all the time . . . and he tells everyone he knows to fly us." In short, this is not just a satisfied customer; he is an exemplar of Malcolm Gladwell's *Tipping Point* theory, spreading the JetBlue gospel like a particularly virulent strain of flu. "And so I always say that's why we have to have sixteen flights a day in this market, because we have to fly this guy."

It was a Neeleman tour de force, all compelling sincerity, of course, but with a master salesman's sense for timing. So, back to the CASM, for this is the key, the explanation for the mystery of how JetBlue can succeed where so many others have failed.

Each one of those flights to Florida is about 1,000 miles, and with 162 seats on each plane, that equals 162,000 CASMs. The airline is flying about one billion a month now. To arrive at the CASM, you take those billion CASMs and divide them by the company's monthly expenses.

So you want to know the real reason why Delta is in such trouble? he asked.

This morning, he said, it cost us $63 to fly each seat on that plane; you divide it by our average fare, that's $108, to get the break-even load factor: 58 percent. Anything over that, you make money; anything under that, you lose money.

Then there is Delta, with its CASM of nine cents a mile. So at Delta it would cost $90 for the same seat to Florida. And its average fare is $82. So what is its break-even load factor? Everyone hesitated, figuring this had to be a trick question.

"It's 110 percent!," he crowed, to general laughter. "It sucks for them!"

Then it was time to wrap up, with a draught of the Kool-Aid: "And, you know, I'm the luckiest guy in the world to be the CEO of the airline with the best product and the lowest costs . . . and that product is you."

He almost missed the flight back because after he finished speaking, he was mobbed by those who just wanted to shake his hand, to thank him for coming, and Neeleman can see ahead, to the payoff, to the time these people will be serving customers, keeping that equation he has just outlined going. When he finally got to the airport at 1:45 P.M., there was a long line at security, and it was looking bad. If he missed the 1:55 P.M. departure, every other JetBlue flight that day was fully booked, and Neeleman would be loath to eject a paying passenger for his convenience. Then a Transportation Security Administration screener spotted Neeleman and momentarily dropped his officious demeanor: "Hey, I know that guy!" He beckoned to one of Neeleman's companions. "Wasn't he on *60 Minutes?*"

He made the flight.

One week later, on February 11, Neeleman decided to have a little fun at Delta's expense. At an airport ceremony celebrating JetBlue's third year in business, Neeleman cracked a bottle of Champagne on a new Airbus A320 that had been named *Song Sung Blue,* in mock honor of its newest rival. All JetBlue planes are named by employees, and those who submit the winning entries get to accompany the jet from the Toulouse factory. "Let the competition begin!" crowed David and Dave in their first "Blue Note" to employees after the news broke. The letter went on to assure JetBlue workers that, after all, Delta's Song was just a feeble attempt to imitate JetBlue's amenities while failing miserably to grasp the subtleties of its culture. As such, they said, it was inevitably doomed to failure. But still, it was clear that David and Dave had been taken aback by just how much money and effort Delta was putting into the whole enterprise. "We didn't know how closely they were going to try to imitate JetBlue," they admitted. Lest that discourage anyone, they attempted an upbeat flourish: "Competition will make us even better," they wrote.

In comments to the press, however, Neeleman was a little more direct. "You know, first they said our formula wouldn't work, and now they are trying to copy us," he complained to a BBC interviewer.

But Neeleman was apparently so confident that his substantial profits and cash on hand would cushion the blows that he did something unusually provocative. In short order, he declared that JetBlue would begin daily nonstop flights from Atlanta to Long Beach. It was gutsy, to put it mildly, to attack Delta on its home turf, a city that it had owned for decades. Atlanta was Delta's lifeblood, accounting for the lion's share of its revenues, and few airlines had had the temerity to challenge its grip on Hartsfield Airport, where Delta carried more than 60 percent of all passengers. Delta also had a virtual monopoly on many routes out of Atlanta, and the flight to Los Angeles was a prime example. But JetBlue's planners in Darien had studied the route for a while and it seemed just the sort of market where they come in, charge fares as much as 65 percent off the market rates, and still make money. As always, it had considered all the possible scenarios. Delta, of course, would respond in typical fashion by lowering its own fares and adding lots of flights, but it would lose a bundle if it did so.

There was, however, a complication. Delta already had a low-fare competitor: AirTran, the successor to ValuJet, had built a niche as the low-fare, and low-key, alternative to Delta at Atlanta. Perhaps because it had grown more slowly and had a much lower profile, AirTran had survived the sorts of crude attacks from Delta that JetBlue was provoking. But AirTran had no planes in its fleet capable of flying for six hours across country, and so it was not a likely challenger on most of Delta's money-making long-distance runs. So JetBlue, it appeared, had an open field.

On May 8, a JetBlue plane took off from Kennedy, headed for Georgia for a bit of in-your-face revelry, in advance of the first scheduled flight out of Delta's redoubt. The plane, which was flying empty save for a small contingent of senior JetBlue officers, would arrive in Atlanta where it would be greeted by no less than the mayor of Atlanta, Shirley Jackson; a gaggle of local politicians; a local a cappella youth chorus; and assorted hangers-on. An advance team of JetBlue guerrilla marketers (usually flight attendants who volunteered for the cause) had been at work for the last few days, handing out blue chips and other JetBlue paraphernalia to strangers on city sidewalks, and otherwise making their presence known.

It would have spoiled the mood that day, perhaps, to point out that in the last few weeks, JetBlue had been blindsided again. This time, it was by AirTran, which had moved quickly to prevent JetBlue from stealing its thunder, leasing a couple of longer range planes so it could be the first to offer low fares from its home base to Los Angeles. Delta had also pounced with a raft of additional flights to the West Coast and fares that sank to JetBlue's introductory price of $99 one way. So, yes, the people of Atlanta were getting a much better deal on air travel, and it was JetBlue that had set it off. But, for once, JetBlue might not be the primary beneficiary.

On the surface, Delta was a strange adversary. Of all the big airlines, it had long stood out as a paragon of a well-managed company, and its southern roots and paternalistic in-house culture had paid off in an unusual loyalty. It had begun life as a Louisiana crop duster in the 1920s, and during the postwar aviation boom, it had remained apart from the industry club, staying in Atlanta rather than relocating its headquarters to Manhattan, as most of the others had done. It was known for never having laid off employees during the worst of the postderegulation era, and its workforce remained largely nonunion—only the pilots and dispatchers had organized. The morale was so high that during one of the industry's periodic downturns in the early 1980s, Delta employees pooled contributions from their paychecks and purchased a new plane for the company as a show of gratitude for their job security.

All that changed during the mid-1980s, when Delta got caught up in the merger and acquisition craze of the era. Delta had become the fourth largest airline in the United States when it merged with Western Airlines in 1987. Then in 1991, it scooped up the European routes and other assets of the ailing Pan Am in a fire sale. Pan Am's workers had been led to believe they would have jobs with Delta; most, in fact, were laid off. Still, Delta had acquired a host of problems along with Pan Am's choice routes—aging planes, decrepit airport facilities—and morale began to slide. By the late 1990s, Delta had mutated into just another big airline with the attendant labor strife and revolving-door executive suite, to the point where the company's directors finally brought in someone with no airline background for the inevitable housecleaning. He was Leo Mullin, a laconic intellectual with Harvard degrees in mathematics and physics, who had been lured from a longtime banking career with First Chicago. If there was any good ole boy culture left at Delta's Atlanta headquarters, Mullin would be sure to eradicate it.

It was Mullin who made the decision to strike at JetBlue with a new budget clone and stanch the bleeding from Delta Express. To him, Song's premise was simple: Bring costs down and get fares up. The former he'd accomplish by keeping the planes in the air longer, about thirteen hours a day, just like JetBlue. The latter he'd do by improving the product so that customers would be willing to pay a little more. To handle the day-to-day operations, he picked John Selvaggio, a longtime airline marketing official who in the late 1990s had presided over the ill-fated Midway Airlines, which had gone bankrupt after 9/11, after which he had jumped to Delta. Selvaggio thus had experience with an upstart and was a native New Yorker as well. As such he was more than capable of matching JetBlue's put-downs with barbs of his own. In early interviews, he'd been dismissive of the notion that Song was formed to get even with JetBlue. "To think that we are creating something to take on someone who has one percent of the business is ridiculous," he said. "It sort of gratifies their own ego." Some of his other comments revealed a little more of the JetBlue influence than he might have realized. "We want to make flying fun again," he said. "It's all about attitude and friendliness."

But Delta was also big bureaucracy, where ideas had to navigate a succession of committees before they could come to fruition. So it was predictable, then, that the resulting Song product had all the authenticity of a Milli Vanilli performance. Delta created a whole new identity and props to eradicate the shabby old Delta Express. It brought in a team of consultants and outside designers, who concocted an electric color scheme, splashing the newly rehabbed planes with a shade of gaseous green and a squigglelike logo that appeared to some wags to resemble an out-of-control garden hose. The interior of the jet was tarted up with a rainbow of loud hues that Amy Curtis-McIntyre dubbed "Skittles colors." It was attention getting, yes, but, as one commentator put it, "The *Austin Powers* interior may not work for those with hangovers." All told, Delta was rumored to have lavished sixty-five million dollars thus far on this strenuous attempt to copy JetBlue, more than six times what Jet-Blue had spent to publicize its own launch.

Song made its debut on schedule, in mid-April, just as the United States went to war in Iraq, reviving all the fears about terrorist attacks on U.S. targets, of which the airlines were considered among the more likely. Its first flight, from Kennedy Airport to West Palm Beach, carried a contingent of press and Delta executives as well as a payload of customers who had been lured by the $79 one-way promotional fare. Delta was seemingly unaware of the presence of a decidedly less friendly passenger aboard that day: Eric Brinker, from JetBlue's marketing department, had bought his ticket like anyone else, but his true purpose was to glean as much intelligence he could about this new rival.

A few days later, Brinker posted on JetBlue's internal Web site an amusing account of Song's debut. He had the good fortune to be seated next to a Delta marketing executive, he reported, and, playing dumb, had peppered her with questions about how Song would be different from the competition, an interrogation that yielded little of substance. "It's just different—can't you tell?" the Delta marketer had said in apparent exasperation. Brinker was hardly a disinterested observer, of course, and his reviews of the food and drinks that Song was selling were predictably caustic: Sure there were a Song Sunrise and other specialty cocktails served from a shaker, but at seven dollars, a bit of a rip-off; there was also a rubbery bagel that "no self-respecting New Yorker" would accept for the four dollars Song was charging, Brinker wrote. There were some good points, he admitted: more generous legroom and the blank TV screens would someday be ablaze with programming. And Song's cabin crew—plucked from the ranks of its mainline flight attendants— was noticeably trying harder, Brinker noted, a tribute to the additional training it had just undergone.

Song had even held auditions for flight attendants at Manhattan's Studio 54 theater, where applicants were encouraged to display whatever performing talent they might have, raising the somewhat scary prospect of cabin crews' bursting into song if the impulse struck them. How long this sort of enthusiasm could be sustained was another question. For the Song crews would be paid the same as they would be on Delta's other flights, and, given the huge losses Delta was reporting, profit sharing was an unlikely option.

When the Song plane touched down at West Palm Beach, passengers looked out their windows to see a large throng of airline and airport employees standing to greet them. It was, after all, the traditional greeting for a new airline's first flight to an airport. But on closer inspection, this was different. Much of the welcoming committee was from JetBlue—their regalia left no doubt as to their affiliation. From his anonymous perch, Brinker had a close-up view of the distressed faces of the Delta representatives as they realized their party had just been crashed. The competition had indeed begun.

nine
jetblue u

Among the places where the air wars were being fought in that summer of 2003 was inside a drab beige edifice at 118-29 Queens Boulevard in Forest Hills, Queens. This is "FH HQ" to insiders, although there is no sign or other outside evidence that would indicate to passersby that anything remarkable is happening here. Take the elevator to the eighth floor, however, and you will find the nerve center of JetBlue, where David Neeleman and Dave Barger hold court, where Amy Curtis-McIntyre and Gareth Edmondson-Jones and the other marketers stoke the buzz, where the strategic planners map out—in a large conference room covered with aerial photos of JFK and other airports—the outlines of the airline's expanding empire. Every week Neeleman convenes a strategy session to discuss the past week's events and to put JetBlue's performance under the microscope: which flights are doing well; which markets need a little massaging. The makeshift artwork on the walls gives an indication of what the topic of the day will be: It's the refuse from the most recent skirmishes. "Song's Got No Rhythm" was the slogan du jour posted in large letters for the Delta stand-in was getting increasingly aggressive in its assaults on JetBlue turf, even announcing that Song would start vying head to head on the New York to Las Vegas and Los Angeles routes. The tableau was rounded out by a gallery of fatuous remarks from rival executives that Tim Claydon, a sales whiz who joined JetBlue from the Virgin camp, had blown up and displayed prominently. "It is not a question of whether we can compete with JetBlue; it's whether JetBlue can compete with us" was one oddly snarky one from a Song executive.

But it was six floors down, on the south side of the second floor where, Neeleman would have you believe, the fate of the airline was being determined. Several times each month, some thirty-five aspiring flight attendants assemble here, many of them arriving sleepless off a red-eye flight. This is what is known euphemistically as a JetBlue review, a cross between an audition and an auto-da-fé, because its aim is to weed out the neurotics, the cynics, in the words of one JetBlue executive, "the bad apples, who would spread the culture of discontent."

Anyone who's made it to this step has already been vetted numerous times. They've visited the "Work Here" page of JetBlue's Web site, where the first line on the in-flight crew page exhorts: "Please read if your passion is people!" Job requirements are simple and deliberately vague; you must have at least two years' "friendly" customer service experience, be "willing to think outside the box and find a way to say 'YES' to customers." The most promising applicants are interviewed by phone, sometimes several times, and after that, a small number of finalists travel, at the company's expense, to spend a day at headquarters.

There they will need to produce a valid passport on the chance they may someday fly to a foreign destination, they will submit to fingerprinting, and they will agree to open up their personal histories for the requisite background checks. Only then can they enter the classroom where the next six hours will determine whether they get to return someday wearing a JetBlue badge. And there they will find Cathy Westrum, director of in-flight recruitment, who delivers such an effusive welcome as to banish all thoughts of failure. "Thank you for being such *awesome* candidates," she began one such session in the middle of 2003. "And I want you to know this is a really awesome company. It's a family, more than a company . . ." Westrum, one of the first to come over to Neeleman from the Southwest camp, hasn't lost the preternaturally cheery demeanor of the flight attendant she once was, and she's a striking sight, a mass of waist-length chestnut hair flicking against a purple silk top and long skirt.

There were eight long tables arranged around the room, and people could sit wherever they wanted—or so they imagined. Some gravitated to the front of the room; others sought out more space at the emptier tables in the back. Bad move; the "right" thing was to sit at the table that was most full at that moment because, as Westrum put it, "you have to like people. Everyone here *thinks* they're friendly . . . but we're talking about *really* liking people . . .

"And if you get an offer . . ." and she paused, because the odds are that less than half of those present would, "do think hard before you decide, because this is not for everyone. It really isn't. Because we are talking about delivering some *really* awesome service here . . ."

Then there's an exercise: "Look at your face in the mirror, and then look at everyone else," Westrum commanded. "And ask yourself . . . are you approachable?"

Some were definitely more approachable than others. Many had worked as flight attendants for other airlines, but there were a teacher, a bank teller, a former go-go dancer in a Hollywood nightclub; many were midcareer, middle aged, divorced with children. They were geographically diverse: Colorado, Georgia, Michigan, and a hefty contingent from California. One man clearly thought he was a shoo-in, tanned, handsome; he preened extravagantly, flashing a smile of Chiclet-white teeth; trying hard to get a laugh, he sang a ditty as people raced off to the restrooms— "Gotta go, gotta go, gotta go." As the teamwork exercises wore on, however, his act headed south. At one point, he was convinced everyone was mocking him, and during a peroration on customer service, he stopped, grumpily demanding, "What's so funny?"

During a break, Westrum peeled off with other recruiters to hear how they're sizing up the contenders. "I think some of them may be trying to 'game it,'" said one. "Word's gotten out what we're looking for, and they are exaggerating it for effect." Westrum and her team have ways of smoking out the phonies, the fakes, if not in the group session, then in the peer interviews that are conducted by working flight attendants, who are pulled off the line periodically for an added reality check. During another break, the theme from *Austin Powers* boomed from a loudspeaker, but this is no benign distraction: Westrum and her team of interviewers were watching closely for signs of agitation. "Airplanes can be really noisy," she explained later. "And some people just can't take it."

The following week, offers were made to about half of the group that day, higher than normal. ("Joey," the self-styled comedian, was one of those who didn't make it.)

But others had gone through these trials and were awaiting the next step, the call that would summon them to Florida for their three weeks of training. Kim Cox, flying for Mesaba Airlines, a commuter airline in the sticks, was one of them; she had heard good things about JetBlue and didn't want to get stuck in turboprop hell. Eric Alba and Arnel Gama were working side by side at the check-in counters at Terminal Six and had long wanted to break free of the airport grind and fly for a while. Marlies McMackin had sold her yogurt shop in Long Beach; her brother was a pilot for JetBlue and had urged her to try out. Lucinda Hopwood was waiting tables at the corner coffee shop in a tiny hamlet in northwest Pennsylvania, where, she never tired of saying, the cows far outnumbered the people. And all had been tapped to join the next flight training class, which would meet in Florida at the beginning of July.

At around the same time that they were packing up, David Neeleman was boarding a jumbo jet and heading for Brazil. He had been back to the country several times since he'd served as a missionary twenty years earlier, and his father, Gary, was as active as ever in nurturing his Brazilian ties as "honorary consul" in Salt Lake City. But this visit was different; now it was David's turn to be converted. Some months earlier, he had been contacted by someone from the Embraer airframe manufacturer in São Paulo about a brand-new jet it would be building, one that defied easy categorization; it was neither a "regional jet"—the fifty to seventy seaters that Embraer was known for—nor in the league of the A320 or the 737. It held just one hundred seats, which, strangely, was a gap in the market that had never been quite addressed by Boeing and Airbus. The two airframe giants had come up with smaller editions of their standard narrow-body jets, but these used the same basic assembly and thus, on a per-seat basis, were more expensive to operate than the standard-size version.

The more Neeleman learned about Embraer's new 190 jet, the more he was convinced; it was spacious; passengers would sit in two-by-two seating that seemed more civilized than the usual cattle car three-by-three layout. And the jet itself would be only five feet shorter than the A320, which held 50 percent more people. But as always, the details grabbed him and this time it was the jet's unusually shaped windows—square rather than oval and larger than standard—creating a light, airy feel that was unlike anything he'd seen on a commercial jet. Plus, the seats could be a half inch wider, and any increase in the precious space aboard an airliner was welcome.

The jet made sense, for it would give JetBlue an efficient way to reach hundreds of places it couldn't economically serve now, medium-size cities like Richmond, Virginia; San Antonio, Texas; even international destinations like Cancún and Bermuda. These were places where prevailing fares were high enough that JetBlue could charge slightly more per mile than it normally did, to make up for the added costs. Because a second plane type went against a basic premise of JetBlue's game plan, which was to save costs by using only one type of aircraft like Southwest does with its all-737 fleet. Adding a different plane to the mix means that training takes longer, you need to keep spare parts for each aircraft model, and it fosters the very sort of caste system among pilots and flight attendants JetBlue had managed to avoid.

The rapid fleet expansion would help debunk one myth put forward by the skeptics: that Neeleman's profits stood to take a big hit when the Airbus planes he had bought at the outset started aging and when the extensive maintenance required would no longer be covered by warranty. True, the airline's repair costs would start to rise substantially in 2005, but that would be offset, in part, by the influx of newly minted jets from Brazil, which would hold down the average age of the fleet.

On June 10, Neeleman stood before the assembled press in a Manhattan hotel and announced his purchase of one hundred of the new jets. "We'll be able to deliver the JetBlue experience to all these people out there," he gushed.

Or would he? The answer, perhaps, lay in the particulars of JetBlue's flight attendant training class 07-03.

It is the first morning of classes for JetBlue's newest in-flight class and Dean Melonas, who's giving the lecture, is not happy. He had endured what he considered to be substandard service on a JetBlue flight the night before, and the memory of it still pained him. A new flight attendant had seemed oddly disconnected, barely able to go through the motions. "The guy just spaced out," Melonas fumes. "I ordered a Coke and he never brought it." Apparently, Melonas wasn't the only one who was put out; eventually the rest of the crew had to finish the drink orders for the hapless crew member. "He just wasn't really . . . there," says Melonas, trying to put his finger on what he found so disturbing.

"And as I got off, I thought, 'Wow, that was ugly.'"

But this guy didn't do anything bad. He wasn't rude, right? someone asks. Still, Melonas is not someone you want to annoy. He is a longtime airline pro, having worked his way up the in-flight ladder at American to become a purser, or lead attendant, on international flights where there would be as many as twenty in-flight crew members on one plane. He then moved into the training side at American before bolting for a chance to get in on the ground floor at JetBlue. Recruiting and training are his thing, and it disturbed him to think the talent pool might be getting muddied with some unfortunate hires.

So what happened to the flight attendant from the night before? someone wants to know. "Well, we'll take him aside, talk to him, see what's going on. . . . Maybe there's something happening in his life we need to know about.

"After all, no one expects you to be one hundred percent each day."

A palpable relief settles over the room; this is the caring attitude that had led them to JetBlue. Yet it is sobering to realize that the sort of indifferent service that one would take for granted on another airline would gain you some very unwelcome attention here.

This is where it all comes together, where safety protocols meet the service ethic. Nearly 80 percent of the course is mandated by the Federal Aviation Administration; here's where one learns how to evacuate an aircraft in ninety seconds, to administer CPR to a passenger suffering a heart attack, to extinguish a fire in the cabin, and become familiar with all the intricacies of the aircraft. The agenda is a study in contradictions, for it's an admixture of charm school and police academy: one day uniform fittings and hair and makeup, the next, jumping down an escape chute; one minute the class is practicing serving drinks, followed by a lesson in how to hog-tie an abusive passenger with a set of plastic handcuffs.

It is really that nonsafety portion of the program that is the critical component at JetBlue. And here's where it gets tricky, for while JetBlue's whole philosophy practically shouts respect for individualism—and, indeed, echoes through the values—at the same time, the job of an in-flight crew member requires a level of conformity that might strain those used to less regimentation. A packet that arrives in the mail shortly before training begins to set the tone: You're considered to be on duty during training, and there's a long list of verboten behavior—smoking in public, chewing gum, even wearing trendy or overly casual clothing (it's conservative business attire most days); a faux pas so mild as eating or drinking a soda while walking down the hall would draw a reprimand ("the presence of a straw in a beverage cup could create a negative perception"). Everyone is warned about long days and a lot of stress. There is little room for error, and if you score under 80 percent on a written test, you'll need to get a perfect score on the second try or you'll flunk out.

Then comes the kicker: You must "actively live JetBlue corporation values," essentially around the clock. "You will often be recognized whether in uniform or not," the notice explains. "Therefore, it is your responsibility to remember that you ARE JetBlue Airways in the eyes of the general public both on and off duty. We must consistently represent JetBlue in the most positive manner . . ."

In short, it's not a job; it's a cause. There is no divide between the person you are on the job and in your private life.

"At the end of day, it's all about attitude," Dave Barger says, scanning the room to get a feel for what attitude is coming his way. Barger, like

Neeleman and Al Spain, is one of a half dozen company officers who will parachute in the first week, delivering their patented pep talks and trying to memorize as many first names of the new hires as possible. Barger's adept at tempering the JetBlue feel-good message with a dose of reality. He points out that JFK is now the busiest airport serving New York, having just surpassed his old bailiwick, Newark Airport.

"And it's all because of us!" he crows, and JetBlue is now the eleventh largest airline in the country. But then he edits himself: "If you think you are really great, then you're probably getting arrogant . . . in our business, you are only as good as your last arrival."

Orientation is in a windowless classroom in the Airbus low-rise offices on Northwest 36th Street, a dreary strip of airport hotels, greasy spoons, and the odd airline supplies store. Many airlines do their pilot training here, in a cavernous room outfitted with a bank of simulators for the various aircraft Airbus flies.

One aspect of JetBlue training is unusual, if not unique: Flight attendants and pilots are together for much of the first two weeks, and while a lot of the training is in separate classes, there is still a lot of overlap. Most airlines keep the two employee groups strictly apart. Barger says it is all part of attacking the hierarchy in the airlines. Analyses of accidents, in fact, have revealed that lives have been saved when the crews were comfortable with one another—enough so to question decisions, if necessary.

So it is with this hoped-for collegiality in mind that Barger urges everyone to stand up and introduce themselves. The pilots, unsurprisingly, are the more homogenous group, most having come off the traditional feeders of the air force or navy with stops at smaller commuter or cargo airlines. There is one woman among two dozen men. By contrast, the flight attendant camp is an emphatically motley crowd, ranging in age from twenty to fifty-five, and equally varied in education and experience: Some have a high school degree, others attended graduate school. One woman is a former nuclear engineer from Japan; another describes herself as a refugee from Wall Street. A half dozen are already JetBlue employees, working in the customer service jobs at the airport—typically regarded as the most thankless of jobs, and thus a move to the in-flight crew is seen as a definite step up. (In fact, some will later share their sense that the in-flight crews look down on their ground-based colleagues.) Then there are those who've either lost or left in-flight jobs at other airlines, such as Jennifer Cooley, who had just joined American Airlines as a flight attendant a few weeks before September 11 and was one of the first to be laid off.

Pilots and flight attendants don't stay in the same living quarters, however. Mike Barger, who runs the programs, chooses his words carefully. "It's sort of like cats and dogs," he says, groping for the right analogy, muttering something about "interesting situations." In fact, when JetBlue first broke the taboo of training the two groups together, there were reportedly some problems. The pilots' wives complained that their husbands were off in Florida with what they imagined was a throng of nubile stews. Of course, the typical stew these days is often closer to retirement age than to adolescence, and more than a third are male. Eventually it was decided that pilots would be allowed to bring their spouses; after the first few days, most see there's no cause for worry and decamp. Flight attendants, however, share rooms during training and must leave their families behind. There was only so much the company would do to break down these barriers completely.

Next up is Vinny Stabile, the vice president of people who joined JetBlue the morning of September 11, 2001. He tells a little about that day, and how when people started to call in from the places where they were stranded, they were assured that if they followed their conscience and did the right thing, they would not be second-guessed by management.

And those five values again: You're going to be hearing those a lot, he warns, but at least they are easy to remember. And you know a lot of airlines have rules about what you can and can't do to help a customer in a given situation; make a mistake and you might be docked. But here you can rely on your "values filter," and you will be okay. "Ask yourself, 'If this were my company, how would I do it?' and that'll generally drive you to the right decision."

Al Spain arrives, and it appears he is the warm-up act for Neeleman; his stand-up shtick is an amusing riff on how the airline got its name, complete with exaggerated French accents to evoke what he imagines were the horrified reactions from Airbus officials to some of the more bizarre labels that were floated—Taxi, Dairy Air, Egg. It's all good fun but there is a more serious point here, too: "Yes, we're a start-up; yes, we're an airline . . . but we're also a brand."

Around 11:00 A.M. Neeleman breezes in for his Economics 101. It's impossible not to stare as he bounds up to the podium—he is now that well known. This day, his ad-libs are less to do with Song than the other more pressing matter on his mind. "We are going to grow this company and we are going to do it smart, because we have to."

And why is that? He tells them about how he spent the past two months in a frenzied spending spree. Not only did he commit to at least one hundred new 190 jets, but he'd also sent Dave Barger to Toulouse to ink another deal to acquire another sixty-five A320s, with options for an additional fifty. That means, he says, that by 2007 JetBlue will need twenty thousand employees to fly what will be a fleet of more than two hundred planes. The import of that sinks in: The company has just over five thousand employees now, and it's tough to imagine it quadrupling in so short a time.

"And so the question is, How can we keep from screwing this up?" He then talks about profit sharing and keeping costs low, and the fact that last year, employees got 15.5 percent of their gross pay in a profit-sharing distribution, and all the other good things. You can almost hear the quick calculations going on in people's minds: If you make, say, $30,000 a year as a first-year flight attendant, you get a nice $3,550 bonus check in the mail. That's on top of the 401(k), another no-lose deal, he says, because the company matches contributions dollar for dollar for the first 4 percent, "and if you don't sign on, I don't know what planet you're living on. And the stock purchase plan, you can put up to 10 percent of your paycheck aside to purchase company stock at a discount. There is no downside for you in this; there's only an upside." There's only one risk in all this, he says, and that is that some employees might forget the direct connection between the service they give and what ends up in their pocket at the end of the day. "Remember when you get your paycheck, your profit-sharing check . . . every cent of that came from our customers." (It's a connection that Herb Kelleher underscores by having this line printed on every Southwest paycheck: "From Our Customers.")

There were other things on his mind that morning, too. Just three weeks earlier JetBlue had endured a disastrous weekend during which its computers had crashed, forcing it to check in thousands of passengers by hand and to delay many of its flights by four hours. The fracas cost them in lost revenue and untold goodwill but, Neeleman said, they'd make it right: Give put-upon customers vouchers toward future travel, and the reservations systems owners (formerly Neeleman's own company) had promised to split the losses. "Hey, we're not perfect. But all we ask of you is that you show up on time, sober, and with a great attitude."

Much of the first week of training comes under the general rubric of "crew culture," and Mike Barger is talking about an industrywide program known as CRM, for crew resource management (except in JetBlue's lexicon it is "company" rather than "crew" to get across the notion of togetherness). That seems guaranteed to induce a yawn, but then Barger gets into what it was like growing up in an airline family in the 1960s and how the glamorous façade of the business hid some disturbing flaws. "My father was the Antichrist," he cracks, which has the desired effect of riveting everyone's attention. "He was one of those crusty old captains who came out of the military and it was all 'I'm in charge and you'll do it my way,'" he says. In fact, Barger Senior was well known as a rabble-rouser at United. During one especially acrimonious period in United's labor relations, he once refused to admit the-then-CEO of the company, Richard Ferris, into the cockpit of the plane he was going to fly. Barger's dad was just reminding Ferris, in a particularly humiliating way, of course, that as the pilot, he, not the company brass, is legally in charge of a plane. But the anecdote speaks volumes about the distrust that had much to do with the majors' present predicament.

Dave and Mike Barger, however, had pledged to eliminate the very sort of machismo their father reveled in. The program they follow started after a series of airborne mishaps that eluded easy explanation in the mid-1970s. United brought in some behavioral scientists who pinpointed a problem: The captain was essentially barking out orders without consulting with his peers. Although it was too late to reform those of Dave and Mike's father's generation, by the 1980s, a more enlightened approach had gained favor. The point is that everyone in the company is involved at some point in the safety process, whether they are overtly aware of it or not. Mike Barger helpfully translates it into plain English: What CRM really means, he says, is "if I see something I don't like, I do something."

One theme heard frequently in training is what might be called the ValuJet effect: the double standard that exists in the mind of the public that forgives a larger airline like American or United for an aviation disaster, but not an upstart. "We don't have the luxury of being able to recover from even one major accident," Mike Barger says. When you say low-cost airline, he notes, "the customers are probably thinking 'so how are they cutting costs, then?'" It may not be fair, he says, but "we need to be cleaner than everybody else." Yes, we're proud of our on-time performance but if there's something wrong, "then that is not the time to be on time."

It is not just about preventing an accident, Barger says, but about anything where your reality is at odds with company policy. When JetBlue first started up it was determined to stick to its plan of thirty-minute aircraft turnarounds, but when the airline started flying longer routes and planes were filling up, flight attendants complained they couldn't make the on-time goal and make the plane presentable at the same time.

The first response from management was "go back and try it again," Barger admits. "And you did . . . and we were still hearing from you. And you were right." And now the goal is to turn a plane arriving from a short flight in thirty-five minutes and in fifty-five minutes for a cross-country flight, where the aircraft gets more thoroughly trashed.

Apparently the gospel of CRM spills over into off hours. One night that first week, everyone heads over to the pool at the Staybridge Suites, where the pilots are bunking, for a welcome reception. There's free beer and wine, and a company tradition to kick off: a ritual game played by the pilots and flight attendants that revolves around some props—a toy bear, a caboose—that everyone is commanded to fight over during the next ten days. A pilot stands up and reads a lengthy list of rules of engagement that appear to rival the FAA's regulations in complexity. In each group, the youngest and oldest class members are appointed custodians of these fetishistic objects: In the flight attendants, it's Sophia Mo-hammed, a twenty-year-old customer service agent from Kennedy Air-port, and Sung Ou, a gracious Korean woman who good-naturedly accepts her designation at the other end of the age spectrum.

By the next morning, the bonding ritual appears to be working. The pilots have already conducted a raid on the flight attendants' classroom and made off with the bear mascot, after which they send over an emissary to solemnly read the "ransom demand" that the flight attendants host a pizza party for them. As antics go, this is all pretty tame, but it sets off much merriment and plotting to avenge their foray and, perhaps more to the point, provides some welcome distraction from the tedious agenda of the next few days, which deals with FAA regulations and getting familiar with the turgid manuals upon which all crew members must rely.

There are other diversions that first week, too, primarily the "lifestyle" lecture: the vagaries of drugs and booze awareness, and even hair and makeup pointers. Smoking while in uniform is apparently a major cause of angst, and all are urged to kick the habit completely during training to prove they've got the self-discipline to go without nicotine for up to fourteen hours or more while working. As if this weren't suggestive enough of one's school years, it seems that the cliques are already emerg-ing: A group of young singletons sits together, and the two friends from customer service, Arnel and Eric, stick together on the opposite side of the room. The JetBlue veterans are like the upperclassmen, frequently in-terjecting their own take on how things are done at the company. Kim Cox is emerging as a de facto class leader. She is tall and handsome, with ebony skin and short cropped hair and a bearing that betrays her early stint in the military. She and several other woman are divorced and have teenage children to whom they talk on a daily basis. Doreen Lawrence notes wryly that most of those in the room wouldn't have been hired by an airline thirty years ago—they'd be too old, too heavy—

but even so, there are a couple of trainees who would easily fit the stewardess stereotype of yore. During the discussion of drug and alcohol awareness, Devon, a statuesque brunette, raises her to hand to ask with a straight face, "What if I get really ripped?"

The appearance seminar promises to be lighthearted; the only requirement in the manual is to maintain "neat and professional appearance," which doesn't seem to require much explanation. However, everyone is presented with a two-page, single-spaced document setting out JetBlue "appearance standards," leaving nothing to chance, as in:

> ➤ Skirt hem no more than two inches above the knee.
> ➤ No more than two rings per hand.
> ➤ Mustaches must not extend more than a quarter inch beyond the corner of the mouth.
> ➤ Females are allowed not more than two earrings per ear, no earrings larger than a quarter.
> ➤ For males, earrings are not permitted while on duty.

By the fourth day, there is something afoot: The instructors have been watching closely for any unseemly displays of attitude, and one class member has already been called on the carpet for some decidedly un-JetBlue-like demeanor. Most classes lose one or even two members by graduation; even if you pass every test you can still get kicked out for bad behavior. The winnowing process has begun; by the end of the week, the class is down by one. It was one of the younger trainees, in fact, who had lost her job with United after 9/11.

From now until leaving Miami, everyone spends five hours each day doing the door drill; that is, opening and closing the forward and rear doors of the aircraft, using a mock aircraft section that is used by Air-bus for training. This is perhaps the single most critical maneuver one must master, because flight attendants must perform it twice on every flight. In theory, it ought to be a no-brainer, but it is easy to get flum-moxed by grappling with the heavy door and learning a precise series of maneuvers to unlatch it. Inattention to any of these steps can be fatal; an American Airlines flight attendant was killed not long ago when he inadvertently opened the door before the cabin had finished depressur-izing, and was sucked out of the plane and fell onto the runway thirty feet below.

By the second week, many of the pilots' wives have returned home, and the ritual fighting over the bear and the caboose has morphed into a daily excuse for a party. The pilots have promised to cook a farewell dinner for the flight attendants on their last night in Miami, and writ-ing out a shopping list seems to be sapping all their attention.

But first everyone must learn what to do if a plane crashes into the sea.

Ditchings of a commercial airplane in the ocean are rare; survivors are rarer still. The few times a passenger aircraft has been successfully evac-uated in water have been when a plane overshot a runway and landed in a nearby body of water. But it is an FAA requirement that flight attendants demonstrate that they would know what to do in any number of terrifying scenarios: It could be pitch dark; you could be landing in rough seas; you might need to find life rafts in a smoke-filled cabin and will need to know how to inflate them; you might have to erect a canopy overhead to protect from the sun and the elements. You'll need to set off flares and release blue dye into the water to alert rescuers to your presence.

At 8:00 A.M., the class reports in swimsuits to the pool at the Sleep Inn just down the street from Airbus. Everyone dons life vests and prepares to jump into the pool, swim to a life raft, climb in, and assemble the canopy. This precipitates a lot of hand-wringing: Several flight attendants, it seems, don't know how to swim. "Why do we have to do this?" one wails to an instructor, Matt Kliff, confessing she's afraid of the water. Matt is sympathetic but firm: "You will be wearing a life jacket," he says. "But I can't swim." "It doesn't matter," Kliff says, reminding her she'll be expelled from training if she continues to balk.

This is about more than mere adherence to FAA regulations. Dave Barger knew from his experience at Newark Airport that one could escape the thicket of flight paths directly over the city if your plane was equipped to fly over the open ocean, like international airlines. A JetBlue plane bound from JFK to, say, West Palm Beach, could get permission to take off ahead of a line of other airlines' planes headed in the same direction simply because it could jump to a less crowded flight path a mere five or ten miles farther off shore. "It's like getting off Route 1 and jumping on I-95," Dave helpfully explains. All JetBlue aircraft are certified to fly over water for extended periods, and as a result each one carries one hundred thousand dollars' worth of extra equipment, an expense that has been more than repaid in the time saved. So that's what is forcing everyone into the pool this morning.

The last morning in Miami is spent at the Pan Am Flight Academy down the road to practice firefighting. The academy was once part of the real Pan Am, and it's an odd, preserved-in-amber sort of place, with the blue meatball logo on the outside of the building and a large mural depicting Pan Am's once-boundless route system. Upstairs is a gift shop hawking the airline's surplus paraphernalia—pens, cigarette lighters, even some old uniforms—to which customers are lured with a life-size cardboard manikin of a smiling blond stewardess, circa 1965. It is still an active training facility, used mainly by foreign airlines, and during the exercise a platoon of Russian pilots arrives. They give the class a quick once-over and, perhaps disappointed by what they see, head up to have their picture taken with the faux Pan Am bimbo.

Then it's back to Airbus for a final exercise: jumping down the escape slide, which is dangling from a balcony in one of the training rooms. It's no ride at Six Flags, however; everyone is told to wear long-sleeved shirts "to avoid burns" and not to wear pantyhose, which could melt under the friction and sear your legs. The biggest cause of injuries on planes, in fact, is not the emergency that necessitates the evacuation, but the roll down the escape chute. Lenka Brady, a tall, striking blond Czech woman who is the instructor that day, bellows at everyone to "cross your arms . . . jump, jump!" One by one, everyone leaps into the air—the aim is to get everyone off the plane in a minute and a half.

Back in the break room, it is time to bid good-bye to the pilots before heading to New York. Without the inhibiting presence of spouses, there's much hugging and many promises to "See you on the line." Katrien Ceragioli, an instructor who was one of JetBlue's first flight attendants, is pleased: This class really bonded, she says, and you'll see the difference this makes once they're flying.

In the middle of the three-week course, there's a one-day break to take the pulse of the flying public, to get a feel for being "on the line." Everyone is assigned a flight and spends the day observing their future coworkers at work. The next morning everyone gathers on the second floor of headquarters for a debriefing. Matt Kliff urges everyone to be brutally candid: Tell us what you didn't like, what could be better.

Kim Cox raises her hand; she sat next to a man on the flight back from Fort Lauderdale who spent much of the flight in a fury after fighting with the gate agent. Cox wasn't quite sure what had set him off, but it was his comments that stayed with her: "You know this used to be a great airline," he had reportedly said. "But now they're growing too fast and they're becoming like everyone else!" There are nervous titters: Soon these angry passengers are going to be everyone's problem.

And, indeed, there's soon a sobering reminder. Eveyone's expected to check the company intranet every day for e-mail and internal bulletins. There's a disturbing one the first day in New York. The previous evening, a JetBlue flight bound from Las Vegas to New York made an unscheduled landing to off-load an unruly passenger. This will make good material for the lesson on security and all the other aspects of passenger handling.

Frank Corsillo, a former New York City policeman who works in JetBlue's security department, declares solemnly, "You are the cops on the beat." We are really on our own; pilots can radio ahead to an airport for help, but they won't physically be able to help you until landing. He talks about the incident on the Las Vegas flight: The passenger, whom he refers to as an "EDP," for emotionally disturbed person, suddenly became violent and had to be restrained. Everyone gets a set of yellow plastic handcuffs, or "tuff cuffs," and divides into groups, practicing on each other. "Uh, don't use these at home," Corsillo advises, to much laughter.

But there is a serious side here, the awareness that delivering the JetBlue experience won't always be easy. There are a couple of days of "soft skills" training, when everyone takes turns playing the sorts of customers who "will try your patience," as one instructor diplomatically puts it. They fall into some general categories: drunks, fearful or inexperienced fliers (the "Clampetts" in industry parlance), the overly flirtatious, and, finally, the abusive ones, those who are immune to whatever solicitude the crew has to offer. And that is where the delicate business of deciding who is a threat and who is merely annoying comes into play.

There are three levels of disturbance, and when you hit the top level, it's time to radio ahead for help, and maybe even divert the plane, depending on where you are in your journey. The pilots are behind a locked door, but those cameras JetBlue installed after 9/11 allow them to see what is going on.

Much of the emergency training is, mercifully, almost over. There is one skills test left, however: The evacuation protocols that were polished in the aircraft mock-up at Airbus in Florida will be tested by instructors who will throw out a scenario—blind man with dog—and you must respond how you would help that person while evacuating 160 others. You must do it by the book, no ad-libbing. While you get several chances to pass, with each one, the stress level rises. This is one of the parts of the program that is most likely to end one's in-flight aspirations. During a break, several members of the class are on their third try now, and in tears. Lora and Denise, two friends who'd worked the counters at JFK and decided to go into flight training together, are having a bit a of a dustup. Lora has already failed the test twice and she is ready to quit. Denise gives her an impassioned lecture about getting out of the customer service grind and why she can't give up now.

Upstairs on the eighth floor, there's another debate going on. Inside the company it is known simply, and cryptically, as the row 27 question. What it concerned was this: The very last row of seats of the Airbus A320 was by far the worst on the plane; the legroom was pinched, and the seats didn't recline. For these very reasons it was usually the last to fill up, meaning that it would often be occupied by last-minute travelers who, typically, paid the highest fares. Neeleman was cognizant of this paradox and he'd often spoken about it in staff meetings, but it was hard to solve. If he removed one row of seats beyond the exit rows in the middle of the plane, then that would mean those in the back of the plane would get more legroom than those sitting in the front. That, of course, stood the normal airline formula—putting the best seats in front—on its head.

So he dithered awhile about it until one day he received one of the comment cards the airline routinely stocks in the back of the plane. Neeleman makes a point of reading these, and, like his walk down the aisle routine, files these ideas away for further consideration. This one particularly moved him. It was from a self-described business traveler, and it said, as one paraphrased it: "You've really got balls to charge me $300 for this seat." Neeleman stuck the card in his pocket and kept it there for a week, and every time he wavered on whether to remove the infamous row 27, he would pull it out and reread it.

The marketing staff tried to convince him they could handle the problem another way; just don't sell it, they'd say, or reserve it for dead-heading crew members. But Neeleman was bothered: Inevitably, paying customers would end up back there. So give them a voucher or something else to alleviate the misery, he was told. No—"That would seem like we're just apologizing, instead of doing the right thing," he said, according to those present in one of these meetings.

That July, JetBlue announced it would remove the last row of seats on its planes, leaving only 156 seats—and with two-thirds of them getting a very generous thirty-four-inch legroom.

It didn't hurt that Song had been touting the superiority of its thirty-three-inch seat pitch over JetBlue's.

Two days before graduation, Doreen Lawrence comes in to announce that the class has lost another member. It comes as a shock to learn that it isn't Lora, who'd been so discouraged the previous week, but her friend Denise, who'd so forcefully persuaded her to hang in but who apparently froze during the final exam. Lora, who seems sort of stunned that she's the survivor, is crying; it doesn't seem fair, she says. Denise would have been a great flight attendant.

But everyone is relieved that it is over and now it is time to talk about benefits and free travel; some are already planning R&R in Hawaii. Another instructor comes in to give tips on how to find a crash pad in Kew Gardens, one of the few districts in the city where landlords are eager to bend occupancy standards and rent a two-bedroom apartment to ten tenants since few will ever be home at the same time. They learn about gyms that give discounts to airline employees; while there are no insulting weight limits at JetBlue, there is still a more subtle code of presentability. Lawrence comes back in to assure them, though, that things really have changed. "Back when I was at Braniff we were like little kewpie dolls" and the "first thing we had to do was to step onto a scale." And she shares the indignities she endured, the daily grooming sessions where "they'd wax our mustaches and straighten our hair." Matt Kliff comes in with a boom box and to the tune of "Are You Happy?" Lawrence informs everyone they have one last drill to perform: They will have to learn how to "walk the dime" just like she and all the other big-haired bimbos once had to do, presumably with a straight face.

Graduation is July 30.

It is time to rehearse the "class song" that everyone's been ordered to prepare, and Kim Cox, who has displayed an admirable sangfroid during training, is chosen as class speaker. The class files into an auditorium; family and friends are in the audience and a hushed solemnity settles over the assembly.

David Neeleman arrives, a few minutes late, and his efforts to slip unobtrusively into the back fail so miserably that everybody starts laughing. He then lopes up to the front, and in a soft, almost croaking voice says he is late because he had just been to a funeral for a JetBlue employee. "He'd been with the company a month," Neeleman says, "but that doesn't matter because we treat everyone the same here." He continues in this way, softly but cagily weaving it all together: about the soul of the company and how it is "a company that makes us better for having been part of it" and how one measure of a company's success is whether it would be missed if it were to disappear tomorrow.

Then he says how important flight attendants are because they interact with customers the longest of any JetBlue employees and "you have a profound effect" on the future, and, besides, the average JetBlue flight is now three hours long.

"And when you get on a JetBlue flight five years from now or ten years from now, I don't want it just to be as good as it was in the beginning. I want it to be better. Because that is what we are about—to always try to be better, to do things better." He's good—there are audible sniffles in the room.

After the ceremony, everyone heads off with their families to celebrate. But first a lot of checking of watches: Reality is quickly setting in. Many have flights that depart first thing the next morning; they'll have to arrive at the airport at 5:00 A.M. Do a quick calculation: You can't show up if you have consumed any alcohol within the past eight hours. The letdown is palpable; this is not the night for a blowout.

There's been another milestone lately. JetBlue's flight attendant corps has just passed the one thousandth mark. In another few weeks, a new class will start, and then they'll be training two groups a month, cranking out the crew members at the rate of nearly one hundred a month, ensuring, if nothing else, that Neeleman will be spending many hours attending orientations and graduation rituals.

ten
welcome to
my world

On the fifth day of what must have been one of the worst weeks of his life, David Neeleman tapped out an e-mail to his father that began: "Welcome to the world I've been living in." The sarcasm implicit in this greeting would be apparent to anyone opening the attached file, a nearly book-length exchange between Neeleman and one especially exigent tormentor. This was at the height of what the media had christened the "JetBlue Privacy Scandal," which had begun on September 18, 2003, with the revelation that someone inside the airline had given the reservations records of one million individual customers to an army contractor the previous year for a security study. Within days, the story had been picked up by every major news outlet in the country and the airline had been flooded with more than twenty thousand angry messages. Most of these proved to be identically worded form letters that had been generated by a couple of Web sites devoted to whipping up outrage at perceived affronts to the privacy of ordinary citizens. Neeleman was mainly interested in reading the few hundred or so that came from actual customers, and he was staying up through the night to pore over them, responding to the more hysterical ones with lengthy point-by-point rebuttals. It was characteristic of Neeleman that he was, in a strange way, moved by the intensity evident in these outpourings, even if he disagreed with them.

"I learned there's a lot of mistrust out there," he later said. "And I didn't grow up with mistrust of the government; maybe I thought it was a slow-moving bureaucracy, but I didn't think there was some big evil plan to control people. But apparently there are a lot of people out there who do believe that . . ."

All this had been unleashed because of a long-ago transaction, about which few at JetBlue were even aware until a call had come in to Gareth Edmondson-Jones at the beginning of that September week, from Ryan Singel, a Silicon Valley–based reporter for *Wired* magazine. Singel had gotten tipped off that JetBlue's name had come up during a private meeting in Washington between Admiral James Loy, then the Transportation Security Administration chief, and a group of conservative activists who objected to the government's increasing scrutiny of travel records. Loy had confided that JetBlue was considering cooperating with the security agency in developing a new computer passenger-screening system to replace the rudimentary one that had failed to stop nineteen hijackers on September 11. As one of those rare issues that unite people on opposite sides of the political spectrum—the American Civil Liberties Union was also among the government critics—the news seemed certain to rouse a network of self-appointed watchdogs who had been awaiting such an opportunity to rail against anything smacking of Big Brother.

Singel filed a short news item stating JetBlue had been identified as the "test" airline for the so-called CAPPS II (computer-assisted passenger prescreening) program. The new system was an update of the first incarnation of CAPPS, which had been put into place in the mid-1990s to prevent another bombing attack such as the one that downed Pan

Am Flight 103 over Lockerbie, Scotland. The idea was to flag potential terror threats by searching travel records for criteria such as whether a traveler paid for a ticket in cash. By 2002, however, it was clear the system was ineffectual as the passengers it was designed to catch knew how to circumvent it.

But the supposed test of a replacement system, using color-coded rankings to identify potential threats, had been harshly criticized by several influential congressmen in public hearings, for the plan was to use information that passengers routinely provide airlines to search consumer databases that could include financial and other personal details. While it did strike a few observers as odd that JetBlue would consider lending its name to such a controversial endeavor, the first *Wired* story got little traction in the mainstream media.

But the following day, Singel was alerted to a new, and potentially far more disturbing, angle by Edward Hasbrouck, a privacy activist and author who had been using his Web log to track the government's vast data mining programs in the wake of the 9/11 terror attacks. Hasbrouck, with a couple of simple search commands, had unearthed the fact that virtually all of JetBlue's entire passenger database had been handed over in the summer of 2002 to an obscure research contractor in Huntsville, Alabama, called Torch Concepts. Torch had later posted a lengthy discourse on its Web site about its attempts to plumb the airline's customer records for trends that might help the government to identify potential threats to commercial airliners. This document also had a sample of the work it had done, using a passenger's name and address and combining it with information purchased from a credit-checking agency, which had, among other things, produced the customer's Social Security number and all the places he had lived in the last five years—information that was never in JetBlue's possession. Although the passenger's name had been excised from the presentation, the very existence of this decidedly creepy use of an airline reservations record was a startling revelation.

And thus these two separate stories collided to create a full-blown "scandal" in the national news media. That the words "JetBlue" and "scandal" were juxtaposed in the same sentence at all, of course, was the real shocker for many people and that, as much as anything else, was fueling the coverage. For JetBlue had held its perch as a media darling and industry "good guy" for so long that any slip was bound to excite the sort of smug condemnations that would accompany the disgrace of a politician. It was hardly prepared.

An examination of the sequence of events is instructive, because it reveals just how it happened and why it became such a cause célèbre. Ironically, JetBlue got ensnared by three distinct aspects of its culture, which combined to provide fertile ground for just such a blunder.

The roots of the story stretch back to late 1999, when it was decided that all JetBlue fares would be one way—to keep it simple, to get away from punitive rules like the Saturday-night stay that most airlines imposed on their low-fare customers. JetBlue was praised for its innovation at the time, but after 9/11, there was an unintended side effect: The purchase of a one-way ticket was a red flag to government security probers looking for possible terrorists and, suddenly, a disproportionate number of JetBlue customers were being pulled aside at airport checkpoints for additional screening.

In early 2002, less than six months after the attacks, JetBlue raised the problem with the TSA and asked for some relief from the security hassles. As it turned out, the TSA had been approached by the Pentagon for airline records to use as raw material for a study, and so the TSA, naturally, thought of JetBlue as an ideal prospect because it had an added incentive to cooperate. It later emerged that various government agencies had been getting access to a number of airlines' passenger records ever since 9/11—including American's and Northwest's—without the knowledge of their customers. But here, another aspect of JetBlue's vaunted openness would trip it up: The airline's privacy policy was so sweeping and so broadly written that it allowed for no exceptions. It stated, simply, that it will never share your information with any third parties, any time, for any reason.

It was, Neeleman later admitted, naïve to assume that the company would never face a situation that would warrant sharing some information for national security or law enforcement purposes. Indeed, this was one area where JetBlue would have been wiser to follow industry practice, which is to craft a privacy policy with five pages of exceptions and caveats to cover any eventuality.

Then came the third point: the "empower your people" mantra, which granted middle managers authority to make many decisions without clearing them through David Neeleman or Dave Barger. The person who gave the JetBlue records to Torch Concepts (he or she has never been identified publicly) apparently did not have to clear it with superiors, nor even inform them, and thus the conflict with the privacy policy, which is posted clearly on JetBlue's Web site, did not arise.

So David Neeleman learned about this curious transaction, apparently, the same way everyone else did: via the media. For the first few days after the *Wired* story broke, things were fairly subdued. The news got picked up by a few wire services, but didn't get much play. Instead, the leading news story in New York was the impending arrival of Hurricane Isabel and the possibility that Kennedy Airport might have to close. That Friday, September 19, many businesses in the New York area shut down early and Gareth Edmondson-Jones was preparing to spend all weekend on call in case of mass flight cancellations. Edmondson-Jones did, in fact, spend all weekend on call, but not due to weather. On Saturday, the *New York Times* ran a front-page story, headlined JETBLUE GAVE DEFENSE FIRM PASSENGER FILES, that went into considerable and alarming detail, referring to the file transfer as a grave violation of passengers' privacy. By dint of its play on the front page of the newspaper of record, the story was guaranteed to catch fire.

By the next day, it was clear that this would be the true test of what Neeleman and Dave Barger had always pledged to do: to be open, to candidly admit mistakes, and do everything humanly possible to make it right. JetBlue, as any airline must, has a series of contingency plans in place to deal with all manner of crises, but they are crises you would expect an airline to anticipate: an accident, a blizzard, a computer failure. JetBlue had already weathered variations of all three. During the runway mishap in early 2001, it had acquitted itself well, getting out all the information swiftly and owning up to any mistakes. More recently, the company's resolve had been put to a couple of Job-like tests, including the computer meltdown that had resulted in flight delays of four hours.

JetBlue's latest trial had been during the biggest power outage in U.S. history, which began when a tree hit a power line in Ohio on the afternoon of August 14. Within hours, New York City was in total darkness, and air travel throughout most of the Northeast was at a standstill.

Kennedy, like other airports, did have backup emergency generators, but with a limited output, hardly enough to keep anything other than emergency systems going. Everything from air-conditioning to the security screening equipment was deemed nonessential and began shutting down. As temperatures inside Terminal Six climbed over 90 degrees, JetBlue workers handed out free bottles of water and brought in a Mister Softee truck to cool people down. As it became clear that the lights weren't coming back on at all that night, JetBlue still managed to board planes and depart, calling in workers from all over the New York metro area to assist. Although the computers were down, gate agents inspected customers' documents with flashlights and manually wrote out boarding passes. Instead of using jetways, they guided people to the tarmac down a flight of darkened stairs, using battery-powered floodlights to illuminate the way. One of the volunteers was Neeleman himself, who drove to the airport "fuel farm" on a baggage cart to cadge more fuel, arguing that since his airline was the only one that was trying to operate, it should get first crack. The next day, when American Airlines canceled 295 flights, JetBlue only canceled 20.

Some JetBlue workers had walked to Delta's terminal complex to see how Song was holding up, but the terminal was shuttered. "It was like, don't even think about approaching!" reported one spy. Rumors circulated that American Airlines was charging dehydrated customers three dollars a bottle for water. JetBlue workers seemed to take an almost perverse pleasure in proving their mettle in these trials, versus their wimpier counterparts at other airlines. After each crisis had died down, JetBlue would typically trumpet the results—versus the others—prominently on its Web site.

But in the privacy matter, unlike these earlier ordeals, there was a wide disparity between the besieged organization that came across in numerous news accounts and the reality inside the airline. Before the story broke, David and Dave were set to take off on a cross-country tour of JetBlue bases, a semiannual jaunt that gave nearly everyone in the company a chance to speak to the pair in person. They would arrive in Fort Lauderdale on Monday, September 22, flying to Long Beach the next day, and then on to Salt Lake City, returning to New York on Thursday for an end-of-week pocket session back at headquarters. The week would finish off with a ritual company picnic at a ballfield at JFK.

They didn't skip a single appearance, even as the scandal reached fever pitch, with one exception: Only Dave Barger went to Fort Lauderdale while Neeleman huddled with his advisers and lawyers in New York in an all-day meeting. For the one issue that would dog them, the violation of their own privacy policy, was blowing up in their faces. Several large organizations, including the ACLU, were actively encouraging JetBlue passengers to file a lawsuit, inciting a stampede of plaintiffs' attorneys in search of a "class" to represent. An electronic privacy organization filed a complaint with the Federal Trade Commission asking that it look into the company's actions, and the Department of Homeland Security said it would launch an investigation of what went wrong—an interesting position since it was the department's own transportation security arm that had facilitated the data sharing in the first place.

Neeleman wanted to send out an apology immediately, without waiting for a thorough vetting from lawyers; any hesitation, he thought, would be interpreted as confirmation he had something to hide. He drafted a mea culpa that weekend and by Monday it had been sent to all JetBlue customers and was posted online. He also decided to hire the accounting firm of Deloitte & Touche—not his regular auditor, Ernst and Young—to help review privacy policies and to suggest possible changes. The company took the further step of declaring that JetBlue would no longer offer to help test the airline security program at the TSA, effectively bringing the story full circle.

The flaming of the company continued, however. Those answering the phones at JetBlue were reporting hundreds of calls an hour, often someone shrieking abuse into the phone and then quickly hanging up (one Internet privacy activist, Bill Scannell, had posted Gareth Edmondson-Jones's number on his "Don't Spy on Us" Web site and urged people to flood the PR department with calls). That Tuesday, September 23, the *New York Times* ran several follow-up articles—JETBLUE

MOVES TO REPAIR DAMAGE was a typical headline—and also published an editorial titled "Betraying One's Passengers," that condemned Jet-Blue in harsh terms. "JetBlue passengers, more than a million of them, have been unsuspecting guinea pigs in a Defense Department contractors' experiment . . ." the editorial began, adding that "JetBlue's surrender of the information amounts to one of the most serious betrayals of consumers' privacy rights by an American business." While noting that JetBlue had apologized, and conceding that the company had been "praised on this page for sound management and innovative service," the editorial went on to warn darkly that "plenty of questions remain unanswered," and called for a congressional investigation into the matter. Some JetBlue supporters were moved to complain (although JetBlue itself did not). One of the airline's directors, Dave Checketts, the former chief of Madison Square Garden, knew a senior *Times* executive personally and called him up, asking why the *Times* coverage was so excessive. According to several sources familiar with the exchange, the man responded that he felt the treatment of the airline was fair. "It's a really big story," the *Times* man said, adding, almost as an aside, "But we've given them lots of good press."

It was impossible to predict where this would lead. JetBlue's accessibility only seemed to encourage those who needed a place to vent their distrust of the government, whereas the other parties who bore at least equal blame for the mess—the Pentagon, the obscure Alabama contractor it used—hid behind lawyers and refused to comment. To those inside JetBlue who were manning the phones, it was the tenor of some of the irate calls that was notable. It was as if people felt personally let down, in a sense a backhanded tribute to the affection they felt for the company. This was the flip side of the brand syndrome: JetBlue had created so many positive associations in consumers' minds that this off note was amplified far out of normal range. One JetBlue secretary reported that callers were saying things like "I thought you were different—now you're just like any other airline!" as if that were the worst form of insult to level at the company.

Before the news had hit the front pages, David and Dave had sent out a "Blue Note" to everyone inside the company so they wouldn't be caught off guard. The note reconstructed the chain of events that had led up to the fiasco, mentioning that it had begun when the company responded to an "exceptional request" from the Department of Defense to assist its contractor. "Our response was simply in good faith," they wrote, emphasizing that the company did not share any sensitive information such as financial data.

"We had no knowledge of (Torch's) presentation until recently, and we were deeply dismayed to learn of it," the letter continued. "We have received some emails expressing concern over privacy issues and have responded to each individually with a thorough explanation and a message of sincere regret. We know that you will all demonstrate the same degree of caring toward customers who may contact you . . ."

That impulse would be sorely tested by the tone of the e-mails flooding Neeleman's inbox. And so, on the Friday of that week, he stood before employees at a pocket session at the Forest Hills offices to share with them what his week had been like, the all-night sessions over his laptop answering the blistering messages that were pouring in.

"When we make a mistake, we admit it, and we do what we can to make it right," he said. But, in this case, "making it right" was a little more complicated.

"Because the big wrong had to do with our privacy policy, for even if it was for a good reason we still violated it . . . it goes to the heart of the real important thing, which has been difficult for me personally because it is a big part of what we stand for, which is integrity. The fact that our integrity has been called into question goes against the grain of what we are."

That hurts, he said, but it has also shown him something else, that the company is resilient enough to withstand a public battering.

"We will continue to try to repair this. And I was traveling on two flights this week, and talked to every single customer and didn't get one question on it. And, yes, we got some profane messages, but we are focusing on those who are upset with us for what they perceived was a (betrayal). We called them and without exception they understand in every case.

"And I've taken this really personally and I've tried to respond to each one."

And he did, to the point where some of his colleagues, like John Owen, were getting concerned about their leader's well-being. "David is a persuader, and when he believes he is right, he will keep pounding away," said Owen. Neeleman, in fact, frequently answers e-mails from customers himself, and often addresses the specific complaint directly, without routing it to an underling.

But, as Neeleman recounted later, the customer who had inspired the note to his father looked like the one who would get away. The man, a businessman living in Fort Lauderdale, seemed intent on getting Neeleman to admit that he had lied about his role in the whole affair. "He said, 'Just pass Go and go straight to Hell.' . . . And I wrote back and got back an even angrier response," Neeleman recalled. This time, the accusation was that Neeleman had removed his own personal information from the JetBlue database before it was handed over to the government contractor.

That really got him, Neeleman said. "And I said, 'Look, go look me up in Google and you'll see 5,800 hits. And my home address is there for anyone to find. And my phone number was listed in the phone book until six months ago when my wife took it out fearing for the safety of our kids, because somebody tried to get one of my kids to get in the car with them. . . . So, you see, I have nothing to hide.'"

The man wrote back, apparently mortified he'd been so hard on Neeleman: "If I'm wrong I admit it, and I was wrong." And not only did he back off, he invited Neeleman to be his guest at his home the next time he came to Florida. Neeleman, in all seriousness, said he would accept.

The morning of Saturday, September 27, Neeleman arrived at a ballfield on the outskirts of Kennedy Airport with Vicki and four of his nine children for the JetBlue picnic, the last of his press-the-flesh forays that week. He was still exhausted: He had spent the previous night engaged in a lengthy phone debate on the details of the privacy case with Bill Scannell, who had called for a boycott of JetBlue. Like others before him, Scannell failed to grasp that Neeleman would not rest until he'd converted him to the JetBlue cause. "I think I won him over," Neeleman said, proudly, and one got the sense that winning back these cranky consumers was, for him, the greatest conquest.

Among the hundreds who came to eat turkey burgers and corn on the cob and take part in the carnival rides were employees from other organizations who worked alongside JetBlue at JFK. There were Port Authority officials, FAA workers from the control tower, and, yes, even some security screeners from the Transportation Security Administration, the very agency whose actions had led to the flaming that JetBlue had withstood that week. It was a JetBlue tradition to invite airport workers to join company celebrations and to send pizzas or holiday meals to harried workers at security checkpoints or FAA command posts, all part of the menschy world of David and Dave.

Neeleman had another way to show he cared: A table had been set up at the picnic to hand out literature and take donations for the Jet-Blue Crewmember Crisis Fund, a nonprofit foundation he had established to help employees in need. Although the organization was, legally, a separate entity from JetBlue, Neeleman and other executives sat on its board, along with people like Michael DeLorenzo, a flight attendant who had been with the airline since the first day. The fund, supported entirely by donations, gave grants—not loans—to employees who'd suffered a disaster, be it a house burning down, an illness or death in the family. Neeleman had just sent out the word that he would donate his two-hundred-thousand-dollar annual salary to the fund. Ann Rhoades, who continued to sit on the company board, had pledged a like amount.

It was time to move on, Neeleman said, and he had good news to share: The previous Thursday, JetBlue's planes had flown 87 percent full, an "unbelievable" showing for what should be a slow weekday in the middle of September. JetBlue was also about to enter Boston, a prime territory where customers had been long gouged by the likes of American and Delta. Three years earlier, JetBlue had been directed to tiny Worcester Airport. Now it was being welcomed to Logan.

Two days later, as he traveled to Boston to meet with Massachusetts Governor Mitt Romney, Neeleman was clearly sick of the controversy and eager to get back to normal. He'd just been to Salt Lake City to give a speech at the University of Utah, and while the privacy mess had ensured a larger than average press turnout, he'd been received warmly. In what was perhaps a more telling sign that the flap was losing steam, several calls had come into John Owen's offices from investors who were dying to know one thing: the name of the crisis management firm that

JetBlue surely had used to quell the furor so effectively. The team in Darien had been amused by that one: No one in the company had seriously considered going down that well-traveled path. Gareth Edmondson-Jones had handled the public relations side himself while his deputy was in Europe on vacation.

As a media event, the so-called scandal soon subsided; there was another unsavory aspect to the story, however, that lingered: Other airlines had been less than gracious during the episode. Northwest Airlines CEO Richard Anderson had been quoted in the press to the effect that his airline would never have cooperated with such a request to hand over passenger information to a government agency. Months later, it was revealed that Northwest, in fact, had done just that—lending its customer databases for a security study by NASA. A few weeks after that, it was revealed that American Airlines had also supplied the government with millions of passenger records shortly after 9/11. None of these actions was necessarily wrong, or even in violation of those airlines' privacy policies; even so, those who were already convinced of a grand government plot to spy on its citizens were hardly mollified. Those stories, however, appeared on the inside pages of the *New York Times*.

In the end, what was the effect on JetBlue of this public relations disaster? A few weeks after the dust settled, Neeleman checked to see what if any impact it might have had on bookings. In fact, there were 1.5 million reservations on the books when the scandal broke, and only three customers had called to cancel. Two had been talked out of it by a supervisor. And forward bookings, if anything, were higher than normal.

Neeleman was asked by reporters whether he would fire the person responsible for the data sharing: He firmly refused to, and instead went to the individual's defense, saying that if he had been approached in the hallway about the Pentagon request, he'd probably have approved it. "People have forgotten what it was like right after 9/11," he said. "The government asks you for help in fighting terrorism—what would anyone do?"

But this said, JetBlue did blunder—with its privacy policy that few seem to know the details of, with its perhaps overly loose management style. Neeleman's admission that he was unaware of the data transfer was also troubling: Some questioned his sincerity while others interpreted it as a sign that the CEO was out of touch. However, Neeleman was right to come out quickly and apologize, again, something many CEOs would have deferred until they saw the potential legal ramifications.

A few months later, the privacy activists moved on, the calls for a congressional inquiry died down (and, indeed, there was no formal investigation by Congress), and a rash of positive stories about JetBlue appeared in various sections of the *New York Times*. It was again politically correct to admit you liked JetBlue.

eleven
the terminal

In early 2004, John Owen sent out an invitation to investors: Come to Kennedy Airport on the morning of March 10, he said, and you will get a glimpse of what JetBlue will look like in three years. So many accepted the bait that he ultimately had to turn away dozens of people. It was not the expectation of another bullish presentation but the location of the event that was the lure: It would not be at JetBlue's Terminal Six, but at the once-lauded and now empty and dilapidated edifice next door. That was Terminal Five, the forty-year-old Eero Saarinen creation that was one of the rare airport buildings to be deemed worthy of landmark status. That, in effect, was the cause of its abandonment: No significant changes could be made to the building and the conventional wisdom was that it would not continue to function as an airport terminal, given the realities of the post–9/11 world. American Airlines, which had assumed control of the building with its merger with TWA in late 2000, had shuttered it soon after the attacks. The Port Authority had talked vaguely about turning it into a museum or a restaurant; again, a laughable concept, given that Kennedy was, as ever, an intimidating experience that no one would choose to navigate unless he had a pressing reason to do so.

The bankers who arrived in a caravan organized by Morgan Stanley did have a reason: The word was that JetBlue would preserve the terminal and encompass it within a new complex it would soon begin building to house its expanding flights. The terminal would cost around one billion dollars to build, to be borne mainly by the Port Authority, although JetBlue would chip in some four hundred million dollars it would raise on its own. There was, however, a holdup. The plan, as drawn up by Port Authority, would demolish the signature tubes that connected the main terminal with a bank of boarding gates, and, further offending preservationists, also would destroy the panoramic view of the runways as seen from the floor-to-ceiling windows of the Saarinen building. That would reduce the grand space to an irrelevance that spoke volumes about the Port Authority's vision for taming the mess that continued to define the airport.

Still, JetBlue would soon outgrow the space it had at Terminal Six and would require at least twenty-six gates to handle two hundred daily flights in three years. In the eyes of the Port Authority, JetBlue was the only airline with the financial heft to handle such a massive project and smooth over the objections from the New York cognoscenti.

In late 2003, however, it appeared that JetBlue might be heading toward another public relations dustup. In a spate of articles whose main source appeared to be the Municipal Art Society of New York, the airline was identified as the corporation that would destroy an architectural masterpiece. While most of the stories focused, rightfully, their criticism on the Port Authority for its abject lack of vision, this was hardly the sort of achievement for which David Neeleman wanted to be remembered. Neeleman characteristically did not quite share the industry dogma that the TWA terminal had to be mothballed; it had, after all, been used as a viable airport terminal as recently as 2001. While the layout of the space had been a problem for years, even before the advent of massive post–9/11 security checkpoints, Neeleman thought something could be salvaged of the terminal that would maintain its link to the business whose possibilities it had once symbolized so gracefully.

Gareth Edmondson-Jones recalled that one day when a reporter called seeking a comment, Neeleman, in standard fashion, blurted out: "Well, why can't we use it as a terminal?" Everyone groaned, Edmondson-Jones recalled, "because we knew that would send us back to the drawing board." But that was the point. Neeleman sensed what had so stirred the preservationists: Unless the terminal stayed connected to the travel process, the renovation would, as one critic put it, be "like cutting the arms off a baby."

Neeleman also felt the emotional heat of the issue. When asked by another reporter about the plans, he even raised the demolition of New York's old Penn Station as an example of what he wanted to avoid. The destruction of that Beaux Arts terminal in the early 1960s, to make way for a frighteningly mediocre office tower atop Madison Square Garden, was an affront to anyone who cared about urban aesthetics and more than any other event began to turn the tide away from unbridled development. Several preservation groups became much more powerful and as a result, local laws were toughened, and buildings in imminent danger of falling to some crass developer were identified. The TWA terminal was landmarked in 1994 and subsequently placed on the list of Most Endangered Historic Places by the National Trust for Historic Preservation.

The preservationists did have their own problem, however; no airline had any interest in using Terminal Five in its present form, and its deserted state had hardly helped matters. The floor, composed of tiny Italian marble tiles, was cracked and decaying, and the interior was covered with grime. The Municipal Arts group hired an architect who proposed excavating under the building to accommodate state-of-the-art baggage handling and security systems, a plan that drew derision from the Port Authority, which argued that not only would this be prohibitively expensive but also that the water table at Kennedy was too high to permit digging under terminals.

A lawsuit, then, seemed inevitable unless Neeleman could find a way to meet the objections of the preservationists. Frank Sanchis, the head of the Municipal Arts group, was insistent that real passengers—not curiosity-seeking tourists—had to have a reason to enter the old terminal. In one meeting among the parties, Neeleman seized on an angle that had apparently eluded others: The whole process of getting from the airport lobby to the plane had been radically transformed by technology. More passengers were using self-service kiosks to check in or bypassing that step altogether by arriving with a boarding pass they had printed out at home. JetBlue, with its abhorrence of paper, was ideally situated to capitalize on this change and had just rolled out banks of sophisticated do-it-yourself check-in devices at most of its airports. Neeleman figured that what many of his customers really needed the moment they entered the terminal was information: their boarding time and gate and if their flight was on time. What if we set up the Saarinen building as a self-service check-in and ticketing area, with flight information displays and wireless-enabled zones for Internet access? he asked. Throw in a few restaurants and stores—and arriving passengers would then have an inviting place to pass the time before heading for the dreaded encounter with security. Even the older of the tubular tunnels that connect the terminal to the boarding areas would be preserved, except that it would now form a path to the larger terminal JetBlue would erect next door.

Sanchis embraced the compromise: Here was a way to preserve the terminal's function while acknowledging the dramatic changes that had taken place in air travel. While there was still much work to be done—the Port Authority had yet to sign off on the final plan—the deal was nonetheless in place, and JetBlue was now ready to show off yet another tangible sign that it was here to stay. The Wall Street contingent who showed up that day in March was not disappointed. Over bagels and coffee, they gazed at the remains of air travel past: the "Constellation lounge," with a decidedly Rat Pack decor of black leather and shag carpeting; the names of TWA destinations to convey the airline's global reach; a duty-free-shop window displaying cartons of Benson and Hedges cigarettes. Then there was the future: a smaller edition of the Embraer 190 parked conveniently outside so that bankers could get a feel for the jet's potential. For the money men, there was another appealing aspect to all this. JetBlue would get to glom on to the nostalgia invoked by the Saarinen landmark virtually free of charge. The Port Authority, not JetBlue, would assume full responsibility for renovating and maintaining the building; JetBlue's investment was in the new building next door.

To get there that morning, however, the bankers had gotten a decidedly less inspiring view of the contemporaneous airline business. Kennedy Airport was still a mess, despite billions of dollars that had poured into various improvements. Its essential design of individual terminals strung together by a convoluted network of roadways was as illogical as ever. "One good thing that JFK has going for it is that its architecture accurately depicts the present chaos of the air travel system," *New York Times* architecture critic Herbert Muschamp wrote in 2001. American Airlines' complex was a prime example. In 2001, the airline had been in the midst of a massive multibillion-dollar renovation of its aging twin terminals. Work was halted soon after September 11 and three years later, it was still a construction site with no end in sight. Passengers arriving at busy times were occasionally subjected to waits of up to forty-five minutes simply to get from the airport roadway to the entrance of the terminal. Then there was Delta's sprawling and equally decrepit Worldport, another relic, this one of the glory days of Pan Am, which had proudly opened the futuristic, circular complex in 1962; Muschamp had described it as looking like "a skirt flying up doing the Peppermint Twist." Delta, too, had announced grand plans to fix it, which struck many observers as dubious, given the airline's financial troubles. But Delta was first tarting up the gate space for Song, which, by its very proximity, was a constant spur to the JetBlue troops.

If JFK Airport was a metaphor for the troubled airline business, then the wild card in all this was Song. It was difficult to assess how well Song was doing; the results from the unit were folded into those from the parent company. That didn't stop analysts and other pundits from speculating that Song had fallen far short of expectations and that it would be unlikely to recoup the generous subsidy that Delta's top management had rashly approved earlier in the year. That made it all the more frustrating to the JetBlue team as they witnessed Delta's saturation of the New York City market: Huge banners were going up in the East Village, Chelsea, and other hip precincts; advertisements for Song were appearing in subway cars and on commuter trains; glossy ads were filling the pages of magazines to coincide with the rollout of live television reception aboard its planes. Delta had even taken out a short-term lease on a retail space at the corner of Prince and Mercer streets in SoHo, one of New York City's most expensive addresses, to house an "experiential" boutique of sorts to tout Song's services, including selling Kate Spade–designed handbags and other accessories that would soon go on sale on Song flights. Delta had a harder time duplicating one other aspect of JetBlue, however; Song had drawn only a tepid response from the media, in part because of the lack of a powerful personality to sell it. John Selvaggio, Song's president, had gamely attempted to show he was a regular guy by playing in a rock band on Friday nights at the Song boutique, and according to some Song employees, he did strive to duplicate some of the JetBlue esprit de corps, often meeting with the rank and file. However, when the inevitable articles appeared comparing the writer's firsthand experiences on Song and JetBlue, it was clear Delta had not come close to diminishing JetBlue's edge in the image wars. One reporter for the *New York Times* Sunday travel section filed a report that was replete with embarrassing faux pas on the part of the Song crew: A sandwich he'd ordered in advance, online, wasn't available, and the flight attendant had scolded him for not requesting it earlier. Specialty cocktails and other advertised items fell short of expectations. The new crop of JetBlue clones apparently had been rushed into service without close attention to the details. It was much simpler, after all, to copy the adamantly no-frills style of Southwest.

Selvaggio and others did have a point when they grumbled about the inordinate amount of attention the smaller line was getting. Delta was about ten times the size of JetBlue, operating one thousand flights a day at Atlanta alone, to more than two hundred destinations and fifty countries. International services and hub-and-spoke operations are far more complex to manage than the type of point-to-point domestic services that are the hallmark of Southwest, JetBlue, and most other low-fare upstarts. Major airlines had long complained about JetBlue's "cherry-picking" of their best markets, one critic griping that "JetBlue only flies to places where they can make a profit." (Edmondson-Jones's response: "Isn't making a profit what we're supposed to be doing?") Like public utilities, the largest airlines had had to develop their route systems over years of tight regulation, sometimes for political reasons as much as for profits. Some less lucrative flights to small communities continue to receive federal subsidies under the Essential Air Service program, which, like farm price supports, enjoys support in Congress. While it was easy to dismiss the major airlines' problems as stemming from poor management, intransigent unions, or simply the vulnerability of the airlines to forces beyond their control, the fact was that a Delta or American was a different animal and its business model was a far cry from that of a small company like JetBlue. You could almost hear the mutterings from the executive suites of the big guys: Just wait till you get to be our size.

It wasn't as if Neeleman and Barger hadn't thought of that. They needed more than a new terminal to accommodate their growth; perhaps they needed more internal structure as well. One of their most recent top-level hires had been from Delta, of all places: Vicky Stennes, who had worked her way up in Atlanta from flight attendant to a sort of in-flight service doyenne in the late 1990s, was brought in as the new vice president of in-flight service. The personification of the old Delta culture, she is a petite blonde with an ingratiating manner and easy laugh, but she is also quite direct when necessary.

Stennes was told to take charge of the growing in-flight corps and to organize the in-flight supervisors, which, in typical JetBlue parlance, had been known as in-flight support specialists. Stennes had no problem with calling them supervisors. "What's wrong with that? Let's call it what it is." Their role is, after all, to fly around and spot any nascent problems—burnout, erratic service, lack of interest—that threaten to erode the vaunted JetBlue experience. Stennes had seen Delta grow from several thousand flight attendants to fifteen thousand; she knew what it would require to deliver on Neeleman's promise to "preserve this culture."

So it all went back to Neeleman's question: Is JetBlue for real? On its face, that was a ridiculous question. Of course JetBlue is for real, and Neeleman, who hardly needed another encomium to prove it, was, in early 2004, named by *Time* magazine as one of the one hundred most influential leaders in the world. It was an acknowledgment that what-ever happened to JetBlue two years, or even ten years, hence, Neele-man's airline had had an effect far beyond the confines of his own company. A more objective measure of the previous year's results of-fered further proof that JetBlue had bucked the odds and that the as-saults from American and Delta had had little discernible impact on JetBlue's business. Planes were so full—88 percent of all seats in some markets—that JetBlue had had to slow its original plan to have thirty cities on its route map within the first three years and instead concen-trate on adding more daily flights to those where it was scrambling to keep up with demand, such as those golden routes to Florida. True, JetBlue's stock price had dropped down into the mid-20s range; even adjusted for the stock split it was down somewhat from the giddy levels of the previous year. That had precipitated some hand-wringing among the investment crowd and had sparked some sneering among the traders on the Internet about whether the company was heading for a dot-com-style "correction." Neeleman himself was constantly warn-ing employees not to get too caught up in the market gyrations. He even turned this into material for his town hall sessions, recounting the time his own parents had greeted him at the airport by scolding him with "What happened to our stock?" after a sudden drop in the value of their JetBlue investment. "And I said, I'll tell you what hap-pened. . . . It was probably too high!" That would hardly be amusing to a day trader, but Neeleman had a point: More sober-minded analysts would say the stock price was if anything overpriced in relation to the company's size.

The year 2003 was, after all, supposed to be JetBlue's make or break year. It was understood this meant moving from the uncertain realm of a start-up airline to the more respectable territory of an established company

bluestreak

in the field. JetBlue was nearly five years old, and it was nearing the end of the Federal Aviation Administration's probation period for new entrants. It was about to hit another milestone, surpassing the one-billion-dollars-a-year-in-revenue mark that would meet the Transportation Department's definition of "major airline." It was about to break into the top ten companies in the field. Gone would be the constant worrying over the short shelf life of upstarts, the references to People Express, and all the annoyances that a newcomer must accept as the price of entry.

Down the hall from the marketing department, David Neeleman and Dave Barger were pulling together the data that would show whether JetBlue had passed the test. The fact that David and Dave (the reference is, typically, singular) had survived so long was yet more evidence, for the enduring bond between these two diametrically opposed personalities continued to amaze outsiders. While it superficially resembled the traditional Mr. Inside–Mr. Outside teaming that exists at many companies, Dave Barger was such a strong number two (he actually has more senior executives directly reporting to him than does Neeleman) that it seemed they had pulled off that rarity—an equal partnership.

In fact, the men are so joined at the hip that they share an assistant, Carol Archer, who came to JetBlue in 1999 with Dave Barger. Both have modest offices for people of their stature, and Neeleman's is decorated sparely with family photos and memorabilia and has the unlived-in look of someone who abhors structure and routine.

They appear to work well, in part because they operate on parallel tracks; "we can be in the same room but it's as if we were in different solar systems," Barger observed. Each has his interests: Barger frequently talks with the pilots and airport rank and file; Neeleman loves the marketing and sales side, and he still personally reads over mail from customers and responds with personal notes or phone calls. Those who share the corridor with Neeleman—operations head Al Spain, Vicky Stennes, and Nigel Adams, the vice president of customer service—on the east side of the eighth floor are in sync with his style.

A typical week for them would go something like this: Monday morning starts out with a weekly strategy meeting at 10:00 A.M., usually chaired by Neeleman, where everyone reports on the previous week's progress and how advance bookings are shaping up. The Darien team, hooked up on speakerphone, weighs in with its more detailed analyses of demand, of which flights show promise, the laggards. Much of the meeting is also devoted to where they might fly next, all those hundreds of cities that are on their list, now that the trimmer 190 airplane will join the mix.

Monday afternoon, Neeleman, Barger, Tom Kelly, Jim Hnat, and others hold a separate phone conference of the executive crew, an often lengthy discussion of all company business.

Tuesday or Wednesday might find one or both of the Davids on the road; they each continue to travel at least once a week to test if the JetBlue experience is where it should be. Neeleman has many invitations to speak before groups as diverse as business schools and charitable organizations, to the myriad travel organizations that have adopted him as a sort of mascot. Barger is often detailed to handle some of these as well as meeting frequently with the pilots and teaching the now essential "principles of leadership" they had developed to ward off any strains in their growing organization.

Then there are the company events. Perhaps heeding the example of Southwest as it grew, there are parties on Friday afternoons at HQ, on an outdoor deck weather permitting, with beer and wine for a buck.

So this is what it was like, the end of 2003. JetBlue had clocked in as the most full and most profitable of the entire airline business. Forget about buzz for a moment, said David and Dave, here is what we did this year:

> ➤ flew a schedule of 70,000 flights, with only 0.5 percent canceled due to bad weather or other snafus
>
> ➤ had only six maintenance-related cancellations the entire year
>
> ➤ carried a record load factor of 84.5 percent

Any airline veteran knows how hard this is to pull off. Herb Kelleher had long avoided putting Southwest planes into the Northeast for fear that would tarnish his on-time record.

Every morning, in fact, the first thing most JetBlue workers see when they log on to the company intranet is a box labeled BLUE PERFORMANCE, which includes the previous day's results: on-time arrivals, departures, any delays of more than fifteen minutes (which is when the government regards a flight as late). Those who crave more detail can surf to a page called "Flight Clarification Data," which describes the reason behind the delays; for example, "vomit all over seat," "fuel truck arrived late," "medical emergency in-bound DIV to GEG" (translation: a medical emergency forced the plane to divert to another airport).

And for the employees who must deal with this daily there was the most palpable evidence it was paying off at the end of 2003: A profit-sharing check would soon be mailed out, with each person getting 17 percent of his pretax earnings in a lump sum.

It was inevitable, then, that someone would ask the question: What is wrong with this picture? In early 2004, Wendy Zellner, a *BusinessWeek* editor who had followed JetBlue since the outset, was inspired to find out. Zellner accompanied Neeleman and a gaggle of JetBlue executives from New York to Boston in early January for the ritual ribbon cutting to usher in service out of Boston. It was the usual corn-filled extravaganza, with television crews, a fife-and-drum band, and other "characters"—Neeleman preferred to hire people to dress in costumes rather than play the clown himself—and it went smoothly, or so they thought.

Then Zellner's article came out. IS JETBLUE'S FLIGHT PLAN FLAWED? asked the headline, referring to "miscalculations" and "cutthroat competition" as among the many challenges it faced. But the article was more disturbing in its portrayal of Neeleman himself; Zellner had assembled a pile of anecdotal evidence—even obtaining some highly embarrassing quotes from Vicki Neeleman and Carol Archer—that created the impression of an "almost childishly impulsive" executive, who was "easily bored and distracted." Worse, it criticized him for a "lack of humility" that masked the fact that "he is not a guy to run a day-to-day business," according to another damning quote from one of his admirers, Mark Hill of WestJet. And it seemed to imply that Neeleman was neglecting Barger, who, Zellner wrote, was working without a contract because they hadn't gotten around to negotiating it.

Neeleman, close aides reported, was very hurt by this withering profile. Barger moved quickly to reassure people that he wasn't disturbed by the lack of a long-term contract. However, a rumor quickly began circulating that Richard Branson was, in fact, trying to hire away Barger to head up yet another attempt to launch a discount airline in the United States. This time, Branson wouldn't wait for the United States to change its laws on foreign ownership. Poaching Barger would be a coup; the rumor, however, turned out to be baseless.

Perhaps Zellner's tough piece was yet another rite of passage—the price of playing in the big leagues. But a close reading of the story, however, reveals that it was, on balance, quite positive, applauding the company's strong balance sheet, its low debt-to-capital ratio, all the other good objective measures of a company's strength—and proof that after five years, it had finally shed the baggage of the upstart crowd.

The Boston debut was notable for another reason: On that very day, American Airlines announced an exceptionally generous ticket deal, where passengers who flew two round-trips on American out of Boston or New York's JFK to Florida or California—the very routes where it competed with JetBlue—would get a free ticket anywhere in the world. It was "Kill JetBlue" time again.

An internal American Airlines newsletter to its employees in the eastern United States left no doubt what it had in mind. "This is the first in a series of aggressive marketing programs that you'll see this year to remind customers of the good things they get from American," it said, citing those advantages as the scope of its route system, its frequent flier program, and "the experienced employees who deliver it all.

"There are some who expect American to turn tail and run from the limited-choice competitors encroaching on our markets. We think not, especially when these carriers encroach on our important cities. Every employee can remind our customers that flying involves far more than blue potato chips and TV."

When someone leaked them a copy, David and Dave were both amused and appalled. "Wow!" they wrote in a "Blue Note" to employees. "If that isn't a backhanded tribute to JetBlue." The wording of the American message was telling: the sense of entitlement implied in the reference to "our cities," the allusion to "experienced employees," which in airline terms is code for the very issue that was giving them so much grief—the large number of senior employees who were drawing much higher salaries, on average, than at a newer airline like JetBlue—workers who American was at that moment asking to take a large pay cut to restore the airline to financial health. To JetBlue partisans at least, it was a study in arrogance; proof, if any was needed, of the cluelessness of the people running the bulk of the American airline business.

"Make no mistake about it; our competitors would simply like to see JetBlue as part of the history books so that they can revert to their old broken models of high fares, high cost structures, and caring very little for the customer.

"The airline industry has always been one where 'attacks' have been commonplace as a competitive weapon. As others promote their money-losing ideas aimed at us, we'll continue to respond with moneymaking ones."

Those money-making ones were on everyone's minds as David Neeleman called the company's second annual shareholders' meeting on May 26, 2004 in the third floor auditiorium at the Forest Hills head-quarters. There was every reason to be pleased: a healthy net income of $109 million on sales of just under $1 billion. And there were more awards: JetBlue had just won first place in a highly respected airline quality survey, an annual ranking by two midwestern academics who consider only objective standards as reported by the Transportation De-partment: on-time performance, lost baggage, and the like. JetBlue had not, it seemed, succumbed to the sophomore slump that had bedeviled other promising upstarts from People Express on down. There was more promising news: In-flight entertainment was getting a lift from a new raft of offerings, such as on-demand movies and satellite radio, and JetBlue was branching into the Caribbean and other profit-making markets. It was now flying to twenty-seven cities.

There were, however, some less pleasant developments. JetBlue had failed to attract enough business on its Atlanta flights and decided to exit the city altogether, marking the first time in its short history it had retreated from a market. The first quarter of 2004 had also provided dis-turbing evidence that the pummeling from American's and Delta's free ticket deals had had an impact. That, plus a prolonged fare war on the transcontinental routes, had caused JetBlue to report a decline in its profits for the first time. And Neeleman also mentioned that taking out the infamous row 27 had raised costs somewhat, by having fewer seats over which to spread the expenses. "But two thirds of our seats have a thirty-four-inch seat pitch," he noted, pointing out that JetBlue had beaten Delta and American in offering more legroom in coach.

What about all those competitive assaults? he was asked. "We have a strong balance sheet; we've got staying power. It hurts them more than it hurts us."

Later that day, Neeleman jumped into his SUV, accompanied by Rob Land, and Neal Moszkowski, an investment banker for George Soros's Quantum Fund who'd just been reelected to serve on JetBlue's board. Neeleman pulled out onto the Grand Central Parkway and, spying some traffic, jumped off to detour through the wilds of Queens. "Hey, David, you're really a New Yorker now," kidded Moszkowski as Neeleman showed off his driving prowess. Inside the vehicle was more evidence of the week he'd been having: empty Snapple bottles, food containers, and kids sporting equipment strewn over the seats, a mess that had prompted John Owen to crack that "the back of David's car is compost." On the dashboard were a copy of the book of Mormon, CDs of music by the Mormon Tabernacle Choir, and a bobble-headed plastic Jesus, a tongue-in-cheek gift from Gareth Edmondson-Jones.

Neeleman was on his way to the Mormon temple across from Lincoln Center in New York City, which would be briefly open to visitors before closing to all non-Mormons on June 6. Neeleman was spending a lot of his spare time these days giving tours to his non-Mormon friends.

First, however, they had some pressing business to discuss. JetBlue was about to inaugurate its first flight to a foreign destination, Santo Domingo in the Dominican Republic. JetBlue's flights to Puerto Rico had done very well, and this was regarded as a logical extension into the region, especially given New York City's large population of Dominican immigrants. This would mean, however, that JetBlue would have to fly into another terminal at JFK with customs facilities, and it also required delicate intergovernmental negotiations, as do all foreign routes. The Dominican Republic and Haiti, which share the island of Hispaniola, had just been devastated by flooding and several towns on the border between the countries had been nearly wiped out.

"Here we are, this rich company coming in from this rich country," Rob Land pointed out. "We have to do something," Neeleman agreed, he had been especially moved by the story of a little girl who had lost her entire family in the deluge. But how to help? There was the U.S. embassy to be considered, and all the other diplomatic nuances of operating in a foreign nation. Neeleman proposed writing a check for ten thousand dollars, but it would be the U.S. ambassador who would present it to the Dominican government.

As Neeleman zipped along the Long Island Expressway, he spied a billboard with the telltale chartreuse and lemon colors of Song, this one touting the airline's cuisine. Everyone had a good laugh, for while he wasn't going to comment for the record in the annual meeting on the rumors that he'd heard, they all knew that Delta was preparing to dramatically scale back Song flights in September. In fact, Fred Reid, the president of Delta who had been one of Song's most ardent supporters, had just quit the company to head up Richard Branson's latest quest to form a Virgin America in the United States. Several other Song executives were rumored to be jumping ship. And former Delta CEO Leo Mullin, who had been pushed out earlier in the year because of an overly generous pay package he had awarded himself, had been succeeded by Gerald Grinstein, a tough-minded airline veteran who reportedly was less than enamored with the whole notion of Song to begin with. Some Song flight attendants were said to be trying to get their old jobs back on Delta's mainline flights, so worried were they that someone was about to pull the plug.

As Neeleman pulled up to the corner of Sixty-fifth Street and Broadway, his thoughts were not on Song or even the airlines, for that matter: He was checking to see if the gaggle of anti-Mormon protesters who had been congregating in front of the building were in evidence. He was relieved to see they had decamped, for he was expecting a steady stream of visitors that afternoon. A family he had befriended in Connecticut was to arrive shortly; their daughter had converted to the Mormon faith and would soon be married at the Manhattan temple. Her parents, however, were not Mormon and therefore would not be able to attend. Neeleman had reached out to them in their distress over their exclusion from their child's wedding and thought that showing them the room where the ceremony would take place would offer some solace.

As he stood there waiting for his guests, a hulking black stretch limousine pulled up. Out jumped two burly men with walkie-talkies, signaling that some notable person was behind the tinted windows. It was State Senator Joseph Bruno, the majority leader and one of the most powerful politicians in New York State. Neeleman greeted him warmly, and they set off for an abbreviated twenty-minute version of the hour-long tour, punctuated by factoids helpfully supplied for relevance: "Did you know that the Mormon religion got its start in upstate New York?" Or that "there are forty-two thousand Mormons living in the New York area?" Bruno seemed quite impressed by the number, even more so when he learned that the Mormon faith is regarded as the world's fastest growing religion, with twelve million members.

Neeleman had been spending a lot of time in Albany of late. He had been pushing for repeal of an in-state fuel tax that fell most heavily on airlines like JetBlue, which flew many flights within the state. It was of course those very flights to neglected upstate outposts that had helped garner JetBlue's political support in the first place. A friendly relationship with Bruno was to be encouraged.

Bruno soon sped off with his entourage, and Neeleman was back in form, standing outside the temple, chatting on his cell phone, stopping occasionally to greet friends and family. He waved to his twenty-one-year-old daughter, Erica, who was volunteering as a tour guide at the temple; another relative dropped by to say hello.

There were many more who knew him, too: passersby who recognized him and just wanted to tell him how much they liked JetBlue.

There were about twelve million of those customers the previous year. There could be thirty million by 2008. JetBlue was hiring between five and ten people a day to keep up. And David Neeleman would still try to meet every one.

epilogue

"You define a good flight by negatives," Paul Theroux wrote in *The Great Patagonian Express*. "You didn't crash, you didn't throw up, you weren't late, you weren't nauseated by the food. And so you're grateful."

Theroux wrote those words twenty-five years ago, well before he could have encountered David Neeleman's determination to make him grateful for more than having arrived in one piece. Perhaps that, more than anything, is the essence of what JetBlue has done so far: Neeleman has not only succeeded where many others have failed, but he has also changed our expectations in a fundamental way. We no longer have to define a flight in terms of what it wasn't.

So in May of 2004, I paid a visit to David Neeleman at his Connecticut office, to ask him to put, in his own words, what it is he thinks he has accomplished. It is, conveniently, exactly five years to the day I first met him in a barren office suite on Park Avenue, when he was still just another entrepreneur with a big idea and scant odds of succeeding. This seems a decent interval of time upon which to reflect on his company's journey from anonymous start-up to "It" airline. There can't be any doubt now that he is in it for the long haul; surely he will oblige with some sweeping pronouncements about what it all means.

Naturally, he refuses to play along.

"The jury is still out," he says, scowling. "It is too early to say whether we have made it." There is much uncertainty: The big airlines are wounded but, to borrow from Mark Twain, reports of their demise may be exaggerated. They'll continue to seek new ways to beat up on Jet-Blue, Neeleman knows; it's in their DNA. And as air travel continues to recover and some of the big players get their costs under control, they could become formidable opponents yet again. There are other unknowns, too. What, for example, a second successful terror attack could do to the airlines. "It's unthinkable," says Neeleman.

Then when will you be satisfied? I ask. "Ten years, fifteen years . . ." he drifts off because the obvious conclusion is that you can never rest, especially in a business that has seen so many promising launches come to naught.

But isn't what you wrote back in 1997 still true? I ask him, reminding him that in his first business plan he had laid out the foundation that is still serving him today: plenty of cash in hand, a young fleet that grows by a new plane every month, low costs, and the motivated people to keep it that way.

He gives me a look that says "Don't believe what you hear."

"You know, on September 11, we had only forty-two million dollars in cash," he says, which is startling: I hadn't heard that before, although it makes some sense, since the IPO that was to have been announced that morning was intended to raise a substantial amount. "Even National Airlines had more than us. They had fifty million dollars and they lost it really fast. So that isn't why we made it. It wasn't the money."

And so National is gone, as are virtually all the other members of the class of 1999–2000, which had appeared to be one of the more promising groups of upstart airlines to arrive on the scene since deregulation. Why is it, then, that most start-ups continue to fail, even after all the lessons that could be drawn from their predecessors? Is JetBlue just a fluke? There have been almost no true independent start-up airlines of any size since 2000, just a flurry of stand-ins from the big airlines, and even the newest, Independence Air, doesn't quite live up to its name. On closer inspection it's just a renamed, retooled version of a regional airline, Atlantic Coast, that had been a United Airlines feeder at Dulles Airport for years.

No, the approval process in Washington is just too daunting, and the barriers to entry for a new airline more formidable than they have been since the days when the airlines were so tightly regulated that no new airline was allowed to start up for nearly forty years. Many forget how hard it was for JetBlue to succeed, what a long shot it was—and how many people were openly skeptical of its chances.

So, is JetBlue a "destructive innovator" as one pundit put it, a destroyer of what came before? Consider this: In the middle of 2004, the airline business can be divided, loosely, into two types of competitors—low-cost airlines that charge low fares and high-cost airlines that charge low fares. One makes money; one loses a bundle. Simply put, airlines have recognized that they can no longer force the traveling public to accept extortionate prices, even the business travelers who had gone along with this in exchange for convenience. JetBlue had not set out to court the frequent flier set, but it is steadily becoming their airline of choice by offering not just a better coach product but the reliability that these travelers so crave.

So it's no longer just Southwest and a few low-fare lemmings on one side versus the Big Six on the other. The low-fare camp, in just three years, has gone from flying 10 percent to almost 40 percent of all travelers in the United States. The effect upon pricing is enormous. At this writing, it is actually cheaper in real dollar terms to fly across country than it was since People Express stopped serving the New York to California routes in 1986. This was not all due to JetBlue, of course, but one could argue that its entry into these long-distance routes paved the way. The larger airlines, in a sense, are facing death by a thousand fare cuts. Ultimately they may have to decide whether to desert this sector of the market altogether and stick to higher yield premium service on routes where it makes sense.

There is talk about a paradigm shift, away from the larger network airlines that tried to be all things to all people. In this scenario, different airlines would focus on what they do best, be it international service, domestic point-to-point flights, regional service to smaller communities. And if that outcome sounds vaguely familiar, it should if you traveled by air prior to 1978: That's more or less how the regulated airlines were grouped, and they did not stray far from their assigned role.

Then again, the airline shakeout to end all shakeouts has been predicted at least once a decade since 1978. If this time the transition has been prolonged, it is due in no small part to the government largesse and prospect of loan guarantees that has ensured that no large airline fails, especially in an election year.

Neeleman likes to refer to the nontangible side of his success as "all that Kumbayah stuff." It all goes back to what is drummed into JetBlue's flight attendant training: that mix of empathy and execution, that sense for what the customer needs, and then—and that's the hardest part—delivering on it consistently. For all the hype and the buzz JetBlue generates, it's the less sexy stuff—getting the bags to the carousel within twenty minutes, for example—that ultimately seals the deal, creates that bond, that guarantees you'll fly on JetBlue and be treated with dignity. "And for the larger airlines, that's the hardest thing to do—to change that culture," says Neeleman. "Here, what we have is a deep understanding of the customer instead of the passenger. And there's our nomenclature: It is a little thing, but it's also a mind-set. If you are in a meeting and someone says the word 'passenger' the whole room says"—and he lowers his voice to a bass—"'customer, customer' . . . and it's not a mistake you make more than once."

On my way to see Neeleman, I'd made a list of everything I could think of that JetBlue does differently and came up with more than two dozen, from using only home-based reservationists to the crisis fund to the no-overbooking policy and compensating delayed passengers.

One detail—so obscure that I had left it off the list—speaks volumes about Neeleman and his attention to detail. When it came time to start handing out employee identification numbers in 1999, Neeleman told everyone that unlike most companies, where they are assigned sequentially, at JetBlue, the numbers would be scrambled. But it comes up as we talk about what Neeleman likes to refer to as his "covenant" with his workforce. "When I was at Southwest, there was this hierarchy, this class system based on what seniority number you had. And the numbers were in sequence, so if somebody had a number like 30,000, the attitude was like 'You don't really know much, you haven't been around for long.' But someone who has a double-digit number or a triple-digit number seemed to have a certain entitlement.

"So I said we are not going to do that. We are going to randomly assign every single number. And my number came out and it was starting with an eight, 82226. I would have been employee number one, if it was done logically."

It's a symbolic gesture, to be sure, but one I'd heard about from flight attendants and pilots—it obviously had made an impression. "You can tell if someone is grateful. And I think our people are grateful; they want to go the extra mile."

While many people assume it is Herb Kelleher of Southwest who inspired him most, Neeleman says his hero is really Sam Walton, the Wal-Mart founder, who famously studied the competition closely and figured out how to deliver superior service for less money. Even the reference to Walton has a darker side for it raises the question of what happens to a company once the founder has moved on, or passed on.

But to those who wonder if JetBlue could withstand the inevitable changes that will come with maturity, it is Southwest that provides the answer. Yes, Kelleher stepped down from day-to-day management responsibilities in 2001, and there were signs of strain in early 2004, with the departure of Kelleher's handpicked successor and difficult negotiations with the flight attendants. But there is something lasting there that can withstand the inevitable shifts at the top. Of course, JetBlue could hit some rough spots—for example, the prospect of unionizing the employees is always there—but it would be wrong to assume that it in itself would destroy the company culture. One other telling detail: Most of Neeleman's original team was still with him five years later. Dave Barger had just signed a five-year contract and even Usto Schulz, at eighty-two, had been brought back from a brief period of semiretirement to work on the FAA certification of the Embraer 190 jet.

For whatever happens, there is that other covenant with the customer, and it is that that Neeleman is attending to as we speak. He jumps up in midsentence, pulls out a laptop, and starts answering e-mail while continuing an increasingly disjointed conversation with me. He still doesn't kick me out and, in fact, seems to enjoy narrating the exchanges he's conducting. Soon, he's e-mailing with an obstinate customer who's got a beef about boarding protocols. One suspects he enjoys this back and forth with the people who are buying his product, paying his employees, making it all possible.

And he, too, is a customer, and he continues to sample not only his own product but that of his rivals. He recounts a particularly grim experience on another airline, and it apparently still rankles, although it is strangely gratifying, too, to get fresh confirmation for the reason why so many customers are flocking to his company. He won't identify the airline involved, but it is obviously one of the larger companies whose employees are, understandably, demoralized. To Neeleman, though, nothing could explain the hostility that was directed his way on a recent trip. A flight attendant shouted at Neeleman when he got on the plane with his cell phone in hand and wouldn't let up the whole trip, even refusing to give him information about the gate where they would land.

"So I was ready to throttle the guy," he says, chuckling at the bizarre prospect of his being led away in handcuffs. "I consider myself a really nice person, but when I get bad service, I turn into a total jerk, I blow up . . . and one of these days you are going to be reading about me in the newspapers . . ."

Neeleman, it seems, is on a first-name basis with the CEO of that airline. "I was going to write to him to tell him how bad this person is, and then I thought, 'Wait, he's a competitor. Maybe I'll just let this person continue mistreating his customers!'"

So that is what it comes down to, those interactions, the raw material of the service business. And Neeleman mentions a report not long ago about an American Airlines employee who was assigned to fly around on the competition and report back on how their service compared. The report on JetBlue gave it the highest possible marks in all categories and made particular mention of how JetBlue crew members addressed customers by name, looked them in the eye, all those little things. Inevitably it got circulated among industry insiders. "And shortly afterward, they sent out a memo basically telling their people how they should act toward their customers," he says, laughing.

"It's kind of absurd, but if the whole industry is trying harder to be better because one competitor said 'Look, you can't do this,' then that is good for the industry, it is good for the traveling public." Perhaps, then, Neeleman is ready to accept that he has made a difference.

afterword

In the year that has passed since this book was first published, the basic outlines of the JetBlue saga are, for a company in a volatile business, remarkably stable. Well into its sixth year in business, the airline was continuing on its contrarian path, growing while its rivals were shrinking. New planes were arriving at the rate of one every ten days, from Airbus in France and now, Brazilian jetmaker Embraer. And while it was hiring between eight to ten new people each day (whom it still insists on calling "crewmembers" instead of employees), it kept the Kool-Aid flowing; even in a period where the company suffered a spate of delays, consumer complaints remained among the lowest in the airline industry. There had been no Krispy Kreme–style reversals, no major defections at the top—David Neeleman and Dave Barger were ever the odd couple in charge of the day-to-day running of the airline. Even the industry backdrop has remained distressingly familiar: The major airlines in 2005 were on course to lose, collectively, another $8 billion as jet fuel prices spiked. Although struggling US Airways merged with America West Airways in a last-ditch bid for survival, at this writing United couldn't seem to put an end to its protracted bankruptcy case, and it had been joined in Chapter 11 purgatory by Northwest and Delta Air Lines. And Delta continued to pour money into its low fare spin-off, Song, no doubt disappointing those at JetBlue who had expected this brazen pilfering of their formula to vanish fairly quickly. No one in the airlines believed Song made any money; rather, it survived simply by delivering a better alternative to the lackluster service on its parent airline.

The sharp rise in oil prices didn't spare JetBlue, of course: In 2004, JetBlue eked out a profit of nearly $50 million, and while the fact that it made money at all should have been cause for celebration, the newspaper headlines now read JETBLUE PROFITS PLUMMET. Naturally, its share price slid accordingly: In late 2005 it was hovering around its fifty-two-week low of $17 and warning of a fourth quarter loss. Neeleman's response was not to spin the news as much as to ignore it. When I once asked him about JetBlue's sagging stock price, he responded that he couldn't care less. He was not being facetious; his focus, as always, is not on the next quarter, but the next year, the next decade. And now when David and Dave look out of their eighth floor offices at JetBlue's Queens headquarters, they can spy JetBlue planes heading not only for JFK, but to LaGuardia Airport, whose status as the Manhattanites' airport of choice had been eroded by JetBlue's success at Kennedy. JetBlue has now filled out its map by landing at Newark Airport, where Dave Barger once ran the sort of complex operations at Continental that Jet-Blue inevitably will undertake—for its aim ultimately is to have a fleet of more than four hundred planes. (There was also no small satisfaction in expanding into the New Jersey bailiwick of Continental, whose former CEO, Gordon Bethune, had long predicted that JetBlue would tank like most other airline startups.)

But there is another side to the story that does not show up on balance sheets or SEC filings. JetBlue has moved from the fizzy startup stage to a more predictable middle age; in the airlines, getting past your fifth year is a rare achievement. But the company must keep expanding to preserve startup attributes that are so critical to success: low overall costs (it still beats the industry with costs of six to seven cents a seat mile), a relatively junior work force, and more planes flying more hours (they now spend an average of nearly fourteen hours in the air each day), which spreads its fixed costs over more assets.

And therein lies the test of whether JetBlue can ultimately pull it off. As Neeleman himself acknowledged recently when discussing a disappointing quarter (where JetBlue still managed to be one of the few airlines to post a profit), "It isn't easy to grow as fast as we're growing." You don't need to be an industry insider to know that managing an airline with close to one hundred planes, in the treacherous conditions of the Northeast, comes with a risk: that things will start to slip, that customers will get disappointed. Suddenly, the day may come that the public will see you as just another airline. Whether that's a fair perception is almost beside the point.

It is not an exaggeration to say that much of what occupies the top brass at JetBlue is defending against that very prospect. The spring of 2005 provided just such an opportunity; it was, to put it mildly, one of the more trying periods in JetBlue's short history. A succession of storms in the eastern half of the United States, combined with operational difficulties at Fort Lauderdale Airport, resulted in JetBlue plummeting to the bottom of the on-time performance rankings: In one month, it sank to last place among the nineteen airlines whose punctuality is tracked by the Department of Transportation. JetBlue tried to put a positive spin on it, pointing out that it, unlike most other airlines, has a policy of not canceling flights outright (which would get them off the delay list). Somehow that seemed hollow; when JetBlue was at the top of the heap, of course, it found little to criticize in the way the data was gathered.

So what did Neeleman and Barger make of all this? They simply did more of what they've been doing all along: fly their own airline at least once a week and make a point of meeting all new crew members. One day at headquarters last summer, Neeleman stopped by a class of flight attendants about to graduate. "I worry sometimes we focus so much on CPR and not enough on customer service," he told them. He was distressed by a recent incident in which a flight attendant got into a dispute with a passenger that degenerated into an ugly scene, causing a two-hour delay. "You know when that happens, we don't just lose that customer for life, we lose everyone around them. . . . I know you have to follow the rules, but just remember . . . there is a way to enforce these things in a nice way."

As another sign of its maturity, the company no longer has to field questions about whether it will survive: that part of the story seems settled. Its brand is so firmly entrenched that JetBlue is now seen as a desirable partner by companies many times its size: American Express, for example, courted JetBlue to launch a cobranded charge card in the middle of 2005. The brand has also thrived despite the loss of some key people from its startup. Much of the Virgin gang had moved on by 2005; Alex Wilcox bolted for an opportunity as president of a startup in India, Kingfisher Airlines, named for the beer business owned by its tycoon founder. The Mumbai-based airline has styled itself as the JetBlue of the subcontinent, proving, if nothing else, the name recognition of Wilcox's old employer is perhaps more widespread than anyone realized. Amy Curtis-McIntyre left to move to Chicago with her husband and work as a consultant while raising two young sons. Gareth Edmondson-Jones moved back to his native Australia. But on the operations side, arguably as vital to preserving the JetBlue brand, most of the early recruits were still in place—people like Chris Collins, Tom Anderson, Al Spain, and Usto Schulz, the fly boys, the "ops" guys. Their work, by definition, is less visible to the public, except on days like September 21, 2005, when a JetBlue plane with landing gear problems made an emergency landing in Los Angeles under extraordinary circumstances: The plane circled for three hours to burn up fuel, an ordeal that was broadcast without interruption on cable TV networks—and to the passengers themselves via seatback televisions. The smooth landing and deft handling of the situation by the JetBlue crew drew an astonishing amount of positive coverage, almost rivaling the gushy tributes of its first year.

It was a sharp contrast to the privacy scandal of 2003, where JetBlue admitted its mistakes but nonetheless got a thorough drubbing in the press. Even there, JetBlue was ultimately vindicated; a federal judge last summer threw out the class action lawsuit filed by some JetBlue passengers, on the grounds that the plaintiffs could not prove damages.

Stop by Terminal Six at JFK, and you'll get another snapshot of JetBlue present and future: the traffic backing up, the crowds at the check-in counter, and, at times, the lines that Neeleman detests, although they do move smoothly. And the promised new terminal that will double JetBlue's gate space: After the much publicized deal that would preserve the historic TWA terminal next door, the negotiations with Port Authority dragged on for more than a year, but JetBlue was still aiming for a late 2008 opening date.

New terminals and new cities are one thing: Adding a new plane type to its fleet, as JetBlue intended to do in the fall of 2005, was far more dramatic and riskier than anything the company had done since its debut. After all, it went against one of the cardinal rules of the budget airline camp: Keep it simple. Herb Kelleher, after all, had long cited his all 737-fleet as a factor in Southwest's profitability. And JetBlue must convince a skeptical public that the new Embraer 190 plane, which can seat one hundred people, is not a cramped "regional" jet, which, to its chagrin, was how it was mistakenly labeled by the media at first. Crew members who had seen it, however, knew better: The plane was nothing like the puddle jumpers of yore; its fuselage was expanded by using a unique "double bubble" design, overlapping two circles to create more interior space. In fact, the plane was so unusual for its size, with oversize windows and two-by-two seating, that even the more skeptical observers were burbling about the jet's prospects with phrases like "category killer" that seemed more suggestive of a dot-com revival than of an old economy company like an airline.

Neeleman recalled the indignant reactions of some pundits: "They said, 'You're deviating from the Southwest model!' Well, we never were the Southwest model. . . . We took a lot of pages from their book but we wrote our own book." Despite the additional debt JetBlue took on to pay for its new fleet, and the added expenses of maintaining a different aircraft type, the belief was that the new plane would earn its keep by getting into more profitable markets where there was less competition and hence, higher fares.

Still, there will be many things that JetBlue can't alter to its liking: the traffic on the Van Wyck Expressway to JFK, for example, or the rising price of jet fuel, which had abruptly put an end to JetBlue's double-digit profit margins. JetBlue's annual reports inevitably trot out the parade of horribles—terrorism, labor strife, loss of a key person like Neeleman or Barger—that could write a new ending to the story. Neeleman often refers to his benchmark of success as simply this: "If the company disappeared tomorrow, would it matter?" By that modest standard, no one could dispute the durability of what he built.

October 2005

notes

This book is based on hundreds of hours of interviews with all the principal characters and on many hours spent in general observation at the company: at employee gatherings, at training sessions, in crew lounges, at airports, and on dozens of JetBlue flights. David Neeleman and Dave Barger sat for extended interviews and generously allowed me to approach many people inside the company. While this is not an authorized book, I was given access to many internal company communications, letters, e-mails, documents, and internally produced videos.

All interviews are by the author; reconstructions of specific meetings, events, or conversations where I was not present were based on accounts provided by the participants and cross-checked, where possible, with the others present. Where no citation is given for someone's words or thoughts, it is because the source is judged to be evident from the context or from surrounding citations.

For background on the history of Southwest Airlines, of Virgin Group, and of the airlines in general, I also drew on firsthand research from my years of covering the airlines, as well as on several books that are cited below.

Introduction Drinking the Blue Kool-Aid

Page

x   **drinking the blue Kool-Aid:** On November 18, 1978, 913 followers of the People's Temple perished in Jonestown, Guyana, after drinking cyanide-laced punch.

xii   **JetBlue received 130,000 applications:** From interviews and a flight training course July 6–30, 2003.

xiv   **the fifty-eight jet airlines:** Tom Norwood, *Deregulation Knockouts* (Sandpoint, Idaho: Airways International, 1996).

xv   **losses of twenty billion dollars:** Annual report, 2003, Air Transport Association, Washington, D.C.

xv   **Warren Buffett once joked:** Buffett has expressed this thought several times, in slightly differing versions: see *Fortune,* November 22, 1999.

notes

xv **a one-cent rise:** Estimate from the Air Transport Association, Washington, D.C.

xvii **fewer than 10 percent:** Department of Transportation Bureau of Transportation statistics.

One Flying Home

3 **special presidential commission:** National Commission to Ensure a Strong Competitive Airline Industry, 1993.

4 **David Neeleman was born:** Information on the Neeleman family tree from The Church of Latter-day Saints, Family Research Center, Ancestral Files; Sally Hulett born Massachusetts 1787, died 1856 in Iowa, en route to Utah. Her son, Edwin Whiting, had five wives, including Mary Elizabeth Cox, who led to the family line of David Neeleman's mother, Rose Lewis.

5 **grandfather's ten-thousand-acre ranch:** Now the Zion Ponderosa Ranch Resort in Mount Carmel, Utah, run by the Neeleman family, *Deseret News,* September 29, 2002.

6 **mom and pop coffee shops:** MINIATURE MARKET LEGACY LIVES ON, *Deseret News,* October 29, 2001.

6 **"He wanted to please everyone":** David Neeleman lecture at the Learning Annex, New York City, June 16, 2003.

6 **"I couldn't write well":** Interview with David Neeleman, July 2004.

9 **Big Pineapple:** Neeleman confirmed facts in interviews, May 1999 and May 2004.

10 **"I was devastated":** Neeleman talk at the Learning Annex, New York City, June 16, 2003.

11 **To lessen the risk:** Interview with Tom Kelly, February 2004.

12 **"He thinks like the customer":** Interview with Michael Lazarus, March 2004.

13 **"idea of JetBlue":** Interview with Tom Kelly, February 2004.

14 **slapped them with a two-hundred-thousand-dollar fine:** See Department of Transportation certification order December 1992.

14 **first female founder:** Jacquelyn Denalli, "An Airline of Her Own," *Nation's Business,* August 1993.

15 **"can't we be more like a hotel":** Interview with Tom Kelly, February 2004.

16 **"This was heresy":** Interview with Frankie Littleford, June 2004.

16 **"customers will never":** Quote from Chris Chiames, spokesman for Air Transport Association, 1993.

17 **lowest costs:** Jacquelyn Denalli, "An Airline of Her Own,"*Nation's Business,* August 1993.

18 **switch this business to Delta:** James S. Hirsch, "Delta's Bonuses to Travel Agents Spur Inquiry on Anti-Competitiveness Question," *Wall Street Journal* October 11, 1993.

18 **Neeleman's first appearance:** "Morris Air Official: 'Restructure Overrides,'" *Salt Lake Tribune,* June 3, 1993.

notes

18 **Hersh took to flying:** Interview with Dan Hersh, March 2004.

19 **"He's a creative guy":** Ibid.

19 **Delta had been flying:** Denalli, op cit.

20 **"swim with the sharks":** Jesus Sanchez, "Upstart Airline Winning the West," *Los Angeles Times,* December 12, 1993.

20 **highly lethal:** Interview with David Neeleman, November 2000.

21 **"We knew little about":** Interview with John Owen, February 2004.

Two Love Field

24 **"We were in complete shock":** Interview with Frankie Littleford, May 2004.

25 **the Palm Restaurant in Dallas:** Interview with Michael Lazarus, June 2004.

26 **"best place to work in America":** Robert Levering and Milton Moskowitz, *The 100 Best Companies to Work for in America* (New York: Bantam, 1993).

26 **The legend of Southwest began:** For a detailed account of the origins of Southwest Airlines, see Kevin L. Freiberg and Jaquelyn Freiberg, *NUTS!* (Austin: Texas Bard Press, 1996).

29 **"High Priest of Ha Ha":** "Is Herb Kelleher America's Best CEO?" *Fortune,* May 2, 1994.

30 **"That did it":** Interview with John Owen, February 2004.

30 **"fire watchers":** *Journal of Lending & Credit Risk Management,* May/June 1998, article based on Herb Kelleher's presentation at the Risk Management Association's annual conference, 1998.

31 **"David literally came in":** Interview with Ann Rhoades, May 2004.

32 **"Herb and Colleen":** Interview with Cathy Westrum, September 2003.

33 **if he was cut off:** Accounts of Neeleman's firing from interviews with Neeleman and Ann Rhoades in May 1999.

Three The Virgins

37 **on the cover of *Time*:** The January 13, 1986 issue of *Time* featured Donald Burr on the cover for an article entitled "Fare Games; Flying Has Never Been Cheaper."

38 **One day in 1996:** Interview with David Neeleman, May 1999; details confirmed by Burr in a talk at the Yale School of Management, April 8, 2004; notes provided by Louise Story.

39 **"Unwelcoming, unaesthetic":** James Kaplan, *The Airport: Planes, People, Triumphs, and Disasters at John F. Kennedy Airport* (New York: Quill, 1994), from the introduction.

39 **"depot from hell":** Ibid, p. xviii.

40 **"go bowling on the runways":** Interviews with David Neeleman, May 1999 and May 2004.

40 **"first mega-start-up":** Confidential business plan for New Air, August 1997.

41 **paltry ten million dollars:** Interview with Patrick Murphy, Deputy Secretary of the U.S. Department of Transportation, June 1998.

42 **initial seed money:** Details of Neeleman's investment from Confidential business plan, op. cit., and from a later version, dated June 1998.

43 **"I'd promised my":** Interview with Michael Lazarus, June 2004.

43 **Willie Sutton's explanation:** The bank robber is said to have responded to a question about why he chose his particular profession: "Because that's where the money is!"

44 **"ValuJet burned":** William Langewiesche, *Inside the Sky* (New York: Pantheon Press, 1998), pp. 190–232.

45 **They looked at Planet Hollywood:** Details from Confidential business plan for New Air, August 1997.

46 **ninth wealthiest individual:** Branson has made the list of wealthiest individuals in *Forbes* magazine since the 1990s.

46 **business world virgin:** Richard Branson, *Losing My Virginity* (New York: Times Business Books, 1998), p. 56.

46 **Branson had met privately:** Both Kelleher and Branson have confirmed their meetings, Branson in an interview with me, May 2004.

46 **improbable that Virgin:** Details of David Neeleman's initial dealings with Virgin Atlantic and Richard Branson are from several lengthy interviews with Alex Wilcox that took place from 2001 to 2004 as well as from interviews with David Neeleman, Richard Branson, David Tait, Michael Lazarus, Tom Kelly, and Kevin Murphy.

47 **Sky Train across the Atlantic:** The Laker Sky Train began transatlantic flights in 1977 and ceased operations in 1982. For a thorough account see Simon Calder, *No Frills* (New York: Virgin Books, 2003).

48 **Branson sued for libel:** Branson, *Losing My Virginity,* p. 339.

49 **antitrust laws:** Virgin filed a lawsuit against British Airways in U.S. federal district court in Manhattan in 1993; the court dismissed the case on summary judgment in 1999, a decision that was affirmed by the second circuit court of appeals in 2001.

49 **lofty-sounding "alliance":** Michael Meyers, "Is Big Bad?" *Condé Nast Traveler,* March 1997.

50 **an earlier try:** Branson, *Losing My Virginity,* pp. 9–12.

51 **"people think it's eight hundred miles":** Interview with David Neeleman, May 1999.

52 **"I bet you don't":** Interview with Kevin Murphy, February 2004.

54 **new scheduled airline applicants:** Department of Transportation Bureau of Transportation statistics.

55 **around twenty million dollars:** Confidential business plan for Virgin America, March 1998 (this was briefly the name on Neeleman's plan for New Air).

55 **"Branson got what David":** From interview with Tom Kelly, March 2004.

58 **"chick in a guy's world":** Interview with Amy Curtis-McIntyre, November 2003.

62 **spot of president:** Account of Dave Barger's background and subsequent dealings with Neeleman are from interviews with David Barger, May 1999, 2003, 2004, and Dan Hersh, March 2004.

64 **"big bang":** For a detailed account of the "big bang" merger, see Barbara Peterson and James Glab, *Rapid Descent* (New York: Simon & Schuster, 1994), pp. 206–15.

64 **Airports were jammed:** "Texas Air's Rapid Growth Spurs Surge in Complaints About Service," *Wall Street Journal*, February 26, 1987.

68 **Everyone assumed:** Interview with John Owen, February 2004.

70 **Boeing was operating:** The Boeing/Airbus interviews are from previously cited interviews with Owen, Barger, and Neeleman.

70 **memorandum of understanding:** The aircraft order was first reported on April 21, 1999, when the deal was finalized and announced to the press. See "Airbus Industrie Is Close to Winning $1 Billion Plane Order from Start-Up," *Wall Street Journal*, April 21, 1999.

Four Building Blue

Most of this chapter is based on firsthand observation of several meetings in July 1999 and on interviews with numerous participants—Amy Curtis-McIntyre, Alex Wilcox, and Gareth Edmondson-Jones—in the events chronicled.

71 **morning of June 16:** Account of meeting based on firsthand observation by the author.

72 **Pan Am building:** "Why Pan Am Sold the Pan Am Building," *BusinessWeek*, August 11, 1980.

72 **wealthy investor:** "Pan Am Thinks Small," *Business Week*, May 31, 1999.

75 **George Gershwin soundtrack:** "Listen Closely, These TV Ads Might Have a Familiar Ring," *Wall Street Journal*, October 22, 1987.

76 **"We did some research":** Interview with Douglas Atkin, May 2004.

78 **"crazy names in there":** Interview with Amy Curtis-McIntyre, November 2003.

85 **"They knew at midnight":** David Neeleman at a morning strategy meeting, July 1999.

86 **provoked such outrage:** Barbara Peterson, "What's Going on in the Galley?," *Frequent Flyer* magazine, December 1995.

90 **"Blue Notes":** This one was signed by Dave Barger, week of July 21, 1999.

Five Paper Airline

92 **David Neeleman spotted:** "Schumer Tries to Win Over Skeptical Upstaters," *New York Times*, November 9, 1998.

92 **"putzhead":** "When a New York Tough Guy Feels Fear," *New York Times*, November 1, 1998.

92 **met at the Waldorf:** Interview with Rob Land, November 2003.

94 **DAVID NEELEMAN, JETBLUE MAN:** From meetings during July 1999 at the New Air offices.

94 **FAA created a new division:** Based on FAA announcements in 1998; interview with CSET administrator in 1999.

95   **he was the human face:** "Daunting Hunt Begins for Victims of Jet Crash," *Los Angeles Times,* May 13, 1996.

96   **"fanny test":** An author observation of fanny tests, etc., in July 1999; interviews with FAA CSET team.

97   **a list of values:** Interviews with Ann Rhoades and John Owen, April 2004.

98   **He kept on his coffee table:** Interview with Rob Land, November 2003.

98   **first antitrust lawsuit:** "Antitrust Suit Against American Has Aim of Improved Small City Service," *Wall Street Journal,* May 17, 1998.

100   **flying dinosaurs:** Barbara Peterson and James Glab, *Rapid Descent* (New York: Simon & Schuster, 1994), p. 97.

100   **"hardly Einsteinian thinking":** Ibid., p. 60.

101   **"The airlines manage":** Alfred Kahn made this crack numerous times in the author's presence, including in interviews conducted in February 1992 and March 1998.

102   **the top five carriers controlled:** Barbara Peterson, "20 Years After Deregulation," *Condé Nast Traveler,* September 1998.

103   **the mob's role at Kennedy:** See Nick Pileggi, *Wiseguy: Life in a Mafia Family* (New York: Simon & Schuster, 1985).

104   **filed for his exemption:** Filings made by TWA, Delta, Spirit, and IAM (International Association of Machinists and Aerospace Workers) Department of Transportation Docket #OST-99-5085.

106   **"What do you call a West Sider":** Interview with Dave Barger, May 1999.

106   **TWA's Terminal Six:** This was built in 1969 and opened as the National Airlines terminal in 1970. See Geoffrey Arend, *Great Airports: John F. Kennedy International* (New York: Air Cargo News Inc., 1987), p. 141.

107   **long-awaited air train:** "Last Exit for the Air Train," *Queens Courier,* May 6–12, 1999.

108   **tentative decision:** Department of Transportation tentative ruling issued in May 1999 in the application of New Air Corporation for a certificate of public convenience and necessity.

Six Air Born

110   **luring recruits:** Details on recruiting and staffing are from interviews with David Neeleman, Ann Rhoades, Mike Barger, Doreen Lawrence, and Michael DeLorenzo.

112   **In 1971, the U.S. Supreme Court:** Johanna Omelia and Michael Waldock, *Come Fly with Us!: A Global History of the Airline Hostess* (Portland, OR: Collectors Press, 2003), p. 116.

115   **practitioner of Verbal Judo:** Interview with Lee Fjelstadt, and George J. Thompson, Ph.D., and Jerry B. Jenkins, *Verbal Judo: The Gentle Art of Persuasion* (New York: William Morrow, 1993).

115   **People Express, for example:** Philip Holland with Professor Michael Beer, *People Express Airlines: Rise and Decline* (Boston: Harvard Business School, 1990), p. 9.

116   **"I'd grown up in the industry":** Interview with Mike Barger, July 2001.

119   **Those who huffily refuse:** Kevin L. Freiberg and Jaquelyn Freiberg, *NUTS!* (Austin, TX: Bard Press, 1996).

120   **They first experimented:** Interview with Al Spain, May 2004.

123   **Ralph Nader was denied:** "Allegheny Air Loses Damage Suit for Bumping Ralph Nader," *Wall Street Journal,* October 19, 1973.

124   **"he was right":** Interview with Dan Hersh, March 2004.

128   **safety violations:** Information on safety violations from interviews by the author with former Tower Air employees.

128   **Tower Air:** "Tower Air, Bankrupt, Abruptly Ends Service," *New York Times,* May 14, 2000.

130   **"anything more boring":** While the Conquistadores have managed to maintain a semblance of secrecy, several articles have noted their existence; see a cover piece on Herb Kelleher, "I Did It My Way," *Forbes,* May 28, 2001.

132   **JetBlue had its first test:** Brief mentions of the JetBlue runway mishap made it onto the television news on January 21, 2001; a few weeks later a *BusinessWeek* article mentioned the airline's handling of the incident.

134   **closer look at Long Beach:** The account of the Long Beach negotiations is from interviews with Rob Land in May 2001 and May 2003.

Seven 9/11

Most of this chapter is based on first-person accounts of September 11 and the aftermath by the JetBlue people who were there: David Neeleman, Dave Barger, Al Spain, Ann Rhoades, Amy Curtis-McIntyre, Vinny Stabile, Jim Hnat, Gareth Edmondson-Jones, Fiona Morrison, Doreen Lawrence, and Brian Manubay.

139   **The prospectus:** Details were provided by JetBlue officials John Owen and Rob Land.

140   **Levin, a one-time protégé:** Melanie Leftkowitz, "Farewell to Port Authority Leader," Newsday.com, September 26, 2001 account of/obituary.

140   **the magazine's annual roster:** *Vanity Fair* had established a tradition of publishing an annual list of notable people in the December issue; because of 9/11, the issue instead focused on the terror attacks and the aftermath.

147   **"We are not out of the woods":** A Blue Note from David Neeleman and Dave Barger, October 2001.

149   **A JetBlue plane:** This was reported in *The Wave,* Rockaway Queens, February 23, 2002.

154   **Congress rammed through:** "Airline Bailout Status," Reuters, September 24, 2001.

154   **JetBlue went ahead with the IPO:** "JetBlue Airways Stock Soars After IPO," *USA Today,* April 12, 2002.

157   **"I don't think JetBlue":** Cathy Booth Thomas, *Time* magazine, June 10, 2002.

Eight Blue Envy

158	**"Is JetBlue the next":** *Forbes* magazine cover story, October 14, 2002.
160	**Although LiveTV:** From a JetBlue press release.
164	**TIPS:** Stanford Graduate School of Business, case study on JetBlue, November 4, 2003.
164	**had gone public:** "Take 2 for Delta and Its Low-Cost Carrier," *New York Times,* January 29, 2003.
165	**Discovery Channel:** The series the producers were working on, *Head to Head,* proposed to chronicle competitive battles in a number of industries, including newspaper publishing. As of July 2004, the series still had not aired.
170	**complained to a BBC:** A Neeleman interview on the BBC aired in February 2003.
172	**It had begun life:** R.E.G. Davies, *Delta: An Airline and Its Aircraft* (Miami: Paladwr Press, 1990), p.10.

Nine JetBlue U

Most of this chapter, as should be apparent from the narrative, is based on the three-week training course I observed from July 6 to July 20, 2003.

188	**crew resource management:** H. C. Foushee and R. L. Helmreich, "Why Crew Resources Management? Empirical and Theoretical Bases of Human Factors Training in Aviation," in *Cockpit Resource Management* (San Diego, CA: Academic Press), pp. 3–45.
189	**even one major accident:** Statistics cited by Mike Barger in his presentation show that overall the safety of air travel in the United States has improved steadily over the years; see the annual report of 2004 from the Flight Safety Foundation, Alexandria, Virginia.
192	**American Airlines flight attendant:** "Cabin Door Fatalities Lead to NTSB Recommendation," *Commuter/Regional Airline News,* Potomac, MD, August 12, 2002.

Ten Welcome to My World

200	**twenty thousand angry messages:** From internal company tabulations.
201	**so-called CAPPS II:** "TSA's CAPPS II Gives Equal Weight to Privacy Security," Transportation Security Administration press release dated March 11, 2003.
204	**On Saturday:** "JetBlue Gave Defense Firm Passenger Files," *New York Times,* September 20, 2003.
205	**biggest power outage:** "Airports Operated, But Barely," *Newsday,* August 22, 2003.
207	**drafted a mea culpa:** "JetBlue Chief Says He Wasn't Told About Release of Data," *New York Times,* September 25, 2003.
211	**The man wrote back:** Interview with David Neeleman, September 2003.

213   **Those stories:** The *New York Times* published these stories on other airlines following the JetBlue scandal (page number noted), "Airline Gave Government Information on Passengers" (Section 1, page 16); "American Airlines Admits Disclosure of Passenger Data" (Section C, page 6).

Eleven The Terminal

Most of this chapter is based on interviews and meetings observed at the end of 2003 and in the first half of 2004.

215   **Terminal Five:** See Ezra Stoller, *The TWA Terminal* (New York: Princeton Architectural Press, 1999).

218   **Sanchis embraced:** "JetBlue Plans to Preserve TWA Terminal at Kennedy," *Times Ledger* Queens edition, October 9, 2003.

219   **present chaos:** Herbert Muschamp, "Correcting the Nearsightedness of Airport Designers," August 26, 2001.

221   **One reporter:** Barry Estabrook, "In the Air, On the Cheap," *New York Times,* April 4, 2004.

227   **Zellner's article:** "Is JetBlue's Flight Plan Flawed?," *BusinessWeek,* February 16, 2004.

229   **airline quality survey:** Airline Quality Rating 2004 by Brent Bowen and Dean E. Headley, University of Nebraska at Omaha Aviation Institute of Business, April 2004.

index

index

index

Transportation Department, new airline, requirements for, 95

Trans Texas, 27

Trans World Airlines (TWA), 106

Trevor, Greg, 139–40

Twill, Larry, 63, 67

Ulmer, Dave, 51, 127

United Airlines, 21, 129, 161, 188

United Press International, 5

US Airways, 123, 159, 161

ValuJet, 16, 54, 83, 171

ValuJet effect, 188–89

ValuJet Flight 582 crash, 44, 93

Vanguard Airlines, 98, 161

Virgin America, 52–57

Virgin Atlantic Airways, 45–48

Virgin Express, 46, 55–56

Virgin Records, 46

Vranes, Vicki. *See* Neeleman, Vicki (wife)

Walton, Sam, 240

Washington Reagan Airport, 104

Web site, JetBlue, 83, 122

West Coast flights, 128–29, 134–37, 160

Western Airlines, 19–20

WestJet, 36, 227

Weston Presidio, 20, 67

Westrum, Cathy, 32–34, 177–79

Wilcox, Alex, 47–51, 57, 59, 66–67, 85, 97, 139

Win Air, 134

Wired, 201, 202, 204

Wright, Jim, 28

Wright Amendment, 28, 103–4

Yield management, 101

Zellner, Wendy, 226–27